2F

UNDERSTANDING

Contemporary American
SCIENCE FICTION

Understanding Contemporary
American Literature

Matthew J. Bruccoli, *Editor*

UNDERSTANDING

Contemporary American Science Fiction

The Formative Period (1926–1970)

by THOMAS D. CLARESON

UNIVERSITY OF SOUTH CAROLINA PRESS

Published in Columbia, South Carolina, by the
University of South Carolina Press

Manufactured in the United States of America

Library of Congress Cataloging-in-Publication Data

Clareson, Thomas D.
    Understanding contemporary American science fiction : the
formative period, 1926–1970 / by Thomas D. Clareson.
        p. cm. — (Understanding contemporary American literature)
    Includes bibliographical references.
    ISBN 0-87249-689-9
    1. Science fiction, American—History and criticism. 2. American
fiction—20th century—History and criticism. I. Title.
II. Series.
PS374.S35C57   1990
813′.087620905—dc20
                                                    89–49088
                                                    CIP

CONTENTS

EDITOR'S PREFACE

Understanding Contemporary American Literature has been planned as a series of guides or companions for students as well as good nonacademic readers. The editor and publisher perceive a need for these volumes because much of the influential contemporary literature makes special demands. Uninitiated readers encounter difficulty in approaching works that depart from the traditional forms and techniques of prose and poetry. Literature relies on conventions, but the conventions keep evolving; new writers form their own conventions—which in time may become familiar. Put simply, *UCAL* provides instruction in how to read certain contemporary writers—identifying and explicating their material, themes, use of language, point of view, structures, symbolism, and responses to experience.

The word *understanding* in the series title was deliberately chosen. Many willing readers lack an adequate understanding of how contemporary literature works; that is, what the author is attempting to express and the means by which it is conveyed. Although the criticism and analysis in the series have been aimed at a level of general accessibility, these introductory volumes are meant to be applied in conjunction with the works they cover. Thus they do not provide a substitute for the works and authors they introduce, but rather prepare the reader for more profitable literary experiences.

M.J.B.

UNDERSTANDING

Contemporary American
SCIENCE FICTION

INTRODUCTION

When I agreed to undertake a survey of contemporary American science fiction, the project excited me, although I was aware of the problems inherent in the topic as well as the limitations that I would have to impose to keep the work within a single volume. Now that the study is finished, it remains a challenge.

While much has been said of the "Golden Age" inaugurated by John W. Campbell's editorship of *Astounding*, documentation is largely confined to repetitious anecdotes. Similarly, the supposed revolution that took place in the 1960s—the New Wave—survives in stories of persons and places. As a result the plan of this study took shape as I began to write it: to provide an overview of the period from the 1930s through the 1960s, when science fiction was published primarily in specialist magazines—the publishers'/editors' "ghetto," as many writers have referred to those years. This is the period that editors, writers, and enthusiasts separate from any earlier literary tradition SF may have been a part of. After 1970 the book provided the medium of publication. So I have undertaken an overview limited to what I have called the formative years of science fiction.

I have imposed certain limitations on my work, but I think each can be justified, if need be. Obviously I have included detailed study of American science fiction only, partly because until well after World War II SF remained an American literary phenomenon, although some British authors contributed to the magazines. To avoid a catalogue of titles about which little could be said, I have confined my chief attention to novels published in book form, although even in the 1960s many works saw first publication in magazines. A second reason for this choice: rare as some of the books may be, the magazines are even less available.

First and foremost, I have tried to give attention to those texts which have historical significance either in terms of the ideas they introduced or the narrative strategies of their writers. In short, I have tried to emphasize those works that shaped the field during a crucial period. In making this selection I have tried to follow two basic criteria: first, those books which writers and editors have praised for their influence; second, those books which have received some award, whether voted by the professionals who make up the membership of the Science Fiction Writers Association (SFWA) or those "fans" who are members of the annual world conventions. Whatever their lasting merit, these books somehow captured the imagination of those most interested in the field at a given time. What happens if one emphasizes these groups of novels is that one comes up with the established canon of the field. That concept in itself needs constant reexamination.

Perhaps each decade deserves closer study than is possible here. But that is perhaps impossible—perhaps unnecessary. I hope that my judgments will raise questions, and I am sure that they will draw some protests, particularly because from the vantage point of the late 1980s I have tried to remain as neutral as possible. For just as scholars have made fads of the study of certain writers to the exclusion of all others, thereby distorting what occurred in the field, so the adoption of a rigid political line, like that of the marxist critics, as the means by which to judge the merit of an individual work or evaluate and define the field as a whole introduces a warping bias. All in all, I have tried to produce a study aimed not so much at the specialist SF critic or collector as at the student and general reader.

Be that as it may, I could not have undertaken or completed this project without the guidance that other scholars, the enthusiastic fans of SF, and the writers/editors themselves have provided us all. Specifically, I wish to thank Frederik Pohl and Lois McMaster Bujold, who have listened patiently to my theorizing and have provided information that only active writers could. As always when I needed a rare title, Howard DeVore of Dearborn Heights, collector and dealer extraordinary, has found copies for my use. Donald M. Hassler of Kent

THE FORMATIVE PERIOD

State University, coeditor of *Extrapolation*, has helped me with more than one puzzle. Bart Porter, formerly of the College of Wooster News Service, has given me the insight of a younger fan. And, of course, there are the reference librarians of the Wayne County Library— Alice Roberts Finley, Laurel Baer, and Louise Hamel— who always have answers for even the most nitpicking inquiries. This time around Carolyn Rahnema has turned my scribblings to a word-processed manuscript with great patience and care. Last and most, Alice has again proved that she is a copy editor and interrogator par excellence. It helps to have someone keep you aware that science fiction is part of a larger context, both literary and social. As a teacher and reference librarian she has done that. But she is of most help when the next page won't turn into words.

Thank you, everyone.

CHAPTER ONE

1926–1950: The Flowering of a Tradition

To appreciate the complexities and significance of contemporary American science fiction, one must immediately clear away a number of problems which cloud even such central issues as the definition of the field. On the one hand science fiction belongs to a complex literary tradition going back at least to the medieval travel books; as a result, from the outset it has inherited and cherished certain conventions, both of content and narrative strategy. Almost paradoxically, however, SF has been one of the most topical areas of fiction. What one must recall is that almost nothing has been lost. Once some motif or some narrative technique has been introduced, it may undergo innumerable permutations, but it remains a part of the so-called "science fiction furniture" which writers may rely on. In this sense— and no better example occurs than the "future history" created in the late 1930s and 1940s by such writers as Isaac Asimov and Robert A. Heinlein—the field has developed a kind of code which enthusiasts recognize immediately but to which newcomers must be initiated.

5

Such effort is compounded by the reliance of many writers on exact scientific data, although the debate continues on just how much science SF must contain.

In some ways the greatest obstacle to an understanding of contemporary American science fiction lies in its relationship to the specialized American pulp magazines which came into being between the world wars. These magazines and their early editors, such as Hugo Gernsback and John W. Campbell, took the established tradition and began to shape it into contemporary science fiction during what may be called the formative years of the field. But particularly because its public image has been largely shaped by such early comic strips as *Buck Rogers in the 25th Century* and *Flash Gordon* and, more recently, such TV and film series as *Star Trek* and *Star Wars,* many current readers still think of it as a product solely of twentieth-century American popular culture instead of the continuation of a literary tradition. This mistaken inference undoubtedly explains, at least in part, the uneven critical reception which it still receives from portions of both the popular press and the current literary establishment.

Such critics as Brian Aldiss, E. F. Bleiler, Thomas D. Clareson, James Gunn, Brian Stableford, and Darko Suvin have shown that SF is the latest expression of a long-continuing literary tradition. The first major impetus came, for example, from two areas upsetting the seeming stability of the Western Christian world: beginning with the Renaissance, the nations of western

FLOWERING OF A TRADITION

Europe turned their attention increasingly to the physical world and grew ever more fascinated with the unknown expanses of the terrestrial globe, while the new astronomy of Galileo and Copernicus contributed significantly to the dissociation of sensibility occurring during the seventeenth century. By the end of that century an emerging science fiction had found one of its basic and most enduring narrative structures—the imaginary voyage, whether the journey's destination was the Orient, the moon, or the southern oceans. Sir Thomas More had varied that narrative strategy to provide one of the lasting themes of the field in that his *Utopia* (1516) pictures an idealized society on a hitherto unknown island; it afforded him a vehicle by which he could criticize the social and political condition of England. As Marjorie Nicolson and Philip Babcock Gove pointed out as early as the 1940s, during the seventeenth and eighteenth centuries such voyages became the most popular form of fiction. In these early works—ranging from such well-known titles as *The Man in the Moone* (1638) by Francis Godwin and *The Life and Adventures of Peter Wilkins, A Cornish Man* (1750) by Robert Paltock to the lesser-known *Modern Gulliver's Travels* (1796) by H. Whitmore (Mrs. Susanna Graham?)—the satire of European society remained more important than the scientific content. Not until the American George Tucker, writing as Joseph Atterley, published *A Voyage to the Moon* (1827) did the emphasis change; he gave attention to the ship itself and to the mechanics of the flight, introducing the concepts of negative gravity and a supermetal (*lunarium*). Both innovations became conventions essential to many space flights well into the twentieth century.

Thus the voyage into the unknown and the dream of an ideal state remained central to the field. The Gothic mode added the dimension of horror, moving at its best away from the intrusion of supernatural devices into the external world to the dramatization of the human mind slipping over the rim into madness. Although Mary Shelley's *Frankenstein* (1818) may be read as an updating of the myths of Faustus and Prometheus, despite Victor Frankenstein's insistence that he does not "record the vision of a madman," he does dwell on the "wounds that [his] mind had sustained," thereby anticipating the legion of "mad scientists," who have terrorized the worlds of SF. His nameless creature—rejected by a creator—may well represent the human individual isolated in an uncaring universe, a theme that has characterized much of twentieth-century fiction. Most important to an understanding of science fiction, however, is Mary Shelley's assertion in the preface to the 1818 edition that her novel is no "work of fancy" because its basic premise "has been supposed, by Dr. Darwin and some of the physiological writers of Germany, as not of impossible occurrence." In short, *Frankenstein* is highly topical, drawing on theories and speculations that had not yet been (could not be) tested in the laboratory. It does not seem incorrect to see in Mary Shelley's most famous narrative an ancestor of

FLOWERING OF A TRADITION

that contemporary SF concerned with genetic engineering/biotechnology. Nothing is lost; it simply undergoes permutation as science changes.

Another example of topicality surfaced in the last decades of the nineteenth century. Responding immediately to the Franco-Prussian War and the armaments race among the imperialistic European nations, a wide variety of writers, many of them journalists and pamphleteers, portrayed imminent conflicts between whatever alignment of major powers best suited the individual writer. Quantitatively, as I. F. Clarke has shown so well in *Voices Prophesying War* (1966), these "future wars"—together with the "lost-race" motif—made up one of the two most popular types of SF between the 1870s and World War I (nor have they ever disappeared from the field). Topicality, yes; accuracy of prediction, no. Apparently excited by the sudden advent of the dreadnought—the "ironclads"—most of the writers foresaw the outcome of the next conflict determined by a tremendous sea battle. Before 1914 those who paid any attention to aerial warfare emphasized fleets of dirigibles. As he did so often in that period, H. G. Wells provided a notable exception in *The War in the Air* (1908), in which Oriental aircraft destroy German dirigibles attacking New York City. During the war years in *The Conquest of America* (1916, after serialization in *McClure's Magazine*) Cleveland Moffett was almost alone in permitting "an insignificant airforce" to defeat the German navy as it supports an army occupying the eastern United States. All in all, accuracy of prediction may well be the least important characteristic of science fiction.

No detailed account of science fiction in America at the turn of the century need be given attention here except to show how it prepared the way for those pulp magazines which shaped the beginnings of contemporary SF. For example, Everett Carter has declared as early as *Howells and the Age of Realism* (1954) that during the last decades of the nineteenth century "admiration for the scientist became a commonplace of realistic fiction. As a clear-eyed observer, he was portrayed as seeing through sentimentality to the truth."[1] Such intellectual astuteness made him a noteworthy protagonist, from the village doctor in Oliver Wendell Holmes's *Elsie Venner* (1861) and the young scientist in John W. DeForest's *Kate Beaumont* (1873) to Howells's psychologist Wanhope, Stewart Edward White's Percy Darrow, and Arthur B. Reeve's Craig Kennedy, whose exploits as a "scientific detective" were featured almost every month in *Cosmopolitan* from 1910 to 1916.

How much greater his heroic stature became when, like Edison, Marconi, Morse, Bell, Tesla, the Wright brothers, and Ford, the scientist transformed the American agrarian world. (Such comparison omits individuals like Bohr, Planck, Roentgen, and Madame Curie, who set up the parameters of modern physics.) Within a single generation the development of the telephone, the electric light, the wireless radio, the phonograph, the airplane, the automobile, and the skyscraper estab-

FLOWERING OF A TRADITION

lished the basic foundations from which twentieth-century—contemporary—society has grown exponentially. Too often present-day readers forget that, as Allyn B. Forbes pointed out in 1927, even before World War I industrialization had become "the greatest single determining factor in all phases of American life."[2]

In addition to such novels as Frank Stockton's *The Great War Syndicate* (1889) and *The Great Stone of Sardis* (1898), the dime novels, weekly papers, and the series books aimed at a juvenile audience prepared the American reading public for a science fiction based on speculations about the new technology and its potential. The scope and popularity of this emerging field have thus far been most comprehensively described in Thomas D. Clareson's *Some Kind of Paradise* (1985). The readers' appetites had been whetted, but no single source directed toward a mass adult audience catered to these tastes until Frank A. Munsey produced *Argosy, The All-Story Magazine,* and *Cavalier.*

One cannot overestimate the importance of these magazines. They shaped SF during the period of World War I and included both SF and fantasy titles until the 1940s. Without them there would have been no ready market for the specialist magazines appearing in the 1920s. Edgar Rice Burroughs revitalized the lost-race motif created by Rider Haggard and thereby "turned the entire direction of science fiction from prophecy and sociology [the utopian romances] to romantic adventure ... and [he] became the major influence on the field" until the mid-1930s.[3] His pattern was followed by a legion of imitators whose exotic settings—complete with beautiful women—ranged from Antarctica and subatomic worlds to the planet Palos circling the star Sirius. Yet of those many writers only A. Merritt achieved a reputation comparable to the creator of Tarzan and John Carter of Mars. His serials saw almost immediate book publication: *The Moon Pool* (1919), *The Ship of Ishtar* (1926), *The Face in the Abyss* (1931), and *Dwellers in the Mirage* (1932). Whether the stories looked back to the lost-race motif or, like Ray Cummings and Garret Smith, pictured marvelous technologies of the distant future, the Munsey magazines gave new vitality to the field. One other writer must be named: Murray Leinster, the pseudonym of the inventor Will Jenkins, began his SF career with "The Runaway Skyscraper" (1919) in *Argosy* and became one of the most dependable writers of John W. Campbell's *Astounding* in the 1940s.

In a recent study of Jack and Charmian London, although Clarice Stasz was not referring directly to London's SF, she explained, at least in large part, the appeal of the new fiction: "The West had been won and the qualities required in that battle served ill in the emerging urban and industrial world."[4] Memories of that frontier were mythologized in the Westerns of fiction and film, but American readers could choose to dream of distant corners of Earth as well as other worlds, to say nothing of the wondrous potential of the future. The importance of these early fantasies endured because

FLOWERING OF A TRADITION

from 1939 to 1953 these stories—A. Merritt's particularly—were reprinted in *Famous Fantastic Mysteries* and *Fantastic Novels*, first by Munsey and then Popular Publications, thereby introducing them to another generation of SF readers, who regarded them as early classics of the field.

Frequently the scientific content—from archaeology, geology, and prehistory to the latest speculations about advanced technology—supplied little more than a colorful backdrop for an adventure story. Most of the early writers had little or no training in science. They were professional journalists looking for a new market, gaining their information from tabloids, Sunday supplements, and such periodicals as *Popular Science*. A. Merritt epitomized these writers, for he had a lifelong career as an editor of *The American Weekly*. Like many of his contemporaries Garrett P. Serviss, who wrote for the *New York Sun* before he syndicated a column on astronomy, often simply dismissed any explanation of the workings of the ships and weapons he introduced into his narratives as beyond the comprehension of his readers.

As a result terms like "pseudoscience," "science fantasy," and "super science" have been applied to the field. Writing in 1949, Melvin Korshak admitted that the early stories "pointed out new themes" for writers and "proved that a reading public, for the sake of the story, would accept a fantastic premise in fiction," but he insisted that "several types of stories that were based on imaginative science . . . were not unified into a single body of literature."[5] He was one of many who excluded these early titles from science fiction, declaring that the field began only with the publication of Hugo Gernsback's *Amazing Stories* in the spring of 1926. Another difficulty concerning the definition and history of the field occurs because of the specialization of the pulp magazines during the 1920s. The Munsey chain, *Blue Book*, and *Adventure* remained general fiction magazines, always including some SF and fantasy. But temporarily and incompletely science fiction and fantasy were split apart by the specialization. Although *Weird Tales*, founded in 1923, did publish SF—perhaps most notably the early stories of Edmond Hamilton—by and large it became the vehicle for the H. P. Lovecraft circle emphasizing fantasy and horror. Between 1932 and 1936 it also provided Robert E. Howard an outlet where he could create the Hyborian world of Conan the Barbarian, thereby begetting the "Sword-and-Sorcery" motif which not only dominates much of contemporary heroic fantasy but has remained a principal ingredient of science fiction itself.

Thus science fiction became the province of those enthusiasts, led by Hugo Gernsback, who were fascinated with the future of technology. One might say that SF expressed their infatuation with the machine. Beginning with *Modern Electrics* (1908) and the novel *Ralph 124C41+* (1911), Gernsback had shown an interest in the field, but not until he published *Amazing Stories*

FLOWERING OF A TRADITION

(April 1926) did he devote a magazine exclusively to "scientifiction," as he then called the field. Its masthead included a sketch of Jules Verne's tombstone, on which a partially veiled man stretches his arms toward the heavens, while a motto asserts, "Extravagant Fiction Today—Cold Fact Tomorrow." In that first issue Gernsback defined the field as the "Jules Verne, H. G. Wells, Edgar Allan Poe type of story—a charming romance intermingled with scientific fact and prophetic vision." He included short stories by the three writers in that issue. During the next several years he reprinted extensively, relying on such favorites as A. Merritt and Murray Leinster. In 1927 he reprinted Burroughs's *The Land That Time Forgot* (already issued in book form in 1924 after its earlier serialization in *Blue Book*) and purchased Burroughs's newest Martian romance, *The Mastermind of Mars*, for the initial *Amazing Stories Annual* (July 1927).

Repeatedly his editorials in *Amazing* indicate that he thought of the magazine as a vehicle of instruction and as a means of promoting further research and experimentation. He obviously thought of himself as a prophet, but he could not turn a profit as the Depression approached. By early 1929 his publishing company was forced into bankruptcy, although in June he released a new title, *Science Wonder Stories*; its motto proclaimed, "Prophetic Fiction Is the Mother of Scientific Fact." By 1933 he was forced from the field, but the magazines he started continued. His impact on the field was profound. At his suggestion readers during the

1930s formed those groups from which contemporary "fandom" has evolved. He was the guest of honor at the 1952 Worldcon in Chicago. The Hugo Awards—SF achievement awards comparable to the Oscar or Emmy—first given in Philadelphia in 1953, are named for him. Sam Moskowitz has repeatedly hailed him as the "Father of Science Fiction." Increasingly, however, beginning no later than mid-century, any reference to Gernsback has become pejorative, a denunciation of gadget-cluttered fiction embalmed in description and exposition.

In assessing his role in the development of the field one again encounters the topicality of science fiction. By the 1920s both the British Interplanetary Society and the American Rocket Society had become active. In retrospect it seems a delightful coincidence that Robert H. Goddard launched his first liquid-fuel rocket in 1926, the same year *Amazing* was first published. For in sharp contrast to earlier concerns in the field, space flight became the heart of SF during the 1930s. Indeed, "space fiction" was briefly considered as a possible name for the specialist field. (Although Gernsback coined the term "science fiction" in an editorial for the first issue of *Science Wonder Stories* in 1929, it did not gain established usage until John W. Campbell incorporated it into the title *Astounding Science Fiction* in April 1938.) From the covers of Gernsback's magazines by Frank R. Paul (story has it that he never duplicated the designs of his spaceships) to the *Starship Enterprise* of *Star Trek*,

FLOWERING OF A TRADITION

the emblem—icon, Gary Wolfe would call it[6]—most widely identified with SF has remained the rocket ship.

Prior to Gernsback, however, the great majority of space travelers were content to journey to the moon or planets of Earth's solar system. Whatever abuse is heaped on Gernsback for his role in relegating SF to the pulp magazines—the so-called "ghetto" of which subsequent writers and editors complained—his principal achievement remains the discovery of E. E. "Doc" Smith, whose "The Skylark of Space" (*Amazing Stories*, 1928) opened the galaxies to the super science of space opera. The struggle between the brilliant Richard Seaton and an ex-colleague, the villainous Dr. Marc "Blackie" DuQuesne, for economic control of an "ultimate metal" sets up the basic dramatic conflict. Both are, of course, outstanding scientists. When DuQuesne kidnaps Seaton's fiancée, Seaton follows them into interstellar space, where he becomes involved in a war between the peoples of a planet a hundred light-years from Earth. He takes sides, overcomes the enemy through his ingenuity, and is proclaimed Overlord of Osnome. Even before the serialization of "The Skylark of Space" was completed, Smith began its sequel, "Skylark Three" (*Amazing*, 1930), in which Seaton resumes warfare against a variety of aliens. Its mile-long spaceships and advanced armaments defy brief description. The action climaxes in a long-range, planet-shattering battle (great ray guns flash bolts of energy across millions of miles of space) between Seaton and the last remnant of the "monstrous civilization" of the inhuman Fenachrone, who intended to conquer the galaxy. "Skylark of Valeron" (*Astounding*, 1934) enlarges even that grandiose stage, for Seaton must contend against disembodied intelligences who have helped DuQuesne take over Earth; he escapes to the fourth dimension, where he is briefly detained while defeating other inhuman aliens on several worlds. Eventually, having absorbed the knowledge of all the cultures he has encountered in the three novels and now a superman able to materialize whatever he wishes by his power of thought, he saves Earth.

From a present-day perspective Smith's Skylark novels remind one of Burroughs's Martian novels—if one substitutes a variety of worlds for the deserts of Barsoom and relies on fantastic hardware instead of Sword-and-Sorcery. One sees in them, too, a permutation of the future war motif that has remained—with few further changes other than tone—a notable part of contemporary SF.

Seaton's actions, however, are as child's play when compared with the titanic struggle between good and evil which governs Smith's saga of the lensmen in *Astounding*: "Galactic Patrol" (1937–38), "Grey Lensmen" (1939–40), "Second-Stage Lensmen" (1941–42), and "Children of the Lens" (1947–48). Kimball Kinnison and his future wife, Clarissa MacDougall, are the key figures among the young men and women from assorted races who train at a special academy to serve

FLOWERING OF A TRADITION

in the Galactic Patrol, the law enforcers of an interplanetary community—a concept apparently originating with Edmond Hamilton in "Crashing Suns" (1928). Each lensman wears a bracelet—a lens—a semi-sentient life form so attuned to the individual that it gives the wearer such paranormal powers as telepathy. Although not understanding their destiny, in "The Galactic Patrol" Kinnison and his companions become involved in a struggle against the pirates of Boskone.

Throughout the novels the lensmen fight their way through a hierarchy of evil which began several thousand million years ago when two galaxies drifted together and coalesced. The ancient races of the Arisians (good) confronted the Eddorians (utterly evil) for the first time; ever since they have struggled for control of the cosmos. Not only have the Arisians provided the lenses, but for ages they have guided a program of selective breeding to assure that "Civilization" will triumph over ruthless power. The five children of Kinnison and MacDougall are the superhuman leaders in the final defeat of the Eddorians. In short, the lensmen make up a physical and mental elite who will act as guardians of the universe, assuring that order and goodness prevail. Brian Aldiss concludes that the lensmen saga is "the biggest game of Cops and Robbers in existence";[7] he might also have said, as others have of space opera, that it represents an adaptation of the American Western to cosmic scale.

One should not be surprised that the lensmen nov-

els were published in *Astounding* during the decade
when John W. Campbell guided the magazine through
the so-called "Golden Age," for during the early 1930s
he had been regarded as one of Smith's chief rivals.
With "Piracy Preferred" and "The Black Star Passes"
(*Amazing*, 1930) Campbell introduced the trio made up
of Arcot (physicist), Morey (mathematician), and Fuller
(design engineer).[8] Arcot, especially, may have used the
most expository jargon as he explained the principles
behind their super-science. When they were not saving
Earth from alien hordes, they ranged through time as
well as the galaxies, choosing to fight in whatever wars
they came upon, always taking sides against inhuman
beings deserving extinction. In *Astounding* Campbell began a second series involving intergalactic warfare with
"The Mightiest Machine" (1934), featuring another genius, Aarn Munro, a well-muscled superman, the son of
humans who had settled on the surface of Jupiter. E. F.
Bleiler has both Smith and Campbell in mind when he
judges such extravaganzas "fairy-tale fantas[ies] of
power."[9]

Nor were the two writers alone in such ventures.
Jack Williamson's "Legion of Space" (*Astounding*, 1934)
chronicles the success of the legionnaires against a combination of human traitors and alien Medusae who
threaten Earth in the thirtieth century. Shopworn as the
plotline may be, Williamson created some of the most
notable characters of the period by drawing on the
Three Musketeers as well as Sir John Falstaff for Giles

FLOWERING OF A TRADITION

Habbibula. In another innovation he assigned the keeping of the superweapon AKKA to a young woman, Aladoree Anthar, the only member of her generation who knew its secret. He continued the adventures of these characters in "The Cometeers" (1936) and "One Against the Legion" (1939)—all of which were highly praised by Isaac Asimov. His "Legion of Time" (1938) most clearly shows his indebtedness to A. Merritt. Its protagonist becomes involved in a clash between alternate futures, each of which seeks to alter the past to assure its own existence. The narrative becomes as much a love story as a series of adventures, for each of the worlds is personified by a woman: Lethonee of Jonbar (good) and Sorayina of Gyronchi (evil). Good triumphs, of course, but unlike Merritt's tales, when the protagonist goes forward to join Lethonee, he finds that the two women have merged into one.

In 1939 Clifford D. Simak—now known for his pastoral tone and his encounters with aliens—contributed "Cosmic Engineers" to the parade of adventures. When a billion-year-old race, the Engineers, summons a crew of Earthlings to help save this galaxy from collision with another, the crew joins in the warfare between the Engineers and so-called "Hellbounds"—creatures who can exist outside galactic time and space and thus wish to see Earth's galaxy destroyed so that they can dominate the next. The immortal Gosseyn of A. E. van Vogt's "World of Null-A" (1945) must overcome a galactic conspiracy which would prevent him from leading an enlightened humanity to its full maturity. So popular had "space opera" become—Wilson Tucker gave these extravaganzas that name in 1941—that between 1940 and 1944 Edmond Hamilton celebrated the derring-do of Curt Newton, "Wizard of Science," briefly in a new magazine, *Captain Future*. Newton combated the evil forces of the universe with his staunch comrades, Grag (a robot), Otho (an android), and Simon Wright (his mentor, an aged genius whose brain is kept in a box).

As space flight, catastrophic threats to Earth, galactic warfare, and superhuman heroes became increasingly synonymous with the bulk of science fiction during the 1930s and early 1940s, almost as though to counteract that tendency F. Orlin Tremaine, the editor of *Astounding Stories* before John W. Campbell, suggested that writers submit what he called "thought variant" stories—that is, stories which extrapolate from some scientific speculation instead of relying on some invention or technological "gadget" as a point of departure. Although almost all of these stories have been lost to general knowledge, historians of the field refer at least in passing to the first of them, Nat Schachner's "Ancestral Voices" (Dec. 1933), whose protagonist goes back in time to kill a Germanic barbarian sacking Rome. As a result he and thousands of twentieth-century people from various social classes and races (including a caricature of Hitler) who are descendants of that common ancestor simply cease to exist. Mike Ashley has recently praised the story's effectiveness as social satire because "in a period of intense racism" it points out "that 'racial characteristics' are palpably absurd, given the degree to which genetic lines have been mixed through history."[10] The readers of the 1930s, however, were so obsessed with the improbability of what has been called the "grandfather" paradox of time travel (if he ceased to exist, how could he go back in the first place?) that they overlooked the potential of such a narrative for social and political comment. Yet "thought variant" stories mark a point of transition in SF because they could lead a writer to give more emphasis to character and, especially, to the effects of science/technology on society.

Writing as Don A. Stuart, Campbell himself contributed to that transition. Two stories in particular have been praised for their Wellsian tone. In the widely cited "Twilight" (1934) the protagonist, a time traveler, goes seven million years into the future and finds an Earth where the "hopeless ... wondering" remnant of the human race lives amid vast, brilliantly automated cities. Realizing that in its maturity humanity had "flooded" the other worlds of the solar system for at least a million years, the protagonist is so distraught by the "loneliness" of the subsequent decline that as his last act in that future he turns to the "perfect, deathless machines" and orders one of them to undertake construction of a machine having the intellectual curiosity that humanity had lost. Supposedly this mightiest machine will allow intelligence and progress to continue developing. In "Night" (1935), however, the darkest corner of Campbell's imagination reveals itself, for another time traveler goes even farther into the future, discovering some machines and cities operative only on the outermost planets of the solar system as entropy—the heat death of the Universe—engulfs the worlds.

Much has been written about Campbell's pervasive influence on the field once he took on the editorship of *Astounding* in the winter and spring of 1937–38 (he immediately changed the title from *Astounding Stories* to *Astounding Science Fiction*), and consequently attention has been given to the kind of story he encouraged his writers to develop. All of the writers who worked with him in the 1940s and 1950s praise the manner in which he guided them, often providing them with ideas or asking that they explore all of the implications of their topics. Many have asserted that he wanted SF to show consequences of scientific development in terms of the changes occurring in society. Lester del Rey is one of those who has cited Campbell's statement made in the *1938 Writers' Yearbook* (important because of its date) that he wanted "reactions, not mere actions," even if the character involved were a robot, because "human readers need human reactions."[11] Others have reported that he expected *Astounding* to include stories written by technically trained writers on technical subjects for a technically oriented audience. Speaking of Campbell as editor of *Analog* (the title given *Astounding* in 1960), Donald A. Wollheim, one of the distinguished editors and publishers in the field for a half century, said that Campbell continued the Jules Verne tradition of SF.

Perhaps his widely known "Who Goes There?" (1938) not only shows Campbell at his best as a writer but also represents the kind of story Campbell wanted for his magazine. The initial reaction to "Who Goes There?" is one of horror, for an isolated group of scientists at an installation in Antarctica by accident revives an alien who apparently long ago crash-landed a spaceship; it is a shape-changer able to assume the form of any man (or dog) at the base; if it gets loose in the world, it can assimilate into itself all of the creatures of the earth. Such is the threat. For the scientists the problem becomes how to recognize a creature who can replicate its host, both physically and mentally, so that the personality is unchanged.

Science fiction has often been compared to the detective story because the heart of its intellectual appeal can be the solution of a puzzle/mystery/problem. Thus a basic pattern or narrative strategy of SF is the presentation of a problem of a scientific nature—it may well involve applied science or engineering—which the protagonist can solve, according to Hal Clement,[12] for example, only by drawing on a personal knowledge of natural law. Isaac Asimov has complemented this view when he has asserted that his fiction deals with sane rather than irrational worlds in which crises are overcome by the rational discussions and actions of his characters.[13] As has been said so often, these analyses echo the world view of the Enlightenment that the highest quality of the human mind is reason, that the universe itself is governed by a unified and rational nature, and that if (scientific) knowledge is pursued and attained, both humanity and society are perfectible. However modified, that view has never completely disappeared from Western thought. When coupled with the idea of change (and therefore a concern for the future), it has remained a basic premise of science fiction, so that one way of understanding what has occurred in contemporary SF is to observe what has happened to that view.

This basic pattern/narrative strategy has also caused artistic problems for the SF writer. Whatever narrative perspective the writer may take, the emphasis often concentrates on external action (plot) instead of an intense probing of a complex protagonist torn by inner psychological conflicts. However much the readers are made aware of the protagonist's decision-making, the character remains essentially static. (The problem is complicated because, as in the historical romance, the writer must give attention to settings unfamiliar in their detail to the readers.) Even when colorfully drawn, the character and the action become synonymous because the protagonist has little or no meaning apart from the problem to be solved or the task to be performed. In this way, especially in SF written as late as the 1940s, such stories bring to mind Beowulf and other warrior kings as well as the knights of medieval romance, to say nothing of Ivanhoe and Natty Bumppo. One may argue that, like those earlier figures, the protagonists of SF, whether individuals or members of a select elite, may also be regarded as culture heroes. Indeed, the worlds of heroic fantasy and the galaxies of science fiction may well have been the only epic stages where heroic action could take place in the twentieth century.

Thematically and artistically this narrative strategy and its consequences figured heavily in Campbell's *Astounding Science Fiction*, even during the interval between 1939 and the late 1940s, although, paradoxically, as Barry Malzberg has emphasized, in that decade "the field was, issue by issue, being defined and reshaped by an editor, writers, and readers who became literal collaborators."[14] Brian Aldiss has linked *Astounding* of that period to a "research lab" where many "later problems were foreshadowed in general terms and chewed over excitingly."[15] By general agreement, however, Campbell decided what went into the magazine. He wanted contributors to write fiction that examined the psychological and sociological impact of an ever-changing technology on society. He willingly helped them work out their ideas, as in the case of Isaac Asimov. And he gathered about him such writers as L. Sprague deCamp, A. E. van Vogt, Lester del Rey, Jack Williamson, Hal Clement, Fritz Leiber, L. Ron Hubbard, Clifford D. Simak, Murray Leinster, Theodore Sturgeon, C. L. Moore and Henry Kuttner (often collaborating as Lewis Padgett), Isaac Asimov, and Robert A. Heinlien. Nor should one forget that "Doc" Smith published the lensman saga during those years. The result has been labeled the "Golden Age"—certainly a term reflecting the nostalgia of fans like Alva Rogers as much as it is "self-approving, and quite uncritical."[16]

(Significantly, in the spring of 1939 Campbell brought out *Unknown* as a vehicle for "Fantasy Fiction," the subtitle he soon added. Not only did the authors in his so-called "stable" contribute to both magazines, but *Unknown* contained a number of novels and stories making use of motifs which have played a major role in subsequent science fiction. The first issue featured the British writer Eric Frank Russell's "Sinister Barrier" (March 1939), which drew from the ideas of Charles Fort to expose humanity as *pets* of alien beings, the Vitons, who keep the Earth as their own preserve and feed parasitically on the human nervous system. Robert A. Heinlein pursued the same theme of possession in his memorable "They" (April 1941). *Unknown's* selection ranged from deCamp's light-hearted classic account of accidental time travel, "Lest Darkness Fall" (December 1939), whose protagonist finds himself in sixth century Italy and tries to avoid the oncoming Dark Ages by introducing such practical measures as Arabic numerals, the printing press, newspapers, and a postal system, to L. Ron Hubbard's "Fear" (July 1940), Theodore Sturgeon's "It" (August 1940), and Jack Williamson's "Darker Than You Think" (December 1940), an erotic dream tale reminiscent of A. Merritt which proposes a second line of human evolution to explain the existence of lycanthropy. One of the last novels was Fritz Leiber's "Conjure Wife" (April 1943), a study of modern witchcraft as practiced by the wife of a sociologist specializing in ethnology at Hempnell College. Within months *Astounding* serialized his "Gather, Darkness!" (1943) portraying revolt in a decadent future theocracy where science is misused; telepathy, spaceships, and witchcraft (Mother Jujy) co-exist. Since Campbell's editorials and promotional blurbs show that he took SF seriously and considered fantasy as "fun," one wonders if *Unknown* provided an outlet for fiction which did not project an approved image of what the impact of technology on the future should be. No one has yet fully explored that possibility.[17])

Granted that writers as different as "Doc" Smith and Olaf Stapledon had dealt with the history of the future, the foremost literary accomplishment of *Astounding* during the Golden Age—which has since benefited the field as a whole—was to provide a complex narrative framework which subsequent writers could supplement or modify as they chose. In an editorial (Mar. 1941) Campbell first referred to the "common background of a proposed future history of the world and of the United States" serving as a backdrop to Heinlein's fiction. Two months later as part of another editorial he included a chart Heinlein had drawn up of that "Future History." Beginning with his first story, "Life-Line" (1939) and ending with the serial "Methusaleh's Children" (1941), Heinlein had outlined the period from

1939–40 to 2125, enumerating the many technological advances, sketching a period of imperialism when Earth dominates the Moon, Venus, and Mars before those worlds revolt against oppressive tyranny, including a span in the twenty-first century when a dictatorial theocracy in the United States negates research and technology, and ending late in that century, with a "Renascence of scientific research" and civil liberty as humanity undertakes interstellar travel. Sociologically, Heinlien moved from "The Crazy Days" of the third quarter of the twentieth century (in retrospect, a delightful irony) through the theocracy to "The First Human Civilization" rising from the renascence of 2075. But not until 2600—a final date that seems almost an afterthought—did he remark about "the end of human adolescence, and the beginning of first mature culture."

An examination of Heinlein's twenty-one fictions within the span 1939 to 2125 shows that each period of history is controlled by an elite class, be it the oppressive priests of the authoritarian theocracy or the enlightened "Covenanteers" who help humanity start toward the stars. His principal story line involves the revolt of a freedom-loving elite led by scientists and technicians against a tyrannical, often decadent status quo. He makes use of a long-standing convention in "Methusaleh's Children," for example, in that beginning in the nineteenth century its elite had been secretly bred for longevity; when they make themselves known in the twenty-second century, their leader is the oldest of

FLOWERING OF A TRADITION

them, Lazarus Long, to whom Heinlein returned again and again in his later fiction so that Long may be regarded as his spokesman. Although Peter Nicholls dislikes Heinlein's political and social views, he acknowledges Heinlein as the writer "who domesticated the future for a whole generation of readers; he made them feel at home there, inhabitants rather than tourists." He also touched on the nerve center causing the controversy about Heinlein by saying that "the emotional center of his work has always been the political and social nature of man, and the cultures he builds and lives in."[18] The division of opinion regarding Heinlein may best be underscored by the fact that he was the first writer to whom the Science Fiction Writers of America (SFWA) gave the Grand Master Award (1975), and he has at least twice been voted the "best writer of all time" by SF readers.

Although Heinlein was the first American writer to formalize the concept of "Future History," Isaac Asimov expanded it into the complex narrative framework. Simultaneously, during the 1940s he distinguished himself by liberating the robot from the Frankenstein role to which, with few exceptions, SF had long consigned it. In a series of stories collected as *I, Robot* (1950), Dr. Susan Calvin, the "brilliant roboticist," guides the fortunes of U.S. Robots and Mechanical Men, Inc.; her development of the "positronic brain" leads to robots virtually indistinguishable from humans. With Campbell's aid Asimov formulated the "Three Laws of

Robotics," including them in "Runaround" (1942). Deeply implanted into their brains is the concept that they cannot harm humans.[19] That doctrine has remained a cornerstone of contemporary SF.

In terms of future history Asimov established another cornerstone with those novellas and novelettes written between 1942 and 1949 collected as *Foundation* (1951), *Foundation and Empire* (1952), and *Second Foundation* (1953). Essential to Asimov's work is the idea of the cyclic movement of history. For twelve thousand years a galactic empire has grown to include twenty-five million planets unified in a human civilization. Relying on a newly perfected, exact science, psychohistory, which enables one to predict mass behavior, the psychologist Hari Seldon foresees the collapse of the empire. To shorten the interregnum he sets in motion the Seldon Plan, creating two secret foundations, one of physical scientists and the other of psychologists—unknown to each other. In one sense the novels, covering a span of four hundred years, provide an exercise in social engineering, for the adherents of Seldon's plan avert a predicted thirty-thousand-year lapse into barbarism.

Donald A. Wollheim has declared Asimov responsible for "The Cosmogony of the Future," beginning with the first flights to the planets of Earth's solar system and moving through the fluctuations of empire and isolated barbarism to the "Rise of a Permanent Galactic Civilization" and, finally, to "the Challenge to God"—a time of final harmony and creativity.[20] Brian Aldiss may lack something of Wollheim's fervor and mysticism, but he reinforces the importance of the historical framework when he asserts that as a result, SF writers "could depict a technological culture as a continuing process—often continuing over thousands of millions of years."[21] As noted elsewhere, a story can deal with any portion of the cycle the writer chooses, and by noting certain established conventions, readers immediately recognize the necessary context. Thus, by the end of the 1940s science fiction had created a mythos as complex as those of classical Greece and Rome, the Norse, or medieval Europe. It has been able to contain the variations introduced by an increasing number of writers since midcentury.

From space opera to future history, the SF of the 1930s and 1940s had major importance in at least two ways. First, when the marketplace demanded that SF reach a wider audience than that provided by the pulps, serials and collections of stories from the specialist magazines made up the majority of books offered to the public. Even more importantly, these stories brought to a fullness a tradition which had begun in the nineteenth century and reached its first flowering in the utopian fiction at the turn of the century. In 1971 the essay "SF: The Other Side of Realism" suggested that science fiction involved a different—an opposite—response to the new sciences than did literary realism and naturalism.[22] That contrast needs only brief rehearsal. Drawing on the contemporary thinking of such men as Claude

Bernal, Emile Zola argued, as in *Le roman expérimentale* (1880), that the novel should be regarded as a carefully controlled experiment from which its writer could at least begin to discern those natural laws making exact sciences of psychology and sociology. This would lead, of course, to a just society. His test tubes, so to speak, were the major characters of the Rougon-Macquart series. A century later he sounds, on the one hand, as utopian as any of the dreamers of his day; on the other, he reduces humanity to little more than chemical responses to external stimuli. He wanted very much to believe that subjective art could reproduce the supposed objectivity of a laboratory experiment and science. Novelists like William Dean Howells and George Gissing thought of the world as a mass of phenomena which should be replicated in fiction as closely as possible; Howells, especially, reveals the depth of his yearning when he asserts that such effort will somehow reveal the "beauty . . . truth" of human experience.[23]

As the deterministic implications of nineteenth-century science undercut traditional values and religious systems, such writers as these sought desperately to find a basis for morality in science. Their failure resounds throughout the twentieth century. It echoes through Catherine Barkley's protestations regarding the "biological trap" in Hemingway's *A Farewell to Arms* (1929). It leads through a growing sense of isolation and fragmentation ("alienation" and "estrangement") to the

FLOWERING OF A TRADITION

French existentialists and the concept of the Absurd, where humanity cannot be certain that it has the innate ability to understand a universe which in itself seems to be incomprehensible. It leads to an obsession with cognition and a quest for a methodology. In fiction, where humanity is studied in the throes of everyday life, it leads to the antihero. Of the novelists writing by mid-century perhaps Robert Penn Warren captured the dilemma most effectively in *All the King's Men* (1946) when his protagonist, Jack Burden, faces "the Great Twitch" and finally is able to accept "the convulsion of the world . . . and the awful responsibility of Time."

The key to the difference between literary naturalism and science fiction lies in a passage in Frank Norris's *McTeague* (1899). After McTeague has killed Trina and fled to the mountains, Norris asserts that "in Placer County, California [nature] is a vast unconquered brute of the Pliocene epoch, savage, sullen, and magnificently indifferent to man" (chap. 20). Thus Norris explicitly names the cornerstone of the dark vision of naturalism: a brutal, indifferent nature. Caught amid external forces over which the individual has no control and buffeted by chance, humanity becomes the victim of nature. This condition has persisted throughout twentieth-century fiction.

Although the primitivism ranging from Jack London to Edgar Rice Burroughs may reflect a rejection of the new urban-industrial society, and although much of the American utopian vision at the turn of the century may have been part of the Western confrontation between the capitalist oligarchy and the working classes, nowhere is the basic difference between the cul-de-sac of social realism/naturalism and the vital spirit of early American science fiction more clearly shown than in a final judgment in Clifford D. Simak's *The Cosmic Engineers* (1939, 1950):

Life was an accident. There was little doubt of that. Something that wasn't exactly planned. Something that had crept in like a malignant disease in the ordered mechanism of the universe. The universe was hostile to life. The depths of space were too cold for life, most of the condensed matter too hot for life, space was transversed by radiations inimical to life. But life was triumphant. In the end, the universe would not destroy it. It would rule the universe (206).

Certainly this view serves as the philosophical under-pinning behind Hal Clement when he speaks of nature as the neutral or hostile opponent of his protagonists, for he acknowledges that an intellectual puzzle—which his characters solve by reason and their knowledge of natural law—provides the plot and theme of his fiction.[24]

From the boy inventors and "scientific detectives" to the space operas and future histories of the 1930s and 1940s, the main thrust of the American field projected a single track into the future, whether it be the here-

FLOWERING OF A TRADITION

and-now of next month or a time somewhere in the endless millennia. Most of it was shamelessly optimistic. At the heart of American magazine SF especially lay the dream that the American inventor/engineer would lead the best of humanity outward to the stars. Although undoubtedly elitist in its final stages, it was an extension of the utopian vision rising from the nineteenth-century American dream of the perfection of the individual and society. Recently David Brin has downgraded the early SF as "engineering" science fiction, while earlier Robert Silverberg dismissed much of it as "hollow and pointless adventure fiction," although he conceded that at its best it might reveal "the governing myths of the dawning age of galactic man."[25]

The pessimism which had clouded the European imagination after World War I—from the bitterness of John Gloag and the melancholy of Olaf Stapledon to the angst of Aldous Huxley—had not yet tainted the exuberant American field. That came with the social and political turmoil following World War II.

Notes

1. Everett Carter, *Howells and the Age of Realism* (Philadelphia: Lippincott, 1954) 92.

2. Allyn B. Forbes, "The Literary Quest for Utopia, 1880–1900," *Social Forces* 6 (Dec. 1927): 180.

3. Sam Moskowitz, *Explorers of the Infinite* (Cleveland: World, 1963) 291.

4. Clarice Stasz, *American Dreamers* (New York: St. Martin's, 1988) 43.

5. Melvin Korshak, introduction, *Best Science Fiction: 1949* (New York: Fell, 1949) xi–xii.

6. Gary Wolfe, "Icon of the Spaceship," *The Known and the Unknown: The Iconography of Science Fiction* (Kent, OH: Kent State University Press, 1979) 55–85.

7. Brian Aldiss, *Trillion Year Spree* (Garden City, NY: Doubleday, 1986) 210.

8. In most memoirs and reference books Campbell's trio is referred to as Arcot, Morey, and Wade. The colorful Wade, however, is a space pirate whom Arcot and his friends rescued when he was marooned in space. He is described as having two personalities in one body. Arcot sends in a request to employ Wade. In *Islands of Space* (1931) he is described as "the pirate Wade . . . a brilliant but neurotic chemist" who needs treatment by "modern psychomedical techniques." See *John W. Campbell Anthology: Three Novels: The Black Star Passes, Islands of Space, Invaders from the Infinite* (New York: Doubleday, 1953) 50, 54, 193.

9. E. F. Bleiler, ed., *Science Fiction Writers* (New York: Scribner, 1982) 152.

10. Marshall B. Tymn and Mike Ashley, eds., *Science Fiction, Fantasy, and Weird Fiction Magazines* (Westport, CT: Greenwood Press, 1985) 62–63.

11. Cited in Lester del Rey, *The World of Science Fiction 1926–1976* (New York: Garland, 1980) 153–54.

12. Thomas D. Clareson, personal interview with Hal Clement, regional SF conference, Millenicon -13, Dayton, Ohio, 4–6 Mar. 1988.

13. Thomas D. Clareson, personal interview with Dr. Isaac Asimov, Wooster, Ohio, 2 Oct. 1975.

14. Quoted from James Gunn, ed. *The New Encyclopedia of Science Fiction* (New York: Viking, 1988) 205.

FLOWERING OF A TRADITION

15. Aldiss 225.

16. Robert Scholes and Eric S. Rabkin, *Science Fiction* (New York: Oxford University Press, 1977) 51.

17. For the most complete discussion of *Unknown* to date, see the appropriate entry in Tymn and Ashley.

18. Bleiler 185.

19. The Three Laws of Robotics are:
> "1. A robot may not injure a human being, or, through inaction, allow a human being to come to harm.
> "2. A robot must obey the orders given it by human beings except where such orders would conflict with the first law.
> "3. A robot must protect its own existence as long as such protection does not conflict with the first and second laws."

20. Donald A. Wollheim, *The Universe Makers* (New York: Harper, 1971) 42–44.

21. Aldiss 223.

22. Thomas D. Clareson, "SF: The Other Side of Realism," *SF: The Other Side of Realism* (Bowling Green, OH: Bowling Green University Popular Press, 1971) 1–28.

23. William Dean Howells, "Novel-Writing and Novel-Reading: An Impersonal Explanation," *Howells and James: A Double Billing*, ed. William M. Gibson (New York: New York Public Library, 1958) 7–24.

24. Clareson-Clement interview.

25. David Brin, "Running Out of Speculative Cliches: A Crisis for Hard Science Fiction," *Hard Science Fiction*, eds. George E. Slusser and Eric S. Rabkin (Carbondale, IL: Southern Illinois University Press, 1986) 13; Robert Silverberg, ed. *The Mirror of Infinity* (New York: Harper and Row, 1970) viii, xi.

CHAPTER TWO

The 1950s: Decade of Transition

The atomic bomb and the abrupt surrender of Japan turned the attention of the general public to science fiction, as though Americans thought that they might find in those stories both some simple explanation of what had happened at Hiroshima and Nagasaki and a quick assessment of the consequences of entering the Nuclear Age. After all, the use of atomic power had become a fixed motif in the field between the wars. This interest immediately created a problem of accessibility. Except for the occasional title, like Philip Wylie and Edwin Balmer's *When Worlds Collide* (1933) and its sequel, *After Worlds Collide* (1934)—drawn from a long-established motif—SF had been confined to the pulps; Lester del Rey, for example, has several times said that when he first wrote "Nerves" (1942), there had been no book markets for science fiction.[1] Donald A. Wollheim soon edited *The Pocket Book of Science Fiction* (1943), but his pioneering ten-story anthology not only preceded the market's demand but also did not have the length nor the print run of either Raymond J. Healy and Francis

DECADE OF TRANSITION

McComas's *Adventures in Time and Space* (1946) or Groff Conklin's *The Best of Science Fiction* (1946), both of which drew heavily on *Astounding*. By the end of the decade various SF "fans" became publishers—Gnome Press, Shasta Publishers, and Prime Press among them—and began to issue limited editions of serials or groups of stories reworked into novels, while Ray Bradbury and Robert A. Heinlein placed a few titles in the slick magazines during the late 1940s, Bradbury gaining recognition for several best stories of the year. One measure of public interest in the field came early in 1951 when *Collier's* serialized a new novel by the British writer John Wyndham, a new pseudonym for John Beynon Harris, who had written primarily for the American pulps since 1931. Critics soon named "The Revolt of the Triffids" (book title, *The Day of the Triffids,* 1951) one of the classic tales of catastrophe; it signals a drastic shift in the motif resulting from the impact of the war. A combination of genetic engineering and an unexplained accident to circling missiles armed for bacteriological warfare destroys civilization, although in the manner of Wells, Wyndham implies that some of the survivors may rebuild. The next year, 1952, proved to be a pivotal year, however, for Donald A. Wollheim became the science fiction editor of Ace Books, and Betty and Ian Ballantine founded Ballantine Books. Even though in the 1980s some writers break into the field with short stories in the remaining magazines and even though some longer narratives are first serialized in those magazines, from

1952 onward the novel increasingly served as the primary medium by which SF reached a wider audience.

So far as nuclear matters are concerned, as early as "Blowups Happen" (1940) Robert A. Heinlein had examined the psychological stress and sense of responsibility felt by atomic engineers in breeder plants because detonation of the atomic pile might cause a "complete, planet-embracing catastrophe"; in one of his earliest portrayals of a confrontation between the scientific establishment and corporate businessmen he avoided the terrible danger because atomic and rocket engineers first develop a new fuel and then build a shop which will serve as "an artificial moonlet in a free orbit" some fifteen thousand miles out in space, where beside the ship the pile itself will shine as "a tiny, artificial star."[2] In Lester del Rey's "Nerves" (1942), as public opposition to the location near urban areas of productive industrial atomic plants grows, the action centers on the efforts of a senior physician, Dr. Ferrel, to deal with a seemingly routine accident; a youthful would-be engineer helps to avert a possible major disaster involving Isotope R by piping its magma into an adjacent river and swampland where it quickly disperses. During the early years of the decade the writers of *Astounding* explored the potential of atomic power and, despite its inherent dangers, found it necessary to civilization's future.

John Hersey's *Hiroshima* (1946) documented the events ending the war within a few months of the release of *The Murder of the U.S.A.* by Will F. Jenkins, who

DECADE OF TRANSITION

had long published his SF as Murray Leinster. Although atomic missiles have destroyed all major American cities, retaliation cannot take place until the protagonist analyzes an unexploded bomb to learn what nation manufactured the bomb and perpetrated the initial attack. He succeeds and the enemy is destroyed, but its identity is not revealed. A year later Leonard Engel and Emmanual S. Piller's *The World Aflame: The Russian-American War of 1950* gives an account of a war that has lasted until the mid-1950s and seems without end because atomic weapons per se cannot bring final victory.

Instead of fighting a nuclear war, however, most mid-century writers took it offstage or relegated it to precedent action as they concentrated on its effects. In an effort to unify the world and prevent war, scientists in Max Ehrlich's *The Big Eye* (1949) persuade the general public that Earth faces collision with a new planet. In *Shadow on the Hearth* (1950) Judith Merril focused on a mother and her two young children as New York is bombed and civilization crumples, while the protagonist of Wilson Tucker's *The Long Loud Silence* (1953) survives in an eastern United States ruined by nuclear and biological warfare. Owing much to Norbert Wiener and cybernetics, Bernard Wolfe's *Limbo* (1952) pictures the destruction of both Russia and the United States after an automated war. Motivated by a new religion, men of both countries voluntarily permit amputation of their arms and legs so that they can no longer fight. The quadriplegic is the most honored of men. For their sacrifice volunteers are rewarded with prosthetic limbs surpassing the performance of flesh and blood. Once again the nations fight to gain possession of the rare metal necessary for the construction of the prostheses. Wolfe includes an alternative: refugees flee to a Pacific island where lobotomies cure man of his innate aggressiveness but also destroy his humanity.

Behind such novels a legion of short stories infested *Astounding* at mid-century. A basic premise established itself: inevitable nuclear conflict would transform, if not destroy, the world. The clarion voice among the outcries belonged to Theodore Sturgeon, especially in two stories. Although Grenfell, the protagonist of "Memorial" (1946), shows that he is well aware of the moral responsibility of science and scientists, there is in him something of Faust, for he is one of those who, perhaps unwittingly, tampers with forces which he does not fully comprehend and cannot control. The body of the narrative relies on a series of dialogues juxtaposing Grenfell's dream of creating a memorial which will symbolize the abolition of war with the desire of a close friend, Jack Roway, to have him give his secret to the government for use as a weapon. When government agents intervene, he detonates the atomic pile. The omniscient narrator announces that wars follow and then desolation; a framing device shows that centuries later a seething nuclear reaction—a "Pit"—has become the emblem of "the misuse of great power" and the annihilation of anything remotely human. In another de-

DECADE OF TRANSITION

stroyed America, although she herself is dying of radiation sickness, the lovely performer Starr Anthim, sings of "Thunder and Roses" (1947) as she crisscrosses the country to reach any remaining military establishments anyone knows of in order to plead that no further retaliatory strike be launched. Further action means worldwide extinction; the "spark of humanity" must be given the chance to flourish again—even if only among the descendants of the "temporary enemy." Her suggestion brings raised eyebrows even in the 1980s.

By the early 1950s the examination of postholocaust Earth had become a distinct motif which has never disappeared from contemporary SF. Although its tone has undergone certain changes in the works of individual writers, it replaced the vision of an earthly paradise with the nightmare of an earthly hell. Yet one must remember that both vision and nightmare were linear extrapolations from Western technological culture. The motif itself, however, did not provide the key work shifting science fiction from an enthusiastic adulation of the machine to a criticism of modern urban-industrial society. That occurred with the eight stories Clifford D. Simak fused into the episodic novel *City* (1952). Although Simak repeatedly said that his moral indignation at the events of World War II, especially the bombing of Hiroshima and Nagasaki, fueled his themes, four of the eight tales were published in 1944; they established his basic premises. More accurately, one should say that *City* brought to fruition questions which he had raised in his fiction throughout the 1930s and early 1940s. Like Wells before him, Simak drew on the biological and psychological makeup of humanity to examine its potential. Indeed, instead of celebrating the far-future destiny of the race, he cut it short.

With his first premise, unlike Heinlein's prediction of great road-cities, Simak discards cities as obsolescent in a future shaped by atomic power, robot labor, hydroponics, and helicopters. Humanity disperses (the population sharply reduced) as it attempts to adapt to a life style of "manorial existence, based on old family homes and leisurely acres." In the fifth generation, although Jerome A. Webster suffers from agoraphobia, as a surgeon whose speciality is the Martian brain he reluctantly agrees to journey to Mars to operate on a friend, a Martian philosopher working on a new concept, one that will give all intelligent beings a "new direction of purpose." Acting on its own, Webster's servant, the robot Jenkins, dismisses the ship that comes for the surgeon because his master never goes anywhere. Simak's second premise allows Webster's son, guilt-driven by his father's failure, to experiment with genetic engineering so that dogs can speak and see to read (subsequent introduction of miniaturized robots provides the dogs with hands to work for them); his aim is to assure that humanity will no longer be alone but will have another mind to share experience with, another perspective to learn from.

Simak's third premise is the most devastating. An

DECADE OF TRANSITION

apparently unrelated episode becomes a model of the puzzle story; an engineer must learn why men adapted to survive on the surface of Jupiter do not return to base. He and a pet dog go through the converter which permits them to become "lopers," sensitive animal-creatures on Jupiter; so different—so transcendent?—is their experience that they cannot return to their earthly bodies. Later, given the opportunity to become lopers, all but a few thousand human beings choose immediately to escape their inherited physical and psychological limitations. In this way did Simak clear the world so that the dogs, guarded by Jenkins, can develop a psychically oriented culture, discover a seeming infinity of parallel worlds adjacent to Earth, and establish a brotherhood of animals in which killing and violence have no place because all life is sacred.

Atypical as these tales are of the main thrust of SF in *Astounding* at mid-century, they gain thematic unity and impact through the framing device Simak gave them when he combined them into the novel *City*. In an introduction and notes to the individual stories, a scholarly editor presents the stories as tales surviving through the oral tradition of the doggish culture. No one knows their origin; the editor refers to those scholars who believe that they have a historical basis and those who feel they are pure myth. The intellectual debate turns on the issue that the dogs cannot understand the concepts of city, war, or humanity itself. At one point the editor denounces humanity's "preoccupation with a mechanical civilization rather than with a culture based on some of the sounder, more worthwhile concepts of life" as well as the individual's "inability to understand and appreciate the thought and viewpoint of another"; almost immediately he declares that "man was engaged in a mad scramble for power and knowledge, but nowhere is there any hint of what he meant to do with it once he had attained it." (117, 118). Had the race indeed existed, it would not have gained the "cultural eminence" attributed to it by the stories. "Its equipment is too poor." To reinforce his attack Simak introduces a race of intellectually enhanced ants who, with the aid of tiny robots, undertakes the aimless construction of a building which engulfs all Earth but the Webster property. In the last tale, Jenkins chooses not to advise the dogs to poison the ants, as man would have. Sometime later the dogs retreat to the parallel worlds. From that vantage point far in the future the scholarly editor assembles the tales and his notes.

Not one of Simak's immediate contemporaries condemned Western society so harshly; no one consigned humanity to oblivion. Through his framing device Simak achieved an objectivity which American SF had not previously gained. He created a credible, nonhuman world capable of sustaining metaphors regarding the human condition. *City* must rank with the finest of the beast fables. More than any previous text, either American or British, it released SF from the linear trajectory which had confined it from its beginnings.

DECADE OF TRANSITION

Pivotal as Simak's *City* was, other factors worked in the early 1950s to reshape science fiction. Two magazines challenged *Astounding*. In the autumn of 1949 appeared *The Magazine of Fantasy*, edited by Anthony Boucher and J. Francis McComas; with its second issue (Winter-Spring 1950) it assumed the title *The Magazine of Fantasy and Science Fiction*, which it still retains. In little more than a year Horace L. Gold edited the first issue of *Galaxy Science Fiction* (October 1950), a distinctively alternative voice in the field because of its social criticism and satire. That October issue included the first installment of Simak's *Time Quarry* (book title *Time and Again*, 1951). Its protagonist, killed in a crash-landing on an unknown planet in the Cygni system, is restored to life and fused symbiotically with an alien. His task is to write a book that will change humanity's perspective and its future. His message declares that all sentient beings, however diverse their forms, are united into a single community which gives purpose and meaning to the universe. Even before all episodes of *City* had been assembled in book form, Simak stated the theme which gave unity to his subsequent SF. (The story line of *Time Quarry* turns on the repeated attempts of "revisionists" to keep the protagonist from writing the book, for they would keep man superior to robot, android, and alien.)

Of equal immediate consequence to the early 1950s, two writers brought science fiction to the attention of a much wider audience than it had previously enjoyed:

SCIENCE FICTION: THE 1950s

Ray Bradbury and Kurt Vonnegut. For almost forty years readers throughout the world have made the name Ray Bradbury synonymous with SF. For much of that time his *Martian Chronicles* probably remained the most widely known title in the field. As early as 1937 he became active in the Los Angeles chapter of the Science Fiction League, where he knew such writers as Henry Kuttner and Robert Heinlein; during that same period he saw in technocracy "all the hopes and dreams of science fiction." Such enthusiasm does not characterize his best-known fiction; indeed, many fans of SF still declare him to be antiscientific, dismissing him as a writer of fantasy. He did contribute frequently to *Weird Tales* during the 1940s; from those stories came his first book, *Dark Carnival* (1947). Between 1942 and 1949 he also published in *Planet Stories* and *Thrilling Wonder Stories;* a selection from those magazines made up *The Martian Chronicles* (1950), hailed at once by such critics as Christopher Isherwood and Gilbert Highet.

Repeatedly Bradbury has asserted that he has never had an interest in the future for its own sake; instead he sought to use it as a lens with which to magnify the present. General consensus has praised him for drawing on the myth of the American frontier as a basis for the *Chronicles*. In short, to free himself from the social, political, and literary contexts which could restrict his work if he relied on the mode of realism/naturalism, he projected his stories into the uncharted near future of the twenty-first century. He transformed the American nineteenth-century conquest of the West into a future American conquest of Mars. By doing this, he found a fresh basis for his metaphors.

So careful was he in his parallelism that he used chicken pox to annihilate the last of the Martians, just as smallpox had decimated such tribes as the Blackfeet. He also compressed all of the episodes between January 1999 and October 2026 into a single generation. That compression of the dates emphasizes his concern with metaphor instead of a literal historical account of an expanding future. Yet he was more than an angry political critic of the United States. In a story not written until 1952—"The Wilderness"—and not included in *The Martian Chronicles* until the 1972 edition, two young women dream of joining their husbands on Mars in 2003. As Janice Smith and Leonora Holmes muse over their impending journey, they both call up images and events from the past, thus amusing and perhaps reassuring themselves. In the final image, as Janice drifts asleep, she wonders one last time, "Is this how it was over a century ago?" It ends in quiet affirmation, capturing something of the awe and wonder felt by a young bride—as fiction, journals, and letters have shown—on the eve of her departure westward in a Conestoga wagon. Through Bradbury's minglings of images from past and future, he gives at least a momentary universality to human experience. Small wonder that the literary establishment and the general readers found a new richness in his best science fiction.

Early in *The Martian Chronicles* he seems to play with some of the conventional SF "furniture." A sensitive, perhaps telepathic Martian woman has a premonition of the arrival of the first expedition from Earth. She tells her husband about her dream of a dark-haired, blue-eyed man and asks if he thinks the third planet is inhabited. He rebukes her. As she grows more restless one night, he goes outside and kills the voyagers as they land. She weeps as he tells her nothing has happened. The tale of the second expedition, as Gary Wolfe has pointed out, reads like a parody of "triumphant explorers arriving in a new world."[3] The captain pleads for some recognition, some show of appreciation of the accomplishment. Instead he is first assigned to a lunatic asylum and then shot by a psychiatrist trying to cure him of his hallucination. The telepathic Martians probe the minds of the crew of the third expedition so that the ship sets down in a small country town, where each of the crew recognizes friends or relatives long dead. That night the crew is killed. (Someone, somewhere, might fault Bradbury for inconsistency in handling telepathy. The captain of the second expedition could not be judged mad were the psychologist a telepath. But the humor of the tale more than compensates for any forgetfulness. Better to fault Bradbury for the early-twentieth-century town which young astronauts of 2001 could not personally remember. Such a choice may measure something of the nostalgia Bradbury has always expressed for the midwestern scene of his boyhood.)

DECADE OF TRANSITION

After these false starts, so to speak, the mood shifts abruptly. The fourth expedition finds no "native problem" because the Martians have died of chicken pox. Not only does this in itself call up a number of nineteenth-century journals, but it also removes any need to portray warfare. The first three expeditions have conquered a world with their deadliest weapon: their germs. Thus Bradbury can give his attention to the conduct of the Earthmen. In "—And the Moon Still Be Bright" a crewman voices the anxieties so much a part of the nineteenth and twentieth centuries when he condemns both Darwin and Freud not only for removing humanity from nature but also for destroying religious faith. One infers that he may well speak for Bradbury. This sense of loss lies at the heart of much of his best fiction.

The remodeling of Mars to suit the style and whims of twentieth-century America continues until nuclear war threatens Earth. Conveniently, the threat of imminent conflict causes almost all the Americans to return to Earth so that the later stories in *The Martian Chronicles* are not so much a study of conquest as they are a study of both American materialism and the isolation of a few individuals on a desolate world. Unable to ignore the war itself, Bradbury disrupts the unity of his structure with "There Will Come Soft Rains," published in *Collier's* in 1950, in which an automated house burns after functioning patiently for years after its family has died in the war. The final story, "The Million-Year Picnic"

(dated 2026), focuses on a last family of Americans who
have fled Earth in a private rocket to escape the impending conflict. The narrative has particular interest as a
study of the father in relation to his three sons. As he
hopes that another family will get through—with four
daughters—he eases the children in their transition
from one world to another. He emphasizes the ruined
cities and the contours of the land, as though to emphasize that both are a part of nature. At last he tells them
that Earth is gone and that in blowing up the rocket and
burning a variety of papers, including government
bonds, he has burned a way of life, as has the nuclear
holocaust. He explains that "life on Earth never settled
down to doing anything very good. Science ran too far
ahead of us too quickly" (273). For the "mechanical wilderness" of Earth, he gives them the empty wilderness
of Mars. Then, as he promised, he shows them the first
Martians: their reflections in a canal. In this way
Bradbury's use of the metaphor of the American West
dissolves into the issues which so concerned mid-century science fiction.

Two stories linking *The Martian Chronicles* and *The
Illustrated Man* (1951) do little more than indicate his
awareness of racism in the United States. A community
of Southern blacks in "Way in the Middle of the Air"
(*The Martian Chronicles*) save their money and, according
to gossip, secretly build rockets so that on a given day
in 2003 they can undertake an exodus. Casual reference
to a radio report suggests that this occurs throughout

DECADE OF TRANSITION

the South. The form of the narrative gives it its effectiveness: the dialogue of old white men sitting on the porch of a hardware store as they watch the blacks march and the rockets—"golden bobbins"—rise into the skies.

The black population of Mars in "The Other Foot" (*The Illustrated Man*) tell their children that twenty years ago they "just up and walked away and come to Mars," settling down and building towns just like the ones they left. By implication, in contradiction to "The Million-Year Picnic," no whites inhabit Mars. As the blacks await the rocket, the first to arrive in twenty years since "Earth got in an atom war," the men gleefully plan to invert the segregation so many of them remember. One of them, Willie Johnson, brings a rope with him. From the ship one old white man emerges. Immediately he begins to enumerate the cities which were burned; he has photographs to confirm the destruction. As he speaks of the South, including specific places such men as Willie ask about, they relent, as Willie remembers "the green Earth and the green town" where he lived. Quickly they obliterate the signs they made so hastily. "A new start for everyone," declares Willie's wife. The rhetoric may be hopelessly dated and unacceptable, but Bradbury was among the first in SF to face racism.

While individual stories remain noteworthy, the narrative frame of *The Illustrated Man*—that of the tattooed man—contributes little to structure and nothing to thematic unity. Bradbury seems to have made a hurried selection of stories on hand when the success of *The*

Martian Chronicles called for another volume. In "The Veldt" technology permits parents and children to repli- cate any portion of the world in an automated nursery; the children lure their parents into the veldt, where li- ons kill them. In "The Last Night of the World" a hus- band confides to his wife that he and all the men he knows have dreamed that "it was all going to be over, and that a voice said it was." His wife reports that the women have shared the dream. As though exhausted, they passively accept that everything will stop some- time during the night of October 19, 1969. He assures her that the children know nothing and that he has cared only for her and their two daughters, never liking cities or his work. "The City," completely automated, waited twenty thousand years to avenge the planet Taollan, whose population Earthmen had warred on and destroyed with leprosy. When an Earth rocket re- turns, the City captures its crew, transforms them into automatons, and sends them back to Earth in their ship loaded with "golden bombs of disease culture" so that Earth will be infected. Then the City turns itself off, so to speak, and dies contentedly.

Another Bradbury potpourri collection, *The Golden Apples of the Sun* (1953), contains "The Wilderness." In the same year appeared his widely praised short novel, *Fahrenheit 451*. Begun as early as 1947, it had been pub- lished first as "The Fireman" in *Galaxy* (Feb. 1951), but not until he lengthened it to *Fahrenheit 451* did critics begin to place it on a level with Yevgeny Zamiatin's *We*,

DECADE OF TRANSITION

Huxley's *Brave New World*, and Orwell's *Nineteen Eighty-Four*, some of them seeing in it a protest against the McCarthyism of that era. Few, if any, note explicitly that the central, symbolic action of the novel takes its departure from one of the most appalling incidents of the 1930s: the book burning by Hitler's Nazis. Again Bradbury uses the future as a stage to reveal his deeply emotional reactions to a trauma of his generation: the loss or denial of intellectual freedom. Unlike so many of his contemporaries writing magazine science fiction before the 1950s, he has no need to picture in detail a future society, for Bradbury's world is that of the year-after-tomorrow. From the opening encounter with the Fireman, Guy Montag, the reader knows that an authoritarian government rules, and soon learns that many of its citizens, like Mildred Montag, are reduced to less than human by drugs and the soporific wall-sized TV. Thus Bradbury is free to give his attention to character and a state of mind instead of setting and plot. He concentrates on Montag, following his conversion from an unthinking instrument protecting the status quo of the state to an individual memorizing a book in order to preserve a cultural heritage. The act of memorizing a text exemplifies, for Bradbury and for his reader, how private is the interaction between the person and the continuing intellectual traditions. In Bradbury's satire the modern authoritarian state cannot allow such private, individual relationships.

In his early fiction—on which his reputation must

finally rest—Bradbury shares the anguish felt by American society at the advent of the Nuclear Age. But Bradbury's reaction is emotional rather than intellectual. In *The Martin Chronicles* the voyage of the third expedition, originally entitled "Mars Is Heaven" in *Planet Stories* (1948), captures momentarily in both title and plot the speculation of many Theosophical writers at the turn of the century. In *The Illustrated Man* "The Man" (1949) reiterates the dream voiced by James Cowan in *Daybreak* (1896). After remarking that "not since Darwin" has there been peace and quiet on Earth, the captain of an exploring spaceship learns that Christ visited the planet the day before the ship landed; Captain Hart undertakes a quest to meet Christ on some planet, somewhere, although his companions insist that however long he continues his seeking, he will never achieve his goal. Two priests sent to Mars as missionaries in "The Fire Balloons" (1951) debate whether or not the blue fireballs they encounter have intelligence and souls; they conclude that "Truth" exists on all planets and that one day everything will form into "the Big Truth" like pieces in a jigsaw. Bradbury's most deeply personal expression of this line of thought occurs in the poem "Christus and Apollo" (1969). Unlike so many of his contemporaries in science fiction, Bradbury remains at heart a Christian mystic.

Although their unrest stems from much the same source, Kurt Vonnegut stands in sharp contrast to Bradbury. While Bradbury had come up through Los

DECADE OF TRANSITION

Angeles fandom and had published extensively in the SF magazines during the 1940s, Vonnegut had had no acknowledged relationship with SF before his first novel, *Player Piano* (1952). Almost immediately he began an ongoing protest that neither he nor his work should be identified with the field. (Yet during the next decade, 1953–1964, he placed five stories with *Galaxy* and *F&SF.)* In 1950 he had quit his job as a publicist for General Electric in Schenectady and set about transforming his experience with GE into *Player Piano*, one of the earliest and best-known American dystopian fictions. The depth of his personal involvement shows itself in his choice of setting: the Ilium Works in Ilium, New York, following the reconstruction of the United States after World War III. He makes certain that he evokes even the ghost of Thomas A. Edison, for Paul Proteus, his protagonist, keeps for his private use the "original machine shop" that Edison built in 1886, the same year he "opened another in Schenectady." Beyond that Vonnegut has acknowledged that he drew on both samiatin and Huxley.

Player Piano is the story of Dr. Paul Proteus, the most promising young engineer/executive in Ilium, as he grows disenchanted with a society regimented by technology and bureaucratic corporations. Son of the first postwar Commercial, Communications, and Resources Director, Proteus becomes involved in a revolt against the establishment. Vonnegut adds resonance to his narrative by incorporating the format of the traditional utopia. He introduces the Shah of Bratphur as a visitor to the United States and Ilium. The leader of six million "members of the Kalhouri sect" living in "his military and spiritual fastness in the mountains," the shah seeks financial and technological aid. Unlike the usual passive visitor to utopia who simply listens and absorbs information, the shah becomes a commentator and questioner. As he enters Ilium, he asks who owns all the "slaves" he has seen working since his limousine left New York City, only to learn that they are "citizens, employed by the government." When the workings of American society have been explained to him, he equates citizens and slaves. One suspects that Vonnegut would like him, a representative of primitivism, to play a role similar to that of the Savage in *Brave New World.*

Although everyone in the nation has been classified by job description, the Iroquois River polarizes the citizens of Ilium. To the north, next to the industrial complex—"the machines"—lives an elite headed by managers and engineers. The bulk of the people live to the south in Homestead. All of those who cannot support themselves "by doing a job better than a machine" must serve in either the Army or the Reconstruction and Reclamation Corps. The "Reeks and the Wrecks" have a vital role; they consume "more things for better living." Automation appears to be the villain, for it continues to displace anyone whose job can be done more efficiently, with greater productivity, by machines. It has

DECADE OF TRANSITION

reached as high as an engineer who serves the national Petroleum Board. The master tapes controlling the machines—whether at the Ilium Works or in a Homestead bar—have reduced to electrical impulses the movements of skilled workers, as in the case of Rudy Hurst, at one time the best lathe operator in Ilium. Ironically, apparently without realizing the consequences, the finest machinists allowed their activities to be recorded by Paul Proteus and his colleagues. Now the majority are "employed" by the government in the Reeks and the Wrecks, while a few others survive by performing whatever menial tasks are left.

Vonnegut chose World War II as his culprit; automation, as his means. When men and women had to serve in the military, management discovered that machines could replace them: "production with almost no manpower." Wartime crisis fathered the National Industrial Planning Board. For the past fourteen years, by which time Proteus was at Ilium, a single national Manufacturing Council has unified a complex bureaucratic network dominating all aspects of American life, even education. After the war, when the workers finally returned, riots were put down and antisabotage laws enacted. (In Vonnegut's desire to deal with the here-and-now of mid-century America, his chronology becomes ambiguous, to say the least.) Now resentment, anguish, and idleness simmer in Homestead. When the shah labels the result Communism, his guides assure him that industry remains in private hands. The government simply takes as taxes that portion of income that industry used to spend as wages and redistributes it to the Reeks and Wrecks. Private enterprise and the welfare state coalesce.

In the name of industrial progress automation continues its incursions. An aging barber in Miami Beach, for example, hopes that "barber machines" will not be introduced in that city for another two years—until he retires. Uneasy with the Frankenstein that he has helped create, Proteus speaks of the now dominant Second Industrial Revolution, which has "devalued routine mental work." Citing Norbert Wiener, he suggests that a third one has already begun, when "thinking machines"—like the specialized EPICAC XIV, whose nervous system of vacuum tubes and wires fills Carlsbad Caverns—will "devaluate human thinking." Vonnegut's attack moves between the notion that machines have deprived the individual of a sense of being needed and useful and the suggestion that limits be placed on the scope of machines. He echoes Bradbury when he denounces mass popular culture because it reduces all things to the lowest denominator. The hierarchy, for example, shapes all advertising and writing for one of twelve possible audiences and allows no printed work to exceed a fixed reading quotient. Again paralleling Bradbury, Vonnegut pictures TV as the opiate of the Reeks and the Wrecks.

He dramatizes the plight of a society caught between a dehumanizing industrialism and an equally de-

DECADE OF TRANSITION

humanizing primitivism. The shah visits the home of "statistically average" Edgar Rice Burroughs Hagstrohm in a Chicago housing development. Hagstrohm hates civilization and worships Tarzan as much as his father did. Unfaithful to his fat wife, he finally runs amok, destroying his house with a blowtorch and running naked into a bird sanctuary. Restless with growing questions about the system and wanting to escape modern conveniences, Paul Proteus buys an old farmhouse and its land. He wants to retire as soon as possible and work with his hands. But his wife Anita sees the oldest house in the valley as nothing but a place to scavenge for antiques. Undoubtedly the most comic and razor-edged sequence involves the annual two-week encampment at the Meadows, where the most deserving members of the Ilium elite join together in highly ritualized ceremonies emphasizing team sports and community. They are thoroughly indoctrinated, as in a new miracle play in which God is replaced by "the Sky Manager," who assures them of how much they have done for "John Averageman." The entire matter of the Meadows recalls the satire of Sinclair Lewis in *Babbitt*.

The problem in *Player Piano*—and it may well be the key to its continuing relevance—is that Vonnegut knows there is no easy solution, no end to the dilemma. Abruptly, without seeming to realize the extent of Proteus's discontent, the hierarchy asks him to infiltrate the Ghost Shirt Society. This rebellious group within management takes its name from the Ghost Dance religion of the Plains Indians of the late nineteenth century. A precipitate revolt—touched off by a call to arms signed by Proteus—fails. Neither traitor nor messiah, Paul is arrested. But mobs in Homestead riot, destroying all the machines, even the sewage disposal system. A final scene crystallizes humanity's predicament—and Vonnegut's awareness of it. Defeated and surrounded by the establishment, the brains of the Ghost Shirt Society watch as a skilled workman repairs an "Orango-O" Machine so that everyone can have a can of pop, while a youngster asks if anyone has seen a one-eighth horsepower electric motor that isn't "busted up too bad." America will yet be a player piano.

Vonnegut's first novel is memorable because it exposes the nerve ends of the United States just as the nation entered a period of unequaled industrial expansion and innovation after the war. Particularly in addressing the issue of a third industrial revolution, Vonnegut keyed in on a problem inherent in modern industrial society. Technology never remains static; nor does it go away. It develops exponentially, always confronting society with new tensions as the world develops toward a global Ilium. Yet undoubtedly hurt and angered by his experience with GE, Vonnegut had not yet distanced himself enough from his personal involvement to find the casually nihilistic tone which characterizes his later satire. That would emerge at the end of the decade in *The Sirens of Titan*.

DECADE OF TRANSITION

As Bradbury and Vonnegut enlarged the science fiction audience and gained it new critical appreciation, the new magazines made their contributions. *The Magazine of Fantasy and Science Fiction* showed that while the premises on which SF and fantasy usually build are distinct from one another, both belong to a common literary heritage. By the end of the decade, quietly emphasizing literary quality, *F&SF* was twice named the finest magazine in the field. The impact of *Galaxy* was more immediate and obvious. In 1953, the first year Hugo Awards were given, it shared with *Astounding* the best magazine award. In editorials in its earliest issues (1950) Gold had directly challenged Campbell's concept of the field. *Galaxy* wanted stories "too adult, too profound, or revolutionary in concept" to be sold elsewhere; Gold asked for narratives "extrapolating possibilities, not approving present trends."[4] He abandoned the scientist/engineer/technician as his desired audience, aiming instead at the general public—the average citizen—affected by scientific and technological discoveries and innovations. While he lamented the "gloom and doom" tone of much current SF, he did show a partiality for those stories critical of society. A catalogue of titles, many now regarded as classics, could be named.

Among those writers contributing to *Galaxy* whose works were published in book form during the 1950s, the most successful satirists were the team of Frederik Pohl and Cyril M. Kornbluth. Not unlike Vonnegut with General Electric, Pohl had worked after the war for a

Madison Avenue ad agency and had begun a SF novel about the future of advertising. As Vonnegut had responded to the American expansion of technology, so Pohl reacted to the innovative, newly flourishing field of advertising. Quite simply, he hated it. Yet he could not finish his novel until an old friend, Kornbluth, joined him. (It may be that collaboration with Kornbluth served as a necessary distancing device.) Gold serialized the novel as *Gravy Train* during the summer of 1952, and Pohl gave it a final polish before it was issued as *The Space Merchants* (1953). A success at once, it has never been out of print in English-language editions. Science fiction reviewers compared it favorably to *Brave New World* and *Player Piano*, while in 1960 Kingsley Amis assured it a place in the literary canon by calling it probably "the best science-fiction novel so far."[5] Certainly one reason that it caught on so quickly was that it extrapolated the topical satire of Frederic Wakeman's *The Hucksters* (1946) into the early twenty-first century.

Because the narrative is presented in the first person, the novel never exists outside the consciousness of Mitchell Courtenay, "Copysmith first class" in the major firm of Fowler Shocken Associates. The point of departure for the story line is the appointment of Courtenay as head of Fowler Shocken's Venus Section, a project to colonize an inhospitable Venus with eighteen hundred Americans. In a sense, like Paul Proteus, Courtenay is caught betwixt and between: corporate rivals of Fowler Shocken attempt to kill him so that they

DECADE OF TRANSITION

may have a chance to take over the project, while members of the World Conservationist Association try to keep him alive and convert him so that he will abandon the project. He, of course, does not know who is on which side. An element of pessimism enters because the project must succeed.

Venus must be colonized and opened up by persons who will immediately become consumers if the world trade market is to continue growing. By the early twenty-first century Earth has become heavily overpopulated, while its ecology has been irreversibly damaged. Its resources have been virtually exhausted; its people must be fed with synthetic protein derived from tropical hydroponic farms growing algae. Just as the advertising agencies and corporations have ruined Earth and the moon, so will any one of them ruin Venus. What gives the satire its cutting edge is that corporate business knows full well what it has done and what it will continue to do in order to show a profit and control the market. Since the advertising agencies control the government (they elect Congress and appoint the President), their efforts are enthusiastically applauded. Because Courtenay believes in the system at the outset, he serves as an ideal narrator. More fool than hero, he gives a straightforward, at times almost naïve report of the scene. Although Pohl and Kornbluth dwelt on the problems of overpopulation and ecological imbalance more than any of their predecessors, detailed social criticism for its own sake is conspicuously absent, primarily because of the choice of narrator. Thus the machinations of plot action continue until Courtenay and his wife—secretly an agent of the "Consies," as members of the World Conservationist Association are called—depart on the spaceship for Venus. At best Courtenay's enlightenment and the future of both Venus and Earth are unresolved, ambiguous.

Plot action again takes precedence in *Gladiator-at-Law* (1955), serialized in *Galaxy* (1954) before book publication. In this instance the collaborators focus on the legal profession. Again the backdrop is dystopian. A century in the future monopolistic corporations dominate a polarized society. They control the social structure in that they give their contractual employees climate-controlled, automated homes—the earliest form of the bubble houses and cities so important to Pohl's later fiction. The rest of the people live in decayed neighborhoods terrorized by teen-aged gangs, as is Belly Rave (Belle Reve Estates), a run-down, post-World War II development. The masses are narcotized by Roman circus-like field days, violent pageants carefully planned by "emotional engineers." The story line follows the efforts of a young lawyer to win back control of the homes from the G.M.L. corporation for the heirs of their inventor, who had been forced out of the firm. The evil of the corporations, however, is embodied in the seemingly immortal archvillains, Mrs. Green and Mr. Charlesworth, figures symbolic of the use of power for its own sake. A third work that resulted from a collaboration—

this time Pohl and Lester del Rey—*Preferred Risk* (1955) takes on the insurance business, but shifts its scene to Italy and becomes enmeshed in plot action involving cryonics and a cobalt bomb. Perhaps these latter two works do not have the staying power of *The Space Merchants* because the writers did not have the depth of background (and anger?) that Pohl had in advertising; nor did either novel have the topical impact arising from the flowering of postwar advertising. Yet in all three, against the background of a dystopian future, the pattern of action remains the same: individuals oppose essentially faceless powers of the establishment who are manipulating the public.

For whatever reasons, many critics have slighted Pohl and Kornbluth's *Search the Sky* (1954). Some leftist criticism dismisses the novel as a defense of capitalism and free trade. Its episodic structure gives succinct portraits of a variety of cultures which might arise in a human-dominated galaxy, for the narrative becomes an odyssey as the young protagonist attempts to learn why communication between the planets has broken down. Throughout, its satire is topical. After a perfunctory glimpse of a world destroyed by nuclear holocausts, the protagonist finds a planet venerating its oldsters, who govern in the name of morality and religion, rigorously controlling the sexual behavior of its youth. Part of the satire aims at the efforts of medical science to keep the oldsters alive, whatever their condition. A second world, though no feminist utopia, is dominated by its women, who allow no egalitarianism whatsoever; some of the women—especially the space pilots—are the sexual aggressors. On the planet Jones a totalitarian police state rules a populace bred so narrowly that they replicate one another. They are all Joneses. Although at some indefinite time in the past warfare had produced a communist world state, the authorities have forgotten any political principles and maintain the status quo by not allowing any deviation from the physical norm. But the most telling satire is aimed at Earth itself when the collaborators make use of the premise basic to Kornbluth's "The Marching Morons" (1954). Partly because the less capable have bred more frequently than the intellectuals and partly because the smartest and most daring individuals have for centuries abandoned an impoverished Earth in favor of space exploration and planet colonizing, the intellectual ability of Earth-bound humanity has bottomed out at a level reducing everything to fun and games, to great size and vivid colors. A secret elite—the Guardians—protect the masses from their excesses and their machines (the speedometers of the automobiles, for example, are rigged to suggest faster speeds.) Earth is crowded by ten billion people who play their way through the here-and-now.

In such a picaresque novel the protagonists are caught in a pattern of capture and escape which dominates the story line. Yet the sketches of the societies are memorable, if unfortunately brief, while several basic ideas—overpopulation and conformity—are hammered home. Certainly misuse of power shapes the theme, although the ending suggests that a deliberate mixing of the genetic pool can rebuild and revitalize the community of worlds. At times one senses an almost conscious parody of the field itself as the collaborators somewhat distort familiar SF devices, like the "generation" ship, to effect their satire.

If the satire of Pohl and Kornbluth produces good-natured observers who tend to be antiheroes because they do not control the action—Mitchell Courtenay provides the best example—then the best fiction of Alfred Bester, as in the novels *The Demolished Man* (1953) and *The Stars My Destination* (1957), concentrates on obsessed men driven to, if not beyond, the borders of sanity. He himself has said that he wrote about "Man, contemporary Man, subjected to wild, free, unusual stresses and conflicts."[6] After writing for the pulps, comic books, and radio for some ten years, he returned to SF in the 1950s, publishing almost exclusively in *Galaxy* and *F&SF*. Under the tutelage of Horace Gold—for Bester, "the ideal editor, always helpful, always encouraging"[7]—he completed *The Demolished Man*. Writers like Samuel R. Delany and Norman Spinrad have praised him as a forerunner of the shift in SF that took place during the 1960s and early 1970s. He was an innovator in that he brought to the field an emphasis on psychological study of character that it had not known earlier.

Frequently referring to SF as his "safety valve, an escape hatch, therapy," he brought a Freudian dimension to SF at the time that Campbell was promoting Dianetics.

Although *The Demolished Man* uses a murder as its point of departure, it is not a puzzle story, for one watches the ruthless Ben Reich, head of the interplanetary conglomerate Monarch, plan and carry out the killing of his chief competitor, Craye D'Courtney. The narrative shifts back and forth between Reich and Lincoln Powell as it pits the criminal mind against that of the prefect of police. The novel becomes science fiction because, at Gold's suggestion, the crime takes place in a twenty-fourth-century society whose law, order, and destiny are controlled by Espers—"peepers"—those humans who have developed as telepaths. As the first successful murderer in seventy-nine years Reich must block the powers of Powell, who belongs to that small minority within the Esper Guild who have full telepathic powers. The conflict between Reich and Powell highlights the story line, while it also dramatizes Bester's theme in that the deranged psyche of the killer struggles against the community of mind readers who hold the key to humanity's future. Not only does Reich corrupt individual Espers, but he has long financed a movement which could break the Guild, seeking to keep Espers an "exclusive class, . . . an aristocracy" because of the "unsuitability of the average man for Esper training" (69), although the Guild hopes to educate everyone to use the power latent within each human

DECADE OF TRANSITION

mind. Frequently Reich declares that he will impose his will on the entire system of human worlds; several times he compares himself to God.

While accurate, this summary does not convey the impact of *The Demolished Man*. Fresh from writing mystery scripts, as he admitted, Bester abandoned the mechanical hardware of magazine SF except for an occasional "neuron scrambler" or "harmonic gun" and casual reference to interplanetary travel. Instead, he relied on settings ranging from the Disneylike Spaceland on an asteroid near Jupiter to what seem garish embellishments of urban scenes reminiscent of Raymond Chandler or Dashiell Hammett, as well as satire of a decadent upperclass, to provide background for a flamboyant exploration of Freudian psychology. At times his swift-moving narrative becomes a psychedelic splash of color when he sketches scenes or a typographical jigsaw when he represents the party conversation of telepaths—characteristics more expected from comic books than a straightforward narrative.

These techniques highlight another aspect of both of Bester's novels. Granted that extrasensory powers (ESP) were not new to SF in the 1950s, they had undergone an interesting development. Perhaps best known for "Final Blackout" (*Astounding*, 1940, book publication 1948), L. Ron Hubbard had formulated what he called an exact science of psychotherapy which would "uncover the SUPERHUMAN that is latent" in everyone.[8] In an editorial, "Dianetics, the Evolution of a Science"

SCIENCE FICTION: THE 1950s

(May 1950), Campbell momentarily embraced the field. While Hubbard formalized his beliefs into Scientology, actually opening the Church of Scientology in 1955, Campbell had recanted by the end of 1951. He remained fascinated with parapsychology and the need for an exact science of the mind. Possibly taking the term from a story by Murray Leinster, although one cannot be certain, Campbell published an editorial, "Psionic Machine-Type One" (June 1956). As a result of Campbell's endorsement psi powers became a given attribute of supermen in the 1950s. (Psionics largely replaced the term ESP to describe the ability of a person to manipulate matter or human minds by psychic power; telepathy, teleportation, telekinesis, and precognition were chief among the attributes of those persons having psi powers.) Bester championed psionics in *The Stars My Destination*, although he had included unexplained, "unexpected chemotropisms" (54) to augment the seeming genetic basis of the Freudian ties among his characters in *The Demolished Man*.

One first sees Reich awakening—screaming—from a recurrent nightmare of "The Man With No Face." Although D'Courtney has agreed to the merger, Reich rejects his friendly overtures and shoots the older, voiceless man dying of throat cancer; he several times calls D'Courtney "The Man With No Face." Barbara D'Courtney enters the room and, in shock at her father's death, flees into the night. Only later does one learn that Reich is the illegitimate son of D'Courtney, so that Barbara,

DECADE OF TRANSITION

obviously, is his half-sister. Her apprehension becomes pivotal to the story line. Reich must eliminate her as the only witness, while Powell must force her psychologically to return to infancy and mature again—a process taking some three weeks—so that she can cleanse her psyche of its trauma and supply the eyewitness details needed by the policeman. (In the process of growing up again, Barbara happily accepts Powell as a surrogate father, declares her love for "Daddy," and wants to marry him. The only impediment to this romance vanishes when Powell understands that he may marry her because she is a latent Esper, having come to the scene of the crime because she heard her father's mental outcry. The Freudian ties are knotted.)

Bester's skill is most effective as he peels away the onionskin layers of Reich's mind. Reich leaves his sanity ever further behind as he attempts desperately to escape the consequences of his lust for power. Only after Powell's case based on economic motive (the merger) collapses does Powell "peep" Reich sufficiently to learn how dangerous he is to the future. Immediately Powell asks the Esper Council to allow him to subject the madman to "Mass Cathexsis" because Reich is "the deadly enemy of Galactic reason and reality" and will lead the world to "utter destruction" (145). He is "one of those rare World-shakers whose compulsions might have torn down our society and irrevocably committed us to his own psychotic pattern," thereby chaining humanity to "a dreadful tomorrow" (169). The issue, of course, is power; from the name *Reich* one wonders whether Bester thought of Hitler.

Drawing upon the combined psychic powers of all the Espers, Powell overwhelms Reich psychologically, isolating him in his subconscious mind so that he must confront and acknowledge the identity of "The Man With No Face." Only then can "demolition" take place—the destruction and rebuilding of his psyche so that he can take a positive place in society. Powell declares that the world will be "a wonderful place" when everyone is an Esper; when Reich, halfway through his treatment, calls him "friend," Powell cries out in a passage recalling such writers as Edward Bellamy, who saw in telepathy a panacea for the illnesses of society:

Listen, normals! . . . You must tear the barriers down. You must tear the veils away. We see the truth you cannot see. . . . That there is nothing in man but love and faith, courage and kindness, generosity and sacrifice. All else is only the barrier of your blindness. One day we'll all be mind to mind and heart to heart (175).

Thus does Bester invoke his vision of a unified humanity, freed from the torment of the isolated ego. One may join with those who have questioned the viability of such idealism amid the violence of the novel, but the message may have been what many readers in the United States in the mid-50s wanted to hear. In 1953 *The Demolished Man* won the first Hugo given a novel at a

DECADE OF TRANSITION

Worldcon; in 1954 it was runner-up for the International Fantasy Award.

Essential to Bester's thinking was the premise that humanity "can develop unusual powers—telepathy, teleportation, and physical immortality—under unusual stress, and that once developed, these powers can be taught to others."[9] *The Stars My Destination* (published in Britain as *Tiger, Tiger*) achieves an even fuller statement of his theme because it focuses on a single character, Gully Foyle, who changes the future of the human race. Before turning to his protagonist, however, Bester sketches the "seething background" against which these actions take place. Quite by chance, although the distance varies with the individual, humanity has learned that it has the power of teleportation. The ability to move oneself from one place to another instantaneously ("jaunting") unlocks "yet another resource of [humanity's] limitless mind" so that the solar system trembles "on the verge of a human explosion that would transform man and make him the master of the universe" (8, 13). Whatever its potential, jaunting brings about warfare between the Inner Planets and the Outer Satellites, breaking down a delicate balance between them analogous to the nineteenth-century European nations and their colonies. In the twenty-fifth century the eleven worlds enter "the shooting phase of a commercial struggle" (92). Just as the political backdrop of *The Demolished Man* implies a struggle between great corporations, so *The Stars My Destination* denounces imperialism and the power structure behind it—both views in keeping with the climate of the 1950s.

Granting that Gully Foyle is another superman, some read his history as a tale of redemption. Like Reich, he is a driven man. As Reich was haunted by "The Man With No Face," so Foyle is confronted by "The Burning Man," although the latter is not a manifestation of his subconscious mind. Only Gully Foyle fails to recognize the figure as he himself.

Bester introduces Foyle as a "stereotype Common Man" without education, skills, or merit, a brute who "has reached a dead end. . . . And death's [his] destination" (14, 15). Adrift and near dead on the derelict *Nomad* in the asteroid belt, he "awakens" to be driven to a craving for vengeance only after the *Vorga-T: 1339* ignores his distress signal. That he is little more than an animal is underscored when a "savage" culture on the Sargasso Asteroid tattoos his face, giving him tiger stripes. (A later operation removes the dye, but the stigmata flame blood red whenever he grows violent.) The story line pits Foley against the owner of *Vorga*, Presteign, head of Clan Presteign, a member of the oligarchy made up of the families who own the great corporations dominating the Inner Worlds.

One of Presteign's minions has developed a thermonuclear weapon, PyrE, which can be detonated only by thought—psychokinesis. All existent PyrE was secreted aboard the *Nomad*—together, conveniently, with platinum bullion valued at twenty million credits. Since

DECADE OF TRANSITION

Presteign wants to force Foyle to reveal the location of the *Nomad*, the first part of the novel falls into a routine of imprisonments and escapes climaxing when Foyle gains possession of the PyrE and bullion.

Again Bester played with color and typography/ graphics, but more than anything else the brevity of the narrative and the complexity of the action—the legacy of magazine publication—help to create the "pyrotechnic effect" so praised by subsequent writers. It is as though one is given brief film clips often without transition and necessary exposition. Abruptly, the second part of the novel pictures Foyle as the aristocratic young buffoon Geoffrey Fourmyle of Ceres (an identity given him briefly during "therapy" by previous captors), who gains entry into decadent high society to pursue his vengeance. He jaunts to various parts of the world as he seeks information about the original voyage of the *Nomad*. In addition, he has undergone an operation: "Every nerve plexus had been rewired, microscopic transistors and transformers had been buried in muscle and bone, a minute platinum outlet showed at the base of his spine" (95). No mere cyborg, he has been transformed into "the most murderous machine ever devised . . . the Commando killer" (133). In this image one sees perhaps the earliest form of the complex, augmented being who has grown ever more fascinating to writers from the 1960s to the 1980s.

For much of the narrative he seems incapable of

compassion. Despite the aid of two women—Robin Wednesday and Jizbella McQueen—whom he treats detestably, actually raping Robin during their first encounter, Foyle's most grotesque love-hate relationship involves Lady Olivia, the blind albino daughter of Presteign. They first embrace as nuclear bombs fall on New York, he afraid and cursing her, she hailing the beauty of the radiation. With the aid of "The Burning Man," he learns that Olivia commanded the *Vorga* when the ship ignored his distress signal, for Olivia was about to dump six hundred war refugees from Callisto into space after robbing them. Picking Foyle up in space near Mars, Olivia assures him that only hatred and a desire for revenge because she was blind have ever motivated her private life; she insists that the lives of no one else matter: "We stand apart and shape our own world. We're the strong" (159). Abruptly, even as he protests that he will always love her, Gully Foyle calls them both "loathsome"; the savage—the tiger—in him has been replaced by the compulsion to set things right, for mere "purging . . . with punishment isn't enough"; moreover, any "man who gives his own decision priority over society is a criminal" (167).

Only then is he told that an Outer Satellites raider attacked the *Nomad* and took him, more dead than alive, with them to release in a space suit to act as a decoy attracting ships from the Inner Worlds into ambush. Under such stress he space-jaunted six hundred thousand miles back to the hulk of the *Nomad*, regaining consciousness just before the *Vorga* passed him by. Both sides want him for the PyrE, but his true value lies in his potential to teach humanity to jaunt through the vastness of space. Returning to his base in St. Patrick's Cathedral in New York, he is trapped when minuscule amounts of PyrE explode. The concussion makes him suffer synesthesia—a crossing of the senses—as, coated in flames, he time-jaunts uncontrollably. He becomes/encounters "The Burning Man." While Reich's confrontation with "The Man With No Face" was a necessary part of his demolition because of his crazed ego, Foyle's experience with "The Burning Man" leads to a growth of understanding. Recovered, during a meeting at Castle Presteign when the participants will decide who controls PyrE, Foyle rejects the view that "driven men, compelled men" must make the decisions, hold the power (192). Jaunting to major cities around the world, giving PyrE to people in each of them, he declares that the "common man's been whipped and led long enough by . . . Tiger men who can't help lashing the world before them." He challenges a hostile crowd in Piccadilly either to destroy themselves with PyrE or to seek him out so that he can "give [them] the stars" (194–95). Then he jaunts at will through the galaxy and at last returns to the Sargasso Asteroid, where, curled in a fetal ball, he awaits humanity's decision.

To read the novel as a celebration of individualism or as a tale of personal redemption both ignores the narrative's opening and oversimplifies the ending. *The*

Demolished Man and *The Stars My Destination* are complementary works sharing the same basic vision. Reich's
psyche is destroyed so that it may be rebuilt. Foyle
grows from an animal—a tiger—to a person with understanding. *The Stars My Destination* demonstrates that being a physical superman without wisdom is worthless.
But the narrative is open-ended. Foyle will teach, if that
is humanity's decision. Between book publication of *The
Stars My Destination* and the 1970s, Bester wrote fewer
than a half dozen short stories, working during that
interval as a senior editor of *Holiday*. Although two late
novels, *The Computer Connection* (1975) and *Golem100* (1980),
fell short of readers' expectation, SFWA did give him the
Grand Master Award, posthumously, in 1988 as a measure of his continuing influence on the SF community.

During the same interval that Bester produced his
finest fiction, another writer who had moved from
Campbell's *Astounding* to *Galaxy* was making his distinc-
tive and enduring mark on the field. While Delany has
praised *The Stars My Destination* as perhaps the single
greatest science fiction novel, he has also declared that
Theodore Sturgeon's stories make up "the most important body of science fiction by an American author."[10]
Bester himself remarked that "Ted's writing exactly
suited my taste which is why I thought he was the finest
of us all."[11] To say that Sturgeon has been uniformly
praised as a stylist is one of those often-repeated ver-
dicts needing to be made specific and vivid by such a
judgment as that of Scholes and Rabkin: "He made lan-

guage itself important. He made style count."[12] Since Sturgeon's primary concern was always to capture his characters at a moment of self-revelation which simultaneously spoke to the makeup of human nature and the weaknesses in the facade of modern society, his shorter fiction may provide the basis for his lasting reputation, but during the 1950s he published three novels, all exploring the theme of the superman and human potential, although very differently from Bester.

The most famous of these, *More Than Human* (1953), grew from a novella originally appearing in *Galaxy*, "Baby Is Three" (Oct. 1952). The hasty summary almost everyone used in describing its contents—Sturgeon brings together a number of outcast "freaks" who have a variety of psionic powers and slowly develop into an advanced form of humanity, *Homo Gestalt*—misses both the nuances of his craftsmanship and the full display of his most persistent theme. He crystallizes that central concern through dramatizing the anguish and loneliness of characters isolated within themselves and unable to communicate because of the preconceptions and hypocrisy of society. For Sturgeon, love—almost invariably expressed through sexuality—provides the means of communication. Thus the choice of "freaks" and a SF backdrop simply heighten the impact of this theme.

Nowhere is this better shown than in the opening sequences of *More Than Human*. The first of a series of quick scenes introduces "the idiot . . . purely animal" who has within him "a thing which only received and

recorded" but has no outlet. His latent potential awakens when, telepathically, he hears the outpourings of a
young teen-ager, Evelyn Kew, the younger daughter of
a self-righteous maniac who abhors the human body,
particularly a woman's body, as the source of evil. In
this grotesque context, drawn by Evelyn's thoughts—
"floods of . . . loneliness and expectancy and hunger,
gladness and sympathy"—the idiot and the girl meet
by a forest pool. Suddenly her father comes upon them,
whipping the idiot brutally. When Evelyn attacks him,
he clubs his daughter with the whip handle and flees
to the house, where he shoots himself. Searching for
Evelyn, Alicia, her older sister, finds her dying and assures her that wanting to be touched—"love"—is "madness . . . bad" (1–15).

The flow of emotion between Evelyn and the idiot
has given him a new awareness. Badly beaten, he is
nursed by a farm couple, the Prodds, and remains with
the couple for some five years until Mrs. Prodd is pregnant. Realizing then that they kept him not for himself
but as a substitute for a long-wanted son, he moves on
into the woods, although he does not break off the relationship completely. The narrative shifts to the child
Janie, a telepath, and to the tongue-tied black twins,
Bonnie and Beanie, who have the gift of teleportation.
To escape Janie's uncaring mother, Janie and the twins
run away, joining Lone, as the idiot calls himself. These
four unusual persons assemble at Lone's hideaway in
the woods, but they do not understand their potential.

DECADE OF TRANSITION

When the longed-for Prodd baby proves to be a mongol-oid, Lone takes Baby to his shelter. At once Baby com-municates with the twins, who tell Janie that he is "like an adding machine"—a computer, "a figure-outer brain." Baby accepts this role. Almost incidentally, through Janie, Baby instructs Lone how to build a de-vice turning the Prodd's abandoned truck into an "anti-gravity generator." More importantly thematically, Baby explains that the five of them are a single being, *Homo Gestalt*.

One must remember that only after the success of "Baby Is Three" did Sturgeon write—perhaps "gerry-mander" is an appropriate word—the introductory sec-tion of the novel. From Lone's initial awakening because of Evelyn through the years with the Prodds to his realization that he is part of the new being, the story is his. The rest of the novel concerns itself with the growth of *Homo Gestalt*. Artistically the second portion, "Baby Is Three," is Sturgeon's tour de force: the first-person narrative of Gerry Thompson's session with the psychotherapist Stern. It is a tale of transfer of power. When Lone rescues Gerry, Baby recognizes him as Lone's successor (70, 75). Although Gerry can join in the group's "bleshing" (blending, meshing), he envies them because they can do things he cannot. After Lone's accidental death, Gerry follows his instructions and takes the younger children to Alicia Kew. Alicia's attempts first to segregate the twins and then send Baby to an asylum fail, but when Gerry realizes that she has

imposed her life style on them and they can no longer
blesh, he kills her so that his *"gestalt* organism" will
survive. The turmoil of his guilt leads him to the psychotherapist.

The structure of the third part of the novel parallels
that of "Baby Is Three" in that Janie helps Hip Barrows,
once a brilliant engineer and mathematician but now
an amnesiac, recapture the events of the past seven
years. In both stories the precedent action is offstage so
that Sturgeon can emphasize character. Because Hip
discovered the Prodd truck and realized its potential,
he became Gerry's victim. Already paranoid, sick with
fear that his group will be discovered, Gerry not only
discredits Hip so that he is discharged from the army
but gives him the posthypnotic suggestion that he grow
sick and die. Realizing that the group is no longer
healthy and growing, and tired of Gerry's "casual vi-
ciousness" (170), Janie rescues Hip from jail and undertakes his rehabilitation. Janie holds the key to Gerry's
power, for she is his link with Baby; although the mon-
goloid receives everyone, he does not speak to Gerry
(173, 180). And Janie is torn between her love for Hip
and her loyalty to the *gestalt* group: "We're a single entity, a new kind of human being . . . living on a desert
island with a herd of goats" (170). She frets because
Homo Gestalt is alone, without a morality, with only
Gerry's capricious childishness and fear of discovery.
In a final confrontation Hip shows Gerry the *gestalt's*
potential and provides an ethical basis for conduct: the

DECADE OF TRANSITION

"individual's code for society's survival," always help-
ing humanity as a whole (178, 183). Sturgeon had first
voiced this concept in his earlier novel, *The Dreaming
Jewels* (1950, later entitled *The Synthetic Man*), but in
More than Human he achieves his fullest statement of the
theme. At Janie's behest, Hip realizes that he can be
part of the group—its conscience: "the prissy one who
can't forget the rules" (186). In this rapport between the
nontelepathic Hip and the group, Sturgeon achieved a
reconciliation which stands in sharp contrast to the
often bloody confrontations between human and superman in so many scenarios—from Beresford's *The
Hampdenshire Wonder* (1911) to Stapledon's *Odd John*
(1935) and van Vogt's *Slan* (1946).

At least twice Sturgeon faced backward toward the
turn of the century when he wondered why the next
step in evolution should not be psychic rather than
physical (109, 177), and at one point Hip reflects upon
man much as Simak did in *City* (177). Baby echoes
something of the inflated promises of the period when
he suggests that "gravitics is the key to everything. It
would lead to the addition of one more item to the
United Field—what we now call psychic energy, or
'psionics'" (166). In terms of publication dates in *Galaxy*,
it is intriguing that both Bester's Ben Reich and Sturgeon's
Gerry Thompson are described as "obsessed men."

The final scene anchors *More Than Human* to mid-
century American texts. Once *Homo Gestalt* has gained
its conscience, a voice welcomes Gerry as a new mem-

ber of the immortal circle who have long guided humanity toward its destiny; for them "atomic war is a ripple
on the broad face of the Amazon" (188). Yet even as
Sturgeon echoes this central concern of his contemporaries, he reasserts his uniqueness, and underscores a
mystical humanism, in that the *gestalts* unite into a single "Guardian of Whom all humans know" not separate
from, but identical to humanity. To read *More Than Human* primarily as a science fiction "icon of the monster,"
as Gary Wolfe does,[13] seems to overlook Sturgeon's
themes and mysticism. In 1954, the year that *The Demolished Man* was runner-up, *More Than Human* gained the
International Fantasy Award.

Later in the decade Sturgeon returned to the theme
of human advancement in *The Cosmic Rape* (1958), an
expansion of the novelette of the same year, "To Marry
Medusa." The Medusa, a hive-mind which absorbs all
the sentient beings it encounters, cannot comprehend
the psychological isolation of its host, the man Gurlick.
The story line centers on the efforts of the Medusa to
join the people of Earth into a single unit as a necessary
preliminary to absorption. Fused into a collective mind
of its own, humanity overwhelms the Medusa "with the
Self of humankind" as it floods every corner of the galaxy to survive and love, "full of wonder, full of worship." Despite sketches of confused, lonely humans,
because so much of the narrative focuses on the
schemes of the Medusa, one accepts such abrupt tran-

scendence only because it lies at the heart of Sturgeon's continuing vision.

Too often in the 1950s, in stories ranging from James Blish's *Jack of Eagles* (1952) to Frank Robinson's *The Power* (1956), for example, human mutation involving increased intelligence merely served as another point of departure for such established story lines as a struggle for power. Although many of the actions conventional to SF adventures of the period are present in Poul Anderson's first novel, *Brain Wave* (1954), he downplays them or takes them offstage so that he can explore the social and philosophical consequences of a single premise which in itself sets him apart from many of his contemporaries. For millions of years—going back at least to the Cretaceous Period—the solar system has traveled through an area of space in which a force field inhibited certain electromagnetic and electrochemical processes, most importantly the flow of neurone signals to the cerebral cortex. When Earth emerges, the signals are speeded up so that the intelligence of both humans and animals is quickly and drastically enhanced. Madness often results, for the increase overloads a complex, efficient nervous system which had ages ago compensated for the inhibition. Headlines trace the collapse of organized society; made desperate by revolution, Russia impulsively attacks New York, but a newly developed shield detonates the warheads. Using a starship powered by "psi-drive,"Peter Corinth explores the galaxy, finding intelligent life on fourteen of nineteen worlds hurriedly scanned. An infuriated, antiscientific mob, made up of followers of a new, orgiastic religion, are sent searching for those who built the "big bomb"; a conspiracy of individuals—a scientist, an Indian mystic, and a French philosopher among them—who question the worth of intelligence and long for the old beliefs is quickly ended on a Pacific island.

All of the familiar ingredients are there, but Anderson compresses them, sometimes at a cost to the smoothness of his narrative. Similarly, the presence of a love story indicates his awareness of his audience. But all those elements provide the backdrop, for his interests lie elsewhere. Although he follows the simple-minded farm laborer, Archie Brock, as he grows in understanding and enters a compatible relationship with newly intelligent animals, Anderson gives center stage to his probings of the reflections of Peter Corinth, a physicist whose IQ has escalated to the 500 range. At one point Corinth does toast the passing of "animal man," and at another he hails the advent of "Protean man—intellectual man—infinity" (118), although simultaneously rejecting immortality because a man would be "smothered under the weight of his own experience, the potentialities of his nervous system would be exhausted." Prior to his journey through a portion of the galaxy, his imagination is fired by *the stars! By Heaven, the stars!* (96).

To see *Brain Wave* as the emergence of another su-

perman simplifies the complexities of his speculations
and thereby overlooks concerns that reveal Anderson's
individuality. Corinth's voice also adds another dimension to the mid-century dilemma and anxiety. Most simply, he remains unsure of the future. He stands as
though between two worlds, one dead, the other as yet
unborn—because the change had stripped a humanity
living in fear and superstition of its entire cultural background and, as yet, there had been no time to rebuild
"not only its technology, but its whole value system, all
its dreams and hopes" (77). Repeatedly he denounces a
society which offered " . . . disease, war, oppression,
want . . . from the filthy birth to the miserable grave,"
without "hope . . . vision . . . purpose" (151). At one
point he declares that humanity has no "symbol, . . .
no myth, no dream" (86). But unlike so many of his
colleagues, both in America and abroad, Anderson rejected collectivism. On a distant world he saw a humanoid race "so completely and inflexibly organized that
individuality was lost . . . as antlike routine took the
place of thought" (120). Although, like Arthur C. Clarke
and others, he thinks that "the stars are the answer,"
he rejects either "galactic empire" or a silent guardian-
ship of alien worlds "till their races get too flabby to
stand on their own feet" (161). His journey outward to
the stars is no easy, triumphant progression. In the SF
of the 1950s he offers the most existential future. His
mind cannot "encompass . . . the great silence" of the

cosmos. Even though man may "reach forth till the cosmos itself perished, he would still accomplish nothing
against its unheeding immensity." And yet he is hope-
ful; the universe's "chill hugeness" may draw "men together, seeking each other for company. It might make
them kinder to all life" (119).

The casual reference by one of Corinth's colleagues
to the "neurological-psychological" work dealing with
the change leads to Mark Clifton and Frank Riley's
They'd Rather Be Right (winner of a Hugo in 1955, though
not published in book form until 1957). They offered
still another solution for the uncertainties of the future.
In an earlier story by Clifton and Alex Apostolides for
Astounding, "Hide! Hide! Witch!" (1953), the protagonists—a cyberneticist, the telepathic Joe, and a dean of
Psychosomatic Research—build a complex computer ("a
servomechanism") intended to prevent a moving vehicle from any collision. In a society which equates science
and witchcraft, the public fears that "Bossy"—the name
given the "thing" by the Animal Husbandry Department of the university—will prove capable of "replacing
man." In the face of mounting, nationwide hostility, the
protagonists disassemble the computer and flee the
campus. (Despite a difference in tone and a language
which recalls Campbell and Hubbard, the story deals
with some of the concerns behind Vonnegut's *Player
Piano*.) In San Francisco, as soon as they realize that
Bossy can tell right from wrong, they use the computer

DECADE OF TRANSITION

in psychotherapy. Bossy rejuvenates and regenerates an aging ex-prostitute, Mabel, giving her immortality. At once a complex struggle for control of Bossy takes over the story line, as does a debate insisting that the only persons who can be "cured" are those not holding fast to any restrictive system of beliefs, whether moral, political, or scientific. At the end, however, as "psionic communion" engulfs Mabel and several of her admirers, Bossy helps with a plan to give immortality to everyone.

However dated such novels as these may seem, with their talk of psionics and the like, one must see in them a noteworthy response to the climate of the 1950s. Although a number of writers in various disciplines speak of the mediocrity and complacency of that decade, one must not forget that the postwar years saw as great a change in the American life style as had any previous period. The war had catapulted the entire world from the Great Depression into an era that no one had expected nor fully imagined—not even the early science fiction writers and readers, for SF has never proven to be a means of exact prediction. No list of particulars—from antibiotics to nylon and plastic, to TV and media advertising—can evoke the impact on the United States of those years almost two generations ago, but they let loose the forces that have shaped contemporary life. And over all the newness and potential of everyday life hung the paranoia emanating from McCarthyism. And the bomb! Frederick Lewis Allen may provoke snickers today with his speculations about "The New America" in *The Big Change* (1952), but he spoke to some of the matters addressed by these SF writers. Although they may sound outmoded, they expressed their discontent with postwar America and voiced a hope for the future.

However much subsequent writers have praised Bester, Sturgeon, and Anderson, the three sounded a minor chord. Others had struck the dominant tones when they sketched a dystopian future. Bradbury and Vonnegut were most widely heard. Although, as noted, Gold disavowed tales of gloom and doom, his predilection for satire and his willingness to see "what would happen if any given situation [was] carried to the utmost extremes" imaginable (June 1952) opened up *Galaxy* as a medium of social and political criticism. Kornbluth and Pohl's attack on advertising in *The Space Merchants* was soon broadened by others to include the entire business community. Writing alone, Pohl produced his lighthearted "The Midas Plague" (1954) and his shocking "Tunnel Under the World" (1955), variations of his attack on advertising and those persons controlling the consumer market.

Another advertising man, already famous for his *How to Succeed in Business Without Really Trying* (1952), Shepherd Mead produced a scenario of America in 1992, *The Big Ball of Wax* (1954), in which a public already manipulated by television is completely subjugated by a device allowing an individual to share vicariously the experience of another. Proclaiming the 1990s "the best of all possible worlds" in a memo intended for future executives of his corporation, the protagonist proudly explains how Madison Avenue employed his discovery to enslave the consumer market. The business community of Clifton's *They'd Rather Be Right* itself has taken over the government and keeps a closely supervised public in line with "opinion control." Although Dr. Kusko, the protagonist of Damon Knight's first novel, *Hell's Pavements* (1955), retitled *The Analogue Men)*, invents a device which—implanted in the brain—will modify human behavior, thereby eliminating violence, the conglomerates of the future, like United Merchandise (Umerc) and General Products (Gepro), which have divided North America among them, pervert any potential for good by manipulating the whims of the consumers. Uniformly, these writers pictured the American community victimized by power structures arising from present-day society.

Despite the vividness of these societies, the most effective dramatization of the conflict between the individual and the totalitarian state occurs in David Karp's *One* (1953), a Book-of-the-Month-Club selection. During a routine, periodic interview by a committee representing the department of Internal Examination, an English professor—Burden—is accused of heresies because he does not make the approved responses. At the hands of Lark the Inquisitor the resultant hearing becomes a brutal interrogation. The intensity increases as Karp focuses on the two men to the exclusion of all else, with Lark hammering at Burden: the individual good is identical to the national good; all citizens of the state assume the same obligations; without the state chaos would result. Lark mouths the basic hypocrisy of the political situation when he asserts that "the state, as directed by its citizens, determines reality"; and when he adds, "What one believes to be reality is reality" (238), he anticipates one of the concerns of Philip K. Dick and subsequent novelists. He brainwashes Burden in order to give him a new identity acceptable to the state—that of "Hughes." He is apparently successful, for Burden's funeral takes place at the university, but at the next interview Hughes is detained for interrogation because the deep-rooted sense of individuality in the man reappears. An implication also persists that Lark himself is an individual who does not believe in the doctrine he mouths.

Since the interrogation of Hughes suggests the possibility of a continuing stalemate, the most successful alternative to authoritarian domination came from Clifford D. Simak. Instead of either tyranny or a confrontation between corporations and scientists, as in the early fiction of Heinlein, where the scientists always win, in Simak's *Ring Around the Sun* (1953) a superior race of mutants not only threatens to disrupt world economy by introducing goods—ranging from razor blades to automobiles and houses—of higher quality and greater durability, but they also open up an endless chain of parallel Earths for colonization by persons dissatisfied with the present-day world. Like Heinlein, Simak offered humanity the opportunity to start afresh as pioneers; unlike Heinlein, he provided idyllic pastoral worlds: a fresh Earth "for each generation if need be" (144).

Among regular magazine writers he alone turned to a familiar mythologized past, for, as noted earlier, the great majority of his contemporaries accepted as a given the premise that the world would soon be devastated by nuclear warfare. Since the vision of impending holocaust was by no means limited to SF writers, one may regard it as the most pervasive measure of the psychological climate induced by the Cold War. The story lines fell into three categories. Occasional titles, like Agnew H. Bahnson, Jr.'s single venture into the field, *The Stars Are Too High* (1959), show successful efforts to avert war. Many simply chronicle some variation of the action. One of the most widely known at the time, Philip Wylie's *Tomorrow* (1954), allows at least fifteen American cities to be decimated—twenty million dead and injured, to say nothing of the rioting—before the United States retaliates by converting the first Nautilus atomic submarine into a monstrous hydrogen bomb and detonating it in the Baltic so that radiation sickness causes Russia to surrender. With aid from South America and Europe, the United States will rebuild.

Martin Caidin's *The Long Night* (1956) concentrates on the twenty-four hours after Soviet planes bomb the

SCIENCE FICTION: THE 1950s

city of Harrington, just long enough to show that the civil defense organization is able to contain the damage and begin to rectify the situation, while Robert B. Rigg's *War 1974* (1958) becomes little more than an assortment of battles in which the weapons are "the real characters"[14] during a year-long struggle between U.S. and Russo-Chinese forces who surrender because they are outgunned and outmaneuvered. In *Forbidden Area* (1956) Pat Frank (Harry Hart Frank) avoids a full nuclear war, although Russian submarines are sunk off the American coast after the Soviets impulsively threaten attack in order to prevent U.S. development of a superior ICBM. Frank closed out the decade with *Alas, Babylon* (1959), whose Florida setting escapes unscathed the nuclear attack on other areas of the United States; its protagonist, Randy Bragg, a lawyer and an individualist, organizes the populace of Fort Repose in a manner recalling frontier values. One infers from the title that so long as deeply entrenched American values survive, there may be no real loss.

In such narratives as these one may see the main thrust of the American response to the cold war. Ideologically the U.S. answer came in Taylor Caldwell's *The Devil's Advocate* (1952), in which patriots overthrow a socialist, totalitarian government which has kept the country in a series of wars, and Allen Drury's *Advise and Consent* (1959), the first of his novels to debate the need for firmness in dealing with Communism. Significantly, these novels represent the position by writers who are not identified with the science fiction community. One of the most notable works of the decade, Burt Cole's first novel, *Subi: The Volcano* (1957)—never reprinted—places an American army at its base near the rubble of a port city on the mainland of Asia. Although the Americans had successfully stormed ashore some time ago in a landing at Fish Red Beach, the army is as much a prisoner in its base at the edge of the continent as are the Asiatics within the army's stockades. For showing compassion toward the natives, one of the Americans is imprisoned; to the narrator he symbolizes "the crucified man." Nothing is resolved, although the bulk of the army simply vanishes in the mountains of the interior. In retrospect, *Subi: The Volcano* becomes a chilling anticipation of the Vietnam experience.

More than any other novel *Subi: The Volcano* reflects the major attitudes of the SF community in that no writer in the field during the 1950s pictured an American victory. Probably the closest anyone came was the bittersweet of Cyril Kornbluth's *Not This August* (1955). Russian and Chinese armies have occupied the United States, but in Chiunga County, New York, the American underground finds and raises Military Satellite One, threatening China and Russia with hydrogen and cobalt bombs if they do not immediately surrender. Yet the protagonist, Billy Justin, declares that there has been no victory, only the beginning of an accelerating, worldwide arms race so long as humanity chooses to fight.

Just as David Karp's *One* gave little attention to the

external workings of its totalitarian state, so Algis Budrys's *Who?* (1958) does not concern itself with an act of war. In its own way it reworks the familiar Frankenstein theme into a puzzle of human identity. The story line is deceptively simple. An American physicist, the genius Lucas Martino, works on a project essential to weaponry research; only he knows the nature of K-Eighty-eight, for he first imagined its possibilities while he was a student at MIT. When a lab explosion maims him, a Soviet team gets to him first because the lab is near the border of the American and Soviet zones in Central Europe. Although he was dead "for a few moments" (131), they save him with prosthetic surgery. Budrys structures the narrative so that the moment when Martino returns to a checkpoint serves as a frame for all other action. Faced by a creature with a prosthetic arm, respiratory system, and a metal cranium so that he is "mostly metal" (8), the head of American security does not know whether he confronts Martino or a Soviet impostor. Budrys renders the necessary investigation in chapters alternating between the present and an account of Martino's youth; one learns that his early-budding genius became an escape from his uncertainty about himself and his inability to relate maturely to other people. Released from the project, he returns to the family farm, where he is kept under surveillance. He finds that he has never had an identity separate from his intellectual life and research. Summoned back to the project after five years, he insists that he is only a farmer

DECADE OF TRANSITION

and denies his former existence. His dilemma is perhaps best crystallized in the moment when he terrifies the young daughter of a woman who once loved him and then runs aimlessly through the streets. The implication that Martino has never been fully human is reinforced when the narrative moves into his consciousness as the Russians bring him to the checkpoint, for his obsession with theorizing which enabled him to withstand the Soviet interrogation undoubtedly had much earlier kept him from realizing his potential humanity. In that the novel shifts its concern from public identity to private identity, it anticipates one of the centers of interest in SF beginning in the 1960s.

Although the premises that modern civilization faced a dystopian future and that nuclear war would probably destroy it had become widely accepted givens by the 1950s, many novels used postcatastrophic worlds as a point of departure for some adventure while making only incidental reference, if any, to twentieth-century society. In Wilson Tucker's first novel, *The City in the Sea* (1951), a thousand years after nuclear destruction a hundred women from a military elite dominant in California follow a male guide across the mountains into the interior, where they find an advanced culture whose people have telepathic powers; although they have been lured to the city, which has a shortage of women, they willingly agree to remain. Andre Norton's *Star Man's Son: 2250 A.D.* (1952)—intended for a juvenile audience—reminds one of Stephen Vincent Benét's "By

SCIENCE FICTION: THE 1950s

the Waters of Babylon" (1937) in that several centuries after a holocaust its youthful protagonist seeks out the ruined cities of the Old Ones, finds allies among the peoples of some plains tribes, and hopes to rebuild again. In *43,000 Years Later* (1958) Horace Coon allowed alien explorers to visit Earth and discover that humanity has annihilated itself in an atomic exchange in 1957 (some 240 warheads); they muse over their findings and lament the instability within the species that triggered its extinction.

The most effective and realistic of these novels, Leigh Brackett's *The Long Tomorrow* (1955), pictures a near future in which a Mennonite culture has survived "the Destruction" primarily because it has never relied on technology. Spread thin from the fishing hamlets of the Atlantic coast and the lumber camps of the Appalachians to the Southern hill farms and the Midwest farmlands, the church preaches a hellfire fundamentalism, restricting everything, even the size of towns. Its zealots—the New Mennonites—stone anyone they fear or hate. Eager for knowledge but punished for reading old books and listening to a radio, Len Coulter and his cousin Esau run away from home, lured by voices on the radio at night. The narrative becomes their quest for the mythical Bartorstown, a research center built before the war. They find it in the West, secreted beneath a mountain, complete with nuclear reactor and computer. The boys see a picture of Hiroshima and its survivors before they are told that the mission of the center is to find "a field-type force" which will prevent either fission or fusion from taking place (201, 203). Uncertain, faced by restrictions and discontent, Len flees Bartorstown as he fled his home, but he returns to accept the responsibilities growing out of knowledge.

What these novels share is the rich texture of the imagined societies. Although some of these novels presenting post-holocaust societies, like that of Leigh Brackett, may hew close to the utopian-dystopian axis, the best of them make an indispensable contribution to contemporary American science fiction. They share the rich texture of their imagined society. This characteristic may also explain why the novel—the series of novels—has become the principal vehicle of the field. In the 1950s, according to Delany, perhaps especially under the editorship of Gold, the writer began both "to cluster" wonders into a single narrative, thereby creating "a completely new world, in which the technological relation to ours is minimal," and "to explore both the worlds and their behaviors for the sake of exploration."[15] That approach opens up the field much more than do Isaac Asimov's proposals that science fiction "deals with human response to changes in science and technology" and that a reader should be able to imagine "the set of continuous changes" transforming present-day society into that of the narrative.[16]

Delany and Asimov, of course, assert what seem

to be personal preferences; they are not mutually exclusive because SF by its nature is concerned with the interplay between science/technology and society/the individual. If closely adhered to, both prove too narrow to encompass the field. They also ignore the fact that, once developed, no motif disappears from science fiction. It is adapted, used in new combinations. No motif illustrates that more clearly than the future war.

Since Delany goes on to condemn "the plethora of sloppy romances or boneheaded adventures that make up the statistically vast majority" of all literary texts, one may in all fairness ask him to explain what those explorations "of worlds and their behaviors" are about. However much emphasis is put on the examination of "inner space"—as the psychological probing of character came to be called in the 1960s and after—characters must act on a stage containing "wonderous things," real or imagined. Whatever content the writer selects, what becomes most significant is the richness of texture with which the writer has imagined the new society or world. All that the reader and critic can ask, is that the imagined constructs be consistent within themselves, a characteristic that such critics as Jane Mobley have asked of fantasy as well as SF. In short, societies and worlds become important as a potential symbol/metaphor or they may be used as "realistic surfaces" of the kind associated with literary realism and naturalism. At their best, of course, they serve on both levels.

The emphasis on the dystopian view that arose in

DECADE OF TRANSITION

mid-century American SF—a view that shaped the field during the 1960s as well—can too easily overlook the constant variety existing even in the 1950s. For example, the manner in which Hal Clement (the pseudonym of Harry Clement Stubbs) transformed the long-popular theme of first contact between humans and aliens can best be understood by considering his most famous novel, *Mission of Gravity* (1954). Like all of his novels it explicates his contention that the universe itself is the antagonist in that it presents intellectual problems which must be solved by a knowledge of such areas as mathematics, physics, biology, and chemistry—the "hard" sciences. Even as the serialized novel ran in *Astounding*, Clement published an article, "Whirligig Worlds," explaining with what delight and exactitude he had created the planet Mesklin—sixteen times the mass of Jupiter, rotating in 18 minutes, having a gravity which varies from 3 Gs at the equator to 700 Gs at the poles—the largest inhabited world that Clement's human explorers had yet discovered. Charles Lackland has begun to exchange information with a Mesklinite free-lance trader/explorer, Barlennan—"a cylinder a foot and a half long and two inches in diameter" having thirty-six legs. Although Lackland can survive on the equator protected by armor and a ship like a tank, neither he nor his colleagues at a base on the inner moon Toorey can salvage a research rocket that has crashed at the south pole. From the outset the narrative focuses on Barlennan and the crew of his ship *Bree*, not on the humans. Barlennan agrees to search for the rocket; the result is a travelogue of a bizarre planet—witnessed by Lackland and his colleagues only through film and radio. Like the humans, Barlennan wants to learn; he says as much at the site of the wreck when he agrees to disassemble and return the rocket in exchange for a full explanation of its working. This intellectual curiosity, the use of each other by human and alien to gain knowledge, is the theme binding Clement's works together.[17] The story lines of both *Cycle of Fire* (1957) and *Close to Critical* (1964) repeat this cooperation between human and alien as well as providing excuses for guided tours of his inhospitable, fascinating worlds.

Frequently the shorter fictions in the magazines began to glimpse exotic societies, but of those published in book-length form, few portrayed in depth an alien culture. Philip José Farmer's "The Lovers" (*Startling*, 1952) shocked the SF community when a male human mated with a parasitic, mimetic insect who appeared to him as a beautiful woman, but Farmer did no more than sketch the society where this relationship occurred. In the four stories linked together into James Blish's *The Seedling Stars* (1957), human beings are genetically manipulated so that they can adapt to hostile environments. The most famous of the stories, "Surface Tension" (1952), dealing with microscopic men living in a puddle of water, can be read as a parody of epic SF adventures as the narrator gives an account of their successful efforts to break through the surface tension of the water; indeed, one wonders whether Blish was fully aware of the ambiguity of its ending. Yet this series introduced the concept of genetic engineering so that humanity could spread to the stars. While Ted Kennedy, the protagonist of Robert Silverberg's *Invaders from Earth* (1958), expresses sympathy for the gentle primitives native to Ganymede, the story line becomes a denunciation of the Extraterrestrial Development and exploration Corporation as it undertakes the exploitation of the moon for its radioactive materials. The Corporation's use of a public relations firm in a campaign to falsify reports of native atrocities to gain support for military occupation of Ganymede recalls a variety of satires, just as Silverberg anticipates subsequent themes when Kennedy discovers that "the aliens are people; they provide a perspective from which to measure the conduct and nature of man.[18]

Although such writers as Silverberg and Poul Anderson have attested to the importance of Jack Vance's *Big Planet* (1957), that novel has been almost totally neglected, perhaps because only its severely cut version *(Startling,* 1952) was available until the late 1970s, by which time ethnographic studies had become commonplace in SF. Anthony Boucher praised its "narrative interest and charm" because its shipwrecked survivors set "out on a trek, meeting strange kinds of people . . . and having unexpected incidental adventures [on] an archaic world inhabited . . . by misfits from the conformist culture of Earth" *(F&SF* Aug. 1957: 107).

During the 1950s only Poul Anderson consistently matched Clement's success in creating well-imagined worlds. One of his excursions into future history has been the creation of the Polesotechnic League, a confederation of traders similar to the medieval Hanseatic League "who operate in a laissez-faire galaxy of scattered, independent planets."[19] *War of the Wing-Men* (1958), the first in the series, introduces the merchant prince Nicolas van Rijn, head of the Solar Spice and Liquors Company, whose party is stranded by a never-explained act of sabotage ten thousand kilometers from the only human settlement—his company's trading post—on the planet Diomedes. As Rijn manipulates the two warring cultures, the Lannachska and the Drak'honai, to assure the survival of his party, the novel dramatizes the issues of biological and cultural determinism. Anderson gives as much attention to his planet as Clement gave to Mesklin. A low-density world without heavy metals, with an axial tilt severely affecting the climate, Diomedes has restricted its humanoids to an unending Stone Age, although its atmosphere is dense enough for them to fly. Anderson emphasizes the differences in the resulting cultures. Land-based on an island during the summer, the Lannachska migrate to the equator during the winter to trade and mate with other tribes. The Drak'honai live on their boats and rafts and have no fixed mating season. Each despises the other because of this difference in sexual mores, but the conflict has erupted because the trech—the fish staple of the Drak'honai diet—have migrated to a new fishing ground near the Lannachska's island. Rijn deduces that the two cultures belong to the "same identical stupid race" which long ago migrated from a tropical climate and became dispersed. He intervenes in the war so that he and his party can be rescued before their food supply runs out (Diomedan proteins are poison to the human system), but for the reader, as perhaps for Anderson, the story line is incidental to the vividly pictured cultures.

The alien culture in James Blish's Hugo-winning *A Case of Conscience* (1958) was not so fully realized, perhaps because the planet Lithia functioned as a kind of straw man, so to speak, in Father Ramon Luis-Sanchez's personal theological evaluation of an apparently unfallen world. A Jesuit biologist, he is a member of a commission sent from Earth to determine whether Lithia should be used as a way station for space flights or should be banned. The team physicist, Paul Cleaver, wants it placed under a security seal and used as "a thermonuclear laboratory and production center" both because of its richness in such materials as lithium and because its natives have no nuclear knowledge. It is the natives themselves who torture Father Luis-Sanchez's consciousness throughout the first part of the novel. In their idyllic world "without constraint or guidance" the Lithians conform to the Christian ethic, living the lives of saints. Father Luis-Sanchez sees their way of life as a rebuke to human aspirations; indeed, he sees Lithia as a seductive trap "propped up by the Ultimate

Enemy"—Satan. When he returns to Earth, he brings with him a Lithian egg which grows into Egtverchi, who becomes a kind of "messiah" urging the youth to rebel against the decadent human society cowering in its underground-shelter culture in reaction to the fear of nuclear war. The ending is ambiguous. Lithia's sun goes nova; the planet perishes—whether as a result of Father Luis-Sanchez's spontaneous, desperate exorcism or some error in Cleaver's thermonuclear experiments, one cannot tell. *A Case of Conscience* deservedly remains one of the intellectual puzzles of the field.

While aliens were a staple throughout the decade, both androids and clones were conspicuously absent from the novels. Even with the computer that became a candidate for president in Arthur Hadley's satirical *The Joy Wagon* (1958), artificial intelligence remained the province of Asimov's positronic robots. In the opening chapters of *The Caves of Steel* (1954), a detective story, Asimov shows the pervasiveness of the dystopian mood when he explains the tensions that disturb an overcrowded Earth. Eight billion people crowd into eight hundred automated cities—"steel caves"; the detective, Elijah Baley, describes New York with its population of twenty million as "one building." The city itself is "the environment." For generations the most skilled, courageous humans have fled the world to colonize some fifty worlds. Represented by the few "Spacers" who dwell outside the city in Spacetown, they despise the regimented, scientifically controlled city dwellers whose places in the work force are being taken by robots, but they also fear the imperialistic potential of a modernized Earth. Within New York, reduced to a "desperate minimum" standard of living, many persons riot against their replacements; even Lije Baley dislikes the robots. When a Spacer is killed, Asimov introduces R. Daneel Olivaw, a Spacer robot from an Outer World, to be Baley's partner in the investigation. Unlike the machines "made to know a few simple things," R. Daneel Olivaw can pass as human. Of course the crime is solved, but from the moment R. Daneel faces down a half dozen squabbling women with a "blaster," the distinction between robot and human is questioned. Asimov skillfully complicates the situation: R. Daneel Olivaw has been made in the image of his "designer," a distinguished sociologist specializing in robotics, while Lije Baley becomes the representative of an unwelcome minority in Spacetown. Although at the last moment the central issue may be blurred by human politics, Asimov must be credited with the fullest early treatment of a theme still explored by subsequent writers: What does it mean to be human? That Asimov at the time could not take the theme further seems confirmed by the sequel, *The Naked Sun* (1957), in which the partners solve a crime on Solaria, an Outer World where robots outnumber humans. Pushing the robot into the background, Asimov's denouement emphasizes that Lije Baley has escaped the city and that Earth "would be born again and reach outward."

If through Baley's triumph over the confining caves of steel and the distorting (murderous) isolationism of the twenty thousand human inhabitants of Solaria, Asimov suggests that the hope for the future somehow lies with the free human community, as he suggests in such novels as *The Stars, Like Dust* (1951), and *The End of Eternity* (1955), then Philip K. Dick asserted in such early works as *Solar Lottery* (1955) and *The World Jones Made* (1956) that only in the act of rebellion against any established authority can the individual hope for freedom and identity. Although several of his short stories deal with the robot-human interface, during the 1950s he more often dramatized the abnormalities of the human psyche and the distortion of reality. As a result of an accident during a routine demonstration a party of sightseers in *Eye in the Sky* (1957) are trapped, successively, in the "reality" of the illusory worlds each of the mentally ill persons among them—religious and political fanatics—has created as an expression of a personal power fantasy. One assumes perhaps somewhat uncomfortably that Ragle Gumm, the protagonist of *Time Out of Joint* (1959), lives in a familiar but alternate contemporary world in 1959. A citizen of Old Town, for two years he has been a consistent winner of the national "Where Will the Little Green Man Be Next?" contest in the daily *Gazette*. (There is a quiz game and quizmasters who try to rig the drawing in *Solar Lottery*.) Increasingly suspicious because of small discrepancies, Gumm learns that the year is 1997—he is *Time's* Man of the

DECADE OF TRANSITION

Year 1996—and that the military-dominated world government had confined him in a "safe, controlled environment" where he could continue his essential work. A prosperous industrialist, when civil war had broken out between Earth and its moon colonies, he had volunteered his services to predict statistically the paths of missiles incoming from the moon. Only after he switched allegiance because the "lunatics" in the moon colony had agreed to peace if colonization were continued is he imprisoned in the faked environment. Systematically brainwashed, Gumm had become the centerpiece of a town built upon the memories of his youth. The daily newspaper puzzle provided a code by which he unwittingly continued his accurate predictions. Throughout Dick's fiction the manipulation/destruction of one's personal reality remains a dominant theme.

The twisting of reality lies at the heart of Ward Moore's *Bring the Jubilee* (1953), the mid-century classic dealing with the alternate world/alternate universe motif. A distinction must be made. Whereas the concept of parallel worlds proposes any number from two to an infinite series of Earths coexistent in space but separated by dimensions, as in the fiction of Clifford Simak, the alternate world motif builds on the idea that some event, often hypothetical, has brought a second Earth into existence. The new one may replace the old, or they may coexist. Perhaps the most widely known short story was Ray Bradbury's "The Sound of Thunder" because it was published in *Collier's* (June 28, 1952); a big-game hunter travels back to prehistory and accidentally kills a butterfly, thereby transforming the present world into a totalitarian state. Early treatment of the motif in magazine SF may be typified by the two Earths warring in order to preserve a single reality, as in Jack Williamson's *The Legion of Time*. The first significant exploration of an alternative world for its own sake occurred in L. Sprague deCamp's *The Wheels of If* (1940), in which he posits a contemporary America derived from tenth-century Viking colonization. In *Bring the Jubilee*, Ward Moore began with the assumption that the South had won the Civil War and through the trivial interference of a time-traveling historian transforms that world into the present day. Although a discussion of free will versus determinism figures in the narrative, the success of the novel comes through the first-person narrator's vivid picturing of the decadent North and the triumphant South. Something of a similar reversal by Richard Matheson in *I Am Legend* (1954, filmed as *The Omega Man*) revitalized the vampire myth; in 1976 the protagonist, Robert Neville, struggles for survival in an America where plague has turned everyone but him into vampires. The final turn of the screw, so to speak, comes when he realizes that as "the last of the old race" he is an object of fear and loathing to the new society: a mythic figure. Matheson's subsequent *The Shrinking Man* (1956), though a graphic film, was a predictable treatment of an old theme, although it ends only when the narrator emerges into a submicroscopic universe and understands that nature exists "on endless levels."

In retrospect, significant as these novels and authors were to the subsequent development of American science fiction, in many ways the 1950s belonged to Robert A Heinlein. Even before the eulogies following his death in 1988, critical consensus saw him as the "innovator and developer" who "domesticated the future for a whole generation of readers"[20]—although his social and political conservatism drew the wrath of many. Among the writers to emerge in the 1980s, Lois McMaster Bujold acknowledges that Heinlein's thirteen novels with Scribner intended for a juvenile audience, from *Rocket Ship Galileo* (1947) to *Have Spacesuit—Will Travel* (1958), both provided an essentially comfortable sense of the future and established an easy, familiar style that heightened the acceptability of the future.[21] Granting a slim flexibility for the sake of variation, one may summarize the story lines of these rites of passage easily: a precocious teen-aged boy—often an outsider either among his peers or in his family—takes advantage of an opportunity to visit other worlds than Earth; in doing so, he fulfills a dream and gains entrance into the adult world. Often he witnesses or takes part in a rebellion against a decadent establishment. In any final estimate this may be the area of Heinlein's most telling influence.

But as the publishers scrambled for *books* of SF to

offer the public in the late 1940s and early 1950s, Heinlein's earlier works were reissued—from a piecemeal offering of his future history, such as *The Man Who Sold the Moon* (1950), *The Green Hills of Earth* (1951), and *Revolt in 2100* (1953)—through early novels serialized pseudononymously, like *Sixth Column* (1949) and *The Day After Tomorrow* (1948), to collections like *Waldo and Magic Inc.* (1950), perhaps most important because magic plays a major role in the future society. So again his influence was far-reaching because he introduced the world of magazine SF to a wider audience.

What was to become the controversial Heinlein appeared unobtrusively in his first postwar novel intended for an adult audience: *The Puppet Masters* (1951), a treatment of the familiar theme of aliens possessing human beings. On July 12, '07 some time after "the Disorders" during which atomic bombs were used (Heinlein thus casually keeps the conflict within the framework of his future history), "flying saucers" carrying parasitic aliens invade the midlands of Iowa and the prairie states. The "slugs" soon take over entire communities; they affix themselves between the shoulder blades of humans, thereby reducing their hosts to zombies. Their numbers are not limited because they split, amoebalike, each new "master" seeking another host, not necessarily human. Because preventive measures are not immediately taken—neither presidential action nor "one bomb"—a "fight for racial survival" escalates, with the United States always at the edge of complete defeat. At one point during interrogation, speaking through its host, a captive parasite assures his audience that the "people" hope to bring "peace" to a troubled Earth, a view immediately rejected. The reader learns incidentally that a combination of slugs and plagues has decimated Russia, bringing about a fall of its government. Some Americans declare this a "biological war," wishing for a "bug" with which to exterminate the aliens; others suggest that Americans must learn to live with the parasites as they have with the bomb, for whatever the casualties, survivors among the slugs can hide in such places as the Amazon Valley.

In *F&SF* Boucher and McComas typify the initial reaction to *The Puppet Masters*, praising Heinlein for his technical skills and calling the novel "as thunderously exciting a melodrama of intrigue [as anything] outside an early Hitchcock picture" (Feb. 1952: 105). Most academic critics, however, have been openly hostile: "An effective, if rather hysterical, invasion story . . .";[22] "Heinlein's paranoia-laden tale of sluglike creatures";[23] "a cold war allegory, which . . . warns of the insidious Communist menace."[24]

The first-person narrator, Sam Nivens, gives his allegiance to a special services group separate from the CIA; its chief is the "Old Man," whom Sam praises and the President calls a "genius." When Sam reluctantly serves as a host to a captive slug and asserts that the aliens offer humanity "Nirvana," the Old Man declares that such offers of security and happiness have never

been worth a damn. Only during the traumatic aftermath of being a host does Sam break his usual formality
to reveal that his chief is his father. Finally, possessed
by an alien after a plague has annihilated the parasites,
the Old Man ambushes and kidnaps Sam, asking his
son why he did not reveal how blissful possession was
and telling him that the masters will unite a "mankind
. . . divided . . . warring." After Sam causes a crash, killing the master, father and son are quietly but tearfully
reconciled. The Old Man's final remark insists that "the
race must go on, even if it doesn't know where."

A second line of action involves Sam with another
agent, Mary, whom the Old Man tells Sam to regard as
his sister. From the outset, however, Sam is romanti-
cally inclined toward the attractive redhead. She titil-
lates him, and once he acknowledges that after a kiss
he felt "all tingly . . . like a fifteen-year-old." She is a sex
object; for example, if a man does not respond to her
presence, she can tell unerringly that he is "hagridden"
by a slug. Conveniently, she provides the key to defeating the aliens. Although she has blocked the experience
from her conscious memory, as a child she was a member of a cult which fled to Venus, where invading aliens
possessed everyone until a plague destroyed them.
Mary survived. Military psychologists fail, but when
she sees tapes of the sessions in the presence of Sam,
she remembers that she was immune to "nine-day fe-
ver" which killed the slugs. In the biological war for
survival she has provided the needed bug. In a kind of

epilogue to the main action she and Sam join volunteers about to set out to clean up Titan, the sixth moon of Saturn, the home world of the parasites.

The final passages have been quoted widely and variously as an indictment of Heinlein's political thinking or as a vindication of his idealism. At the heart of the rhetoric, in the context of meetings with further alien life forms, lies Sam's judgment: "Well, if Man wants to be top dog—or even a respected neighbor—he'll have to fight for it. Beat the plowshares back into swords; the other [the dream of peace] was a maiden aunt's fancy." As has been noted often, Sam's tone anticipates the youthful protagonist at the end of *Have Spacesuit—Will Travel* (1958), who challenges representatives of a galactic council to do their worst because humanity will survive and avenge itself. Such critics ignore that one of the councilors asks, "Can any race survive without a willingness to fight?"—as well as the lengthy postponement of any final verdict on a race so young as humanity. Yet the idea of a verdict may simply strengthen the judgment of Heinlein as a social Darwinist.

Heinlein changed pace in *Double Star* (1956), which gained him his first Hugo, by concentrating on the actor Lorenzo Whyte's impersonation of the kidnaped political leader John Joseph Bonforte, who had masterminded the Concord of Tycho, a treaty with the "Martian nests," an important step necessary to the inclusion of nonhumans in Earth's expanding empire in the twenty-second century. Shanghaied to Mars, Whyte must play stand-in at a crucial ceremony in which Bonforte is adopted into the Kkkah nest—important as a foreshadowing of Valentine Smith's background in *Stranger in a Strange Land* (1961). To overcome his own fearful distaste of Martians, Whyte must be hypnotized and conditioned, but once the ritual has occurred, most of the action occurs offstage and is dealt with summarily as this slight narrative becomes the autobiographical reflections of the man who through circumstances—kidnaping, illness, death—had to become Bonforte and carry out his political ideas. The action ends just after Bonforte's deaths as one of the subordinates who arranged the cover-up of the switch tells Whyte: "Chief—one man dies—but the show goes on." In a brief judgment of his effort written twenty-five years later, Whyte/Bonforte concludes both that his father would judge his career a "good performance" and that he has played the role needed if humanity is "to go out to the stars."

The first-person narrative of Daniel Boone Davis in *The Door into Summer* (1957) returns to mundane affairs and reveals as much about Heinlein's political stance as any of the early novels. The plot may seem convoluted as Heinlein makes use of familiar SF furniture. After being swindled by his business partners, Davis decides that he and his cat will undergo the long cryogenic sleep, awakening in the year 2000. The first half of the narrative, a detailed account of how Miles Gentry and Belle Darkin forced him out of their small corporation, masks a celebration of the creative design engineer. After surviving "the Six Weeks War" (the seemingly inevitable reference in these early novels to an inevitable nuclear conflict), Davis and Gentry open a small factory in the Mojave Desert, where Davis invents a variety of household robots—*Hired Girl, Window Willie,* and finally the all-purpose worker, *Flexible Frank.* As Davis recalls his background, the reader learns things about him that give insight into Heinlein. Davis wanted a small shop like those of Ford and the Wright brothers, although people no longer believed "bicycle-shop engineering" was possible. And his father named him Daniel Boone Davis as a "way of declaring for personal liberty and self-reliance" and as a protest against the view that "the individual was on the skids and the future belonged to mass man" (25, 26). Whatever else it may be, *The Door into Summer* is an attack on big business, for Gentry and Darkin want to make immediate profit by selling out to Mannix Enterprises to gain broad production and worldwide distribution. Ousted, Davis nevertheless foils their efforts partially by sending his stock to Bank of America to be held in trust for Gentry's young daughter, Frederica—"Rikkie-tikki-tavi"—who has adored Sam's cat and promised Sam she would marry him when she grew up.

Individualism triumphs rather ingeniously. Awakening in a politically dystopian world where sophisticated descendants of his original inventions make up the labor force, Davis finds himself broke and "unskilled," although he learns that D. B. Davis holds all the patents. Plot takes over. A time machine conveniently allows him to return to 1970. He designs the advanced robots, organizes the Aladdin Autoengineering Corporation to hold the patents in the name of D.B. Davis, explains the situation to eleven-year-old Ricky— who undergoes the long sleep when she is twenty-one—and finally returns to the year 2001, where he marries Ricky and lives happily ever after, working independently as a design engineer in a single drafting room. Of the two corporations he controls, Hired Girl, Inc. and Aladdin, he remarks, "Competition is a good idea. Darwin thought well of it" (183), but the novel ends amid his speculations about time-travel paradoxes and multiple universes. *The Door into Summer* remains Heinlein's most lighthearted, entertaining novel. It marks a major turning point in his career.

Whether or not Heinlein interrupted work on *Stranger in a Strange Land* to reply to the antinuclear testing program, at this point he produced his controversial *Starship Troopers* (1959), intended for his juvenile series for Scribner but rejected by them and serialized in *F&SF*. In *Heinlein in Dimension* Alexei Panshin denounced *Starship Troopers* as a "militaristic polemic" and that view has remained consistent among critics, with only variations in the rhetoric. Undoubtedly not the first to do so, Panshin in his final estimate of Heinlein likened him to Kipling.[25] Heinlein sketches a future in which citizenship is conferred only on servicemen; they

DECADE OF TRANSITION

alone may hold office, vote, or teach a course mandatory to all high school students, "History and Moral Philosophy."

Frequently called a *Bildungsroman,* the first-person narrative of Juan (Johnny) Rico gives an enthusiastic, blow-by-blow account of his career from recruit to lieutenant in the elite Mobile Infantry. Between extensive campaigns the Mobile Infantry often make commando-like raids on planets held by the enemy during the unending, galaxy-wide war between the Terran Federation and the "Bugs," who look like "a madman's conception" of a giant spider, although socially and psychologically they are more like ants or termites, "communal entities, the ultimate dictatorship of the hive." The narrative begins with such a raid before its flashback to Johnny's volunteer recruitment and boot camp. Conspicuously absent from his characterization is any growth of understanding; he remains a static, two-dimensional fighter who leads Rico's Raiders in a commando drop at the end of the novel, thus bringing it, figuratively, full circle. Tactical H-bombs exist on a level with grenades; each trooper is encased in a two-thousand-pound suit of armor that augments his power as a fighting machine. Another repetitious diatribe against *Starship Troopers* may well miss, as so many attacks do, the full impact—and horror?—of Heinlein's basic premises: human morality is based only on duty, and "a human being has *no natural rights of any nature*" (96). Later on Johnny asserts: "Man is what he is, a wild animal with the will to survive. . . . Correct morals arise from knowing what Man *is*" (147). Perhaps the best indication of how far Heinlein had shifted from the 1940s and his vision of that future history may be indicated by Johnny's incidental report that the so-called Revolt of the Scientists failed because the premise that rule by "the intellectual elite" will lead to utopia "fell flat on its foolish face" (143). Whatever the novel may suggest about Heinlein's state of mind at the end of the decade, perhaps in retrospect the most troubling thing about *Starship Troopers* is that a popular vote awarded it the Hugo for 1959.

Throughout the 1950s, as the United States tried to adapt to the complexities of the postwar era, American science fiction writers criticized the establishment, particularly the advertising field and the corporations. The optimism which had characterized the scientific community even through the Depression evaporated before the certainty of a nuclear conflict. Whatever its scale, all the writers assumed that eventuality. Within these parameters a dystopian mood prevailed, Heinlein almost alone in his emphasis on the individual while others, like Bester and Sturgeon, hoped for something that would unite humanity—perhaps the exploration of space, as in Anderson's *The Enemy Stars* (1959). Richard Condon's best-selling *The Manchurian Candidate* (1959) may have best captured the fears of the period with its emphasis on brainwashing and assassination.

The increasingly pervasive mood of the 1950s, always bordering on despair, found its voice in Kurt Vonnegut's *The Sirens of Titan* (1959), perhaps because he refused to identify himself with the field but nevertheless resorted to the motifs and fixtures of SF to express his dark vision: "a nightmare of meaninglessness without need" (8). Although he rejects the outward expansion symbolized by space flight, the irony of Vonnegut, at least in *The Sirens of Titan*, lies in that he himself had to "look outward" to Mars and make use of the imaginary planet Trafalmadore in order to denounce the plight of the human soul. One senses that his personal anguish and bitterness intrude to make much of his satire heavy-handed. He tells his story as though it happened less than a century earlier—during the "Nightmare Ages" before humanity gained "easy access to the puzzle boxes within them" (7, 8). With his emphasis on "inwardness" he sparked the quest for "inner space" which became so much a part of the 1960s.

He focuses primarily on two characters. Identified as "a member of the one true American class" (26)—an aristocratic elite—Winston Miles Rumfoord has flown his private spaceship into a time warp; for nine years at fifty-nine-day intervals he has materialized. Although by implication he has supposedly gained a kind of omniscience, he can only tell Malachi Constant, the richest American and a resident of Hollywood, that "it's a thankless job telling people it's a hard, hard Universe" and that Constant's "destination is Titan" (25, 29). Something of a buffoon, Constant desires "a first class message from God," having earlier declared that "somebody up there likes me" (17, 7). But any effort to find a benevolent purpose guiding human life proves fruitless. If Rumfoord is an instigator, then Constant is his victim.

Rumfoord controls the action. He instigates and finances the senseless slaughter of a Martian invasion of Earth, whose human participants have been reduced to mindless automatons. Whether or not out of guilt, he forms a new religion, "the Church of God the Utterly Indifferent." Repeatedly, through Rumfoord especially, Vonnegut's satire strikes out not only at religion but at all phases of the "military and industrial society" (reverberations of that phrasing echo throughout the 1960s). Although amnesiac, Constant has survived the Martian conflict (as the character "Unc") and has gone to Mercury and returned to Earth (as the "Space Wanderer"); Rumfoord first denounces him as Malachi Constant because he believed "that luck, good or bad, is the hand of God" (252) and then orders him to Titan so that he can be a kind of reviled messiah for Rumfoord's church "to remember and ponder" (255). Increasingly throughout the narrative one realizes that Vonnegut is not interested in story so much as producing situations where he can deride humanity. On Titan, Constant meets the robot Salo, a Tralfamadorian courier, who has waited there since 203,117 B.C. for a spare part to be sent him so that he can carry his message from one rim of the galaxy to the other. Salo—the "best machine" his people could make (299)—tears himself apart in a frenzy when he learns that the message he carries simply says "Greetings." Rumfoord dies, declaring that everything humanity has done has been "warped" by Tralfamadore. Vonnegut reduces everything to an incomprehensible "SERIES OF ACCIDENTS" (229), an existentialist minimum. Far from an affirmation, Constant's assertion just before his death that the "purpose of life, no matter who is controlling it, is to love whoever is around to be loved" (313) seems a plea almost as empty as a minor character's belief that "the magical forces of the universe would put everything back together again" (301). *The Sirens of Titan* seems, on rereading, the centerpiece of Vonnegut's fiction and a lesson in futility. With the sound of his voice the 1950s ended.

Notes

1. Lester del Rey 128–29.
2. Robert A. Heinlein, "Blowups Happen," *The Past Through Tomorrow* (New York: Berkley, 1967) 112.
3. *Dictionary of National Biography*. ed. David Cowart and Thomas Wyner. (Detroit: Gale Research, 1981) 8/1: 66.
4. Marshall Tymn and Mike Ashley 294.
5. Kingsley Amis, *New Maps of Hell* (New York: Harcourt, Brace, 1960) 124.
6. *Dictionary of Literary Biography* 8/1: 30.
7. Alfred Bester, "My Affair with Science Fiction," *Hell's Cartographers: Some Personal Histories of Science Fiction*. ed., Brian Aldiss and Harry Harrison (London: Weidenfeld and Nicolson, 1975) 62.

8. Peter Nicholls, ed., *The Science Fiction Encyclopedia*. (Garden City, NY: Doubleday, 1979) 167.

9. *Dictionary of National Biography* 8/1: 40.

10. Samuel R. Delany, introduction, *The Cosmic Rape and "To Marry Medusa"* (Boston: Gregg, 1977) vii.

11. Bester 64.

12. Robert Scholes and Eric S. Rabkin 64.

13. Gary Wolfe 217–22.

14. John Newman and Michael Unworth, *Future War Novels: An Annotated Bibliography* (Phoenix: Oryx Press, 1984) 24.

15. Samuel R. Delany, "Critical Methods: Speculative Fiction," *Many Futures, Many Worlds*, ed. Thomas D. Clareson (Kent, OH: Kent State University Press, 1977) 289.

16. Thomas D. Clareson interview with Dr. Isaac Asimov, 2 Oct. 1975.

17. See Donald M. Hassler, *Hal Clement* (Mercer Island, WA: Starmont House, 1982) 20–21.

18. Thomas D. Clareson, *Robert Silverberg* (Mercer Island, WA: Starmont House, 1982) 12.

19. Bleiler 260.

20. Bleiler 185.

21. Thomas D. Clareson, interview with Lois McMaster Bujold, Marion, Ohio, 30 Jan. 1988.

22. Nicholls 278.

23. Neil Barron, ed., *Anatomy of Wonder* (New York: Bowker, 1987) 145.

24. H. Bruce Franklin, *Robert Heinlein: America as Science Fiction* (New York: Oxford University Press, 1980) 98.

25. Alexei Panshin, *Heinlein in Dimension* (Chicago: Advent, 1968) 93, 191.

CHAPTER THREE

The Early 1960s: Cul-de-Sac

As the 1960s began, the wars continued, as in Alfred Coppel's *Dark December* (1960), whose protagonist survives in a United States devastated by nuclear conflict. Others came so close to the here-and-now that only in retrospect have they been classified as science fiction. Because of instrument failure in Eugene L. Burdick and Harvey Wheeler's *Fail-Safe* (1962), a single SAC bomber attacks Moscow; to prevent an all-out war the American President orders the bombing of New York City, even though his wife is there on a shopping spree. When a Russian invasion causes the partition of Iran and leads to a possible disarmament treaty with the United States in Fletcher Knebel and Charles W. Bailey's *Seven Days in May* (1962), a clique in the American military attempts an unsuccessful coup. Such expressions of the central fear of the period led through films like the adaptation of Nevil Shute's *On the Beach* (1959) and Stanley Kubrick's *Dr. Strangelove, or How I Learned to Stop Worrying and Love the Bomb* (1964)—that dark comedy starring Peter Sellers and based on a novel

SCIENCE FICTION: EARLY 1960s

by Peter George[1]—to Philip K. Dick's *Dr. Bloodmoney or How We Got Along after the Bomb* 1965), whose guilt-ridden Dr. Bluth Geld is a "thinly disguised" Edward Teller.

In contrast to these nuclear holocausts, Harry Harrison's *Deathworld* (1960) pictures the planet Pyrrus, which has become a "big deathtrap for mankind" because the planet itself responds telepathically to the fear and hostility present in the human minds, beginning with the earliest settlers. Jason dinAlt begins to discern the explanation as he reads the logs of the *S.T. Pollux*, the ship which brought the colonists. The conflict has escalated as each side adapts defensively to the violence of the other. One would like to see the narrative as Harrison's effort to capture the mindset of the 1950s, but a reliance on plot conventions arrests the metaphor. When dinAlt has solved but not fully alleviated the problem, he announces that he hopes to go into the "business of opening up new worlds." The opening sequence in which dinAlt, identified as a gambler, wins some three billion credits at a casino on the planet Cassylia reminds one of Ian Fleming's James Bond, but Harrison did not produce a memorable protagonist until *Bill, the Galactic Hero* (1964), who broadly and effectively parodies the ventures of devoted warriors like Johnny Rico of Heinlein's *Starship Troopers*.

Poul Anderson's *The High Crusade* (1960) is more than a delightful, humorous adventure story. He sets up a framing device in which the captain of a ship from Earth reads a manuscript translated by his sociotech-

nologist, supposedly telling of a great catastrophe occurring a thousand years earlier on this alien world. The
manuscript's first-person narrator is Brother Parvus, a
Franciscan monk, who gives a full account of the
Wersgor Crusade. In the year 1345, as Sir Roger de
Tourneville assembles an army of "free companions" to
aid Edward II against France, the good Lincolnshire
people are astounded by the landing of a dazzling me-
tallic cylinder, denouncing it as sorcery or a French
trick. Running "wild," they massacre the crew, leave
one alien—Branithar—who explains that the ship has
been sent as a scout, and are tricked by Branithar into a
flight to the nearest Wersgorix planet when they
wanted simply to go to France to do battle against a
Christian foe. Their landing on Tharixan marks the beginning of the conquest of the Wersgorix empire and
the establishment of a feudal, Catholic England through
much of the galaxy, though that is incidental to their
desire to return to Earth and Britain.

Just as Jack London's "The Red One" (1918) provided a naturalistic response to the theme of first contact, so Anderson's *The High Crusade* dramatizes a
romantic response. Anderson's understanding that he
borrows the materials of medieval romance makes itself
clear when he introduces Sir Owain Montbelle in the
dual roles of Modred and Lancelot. Although Sir
Roger's Lady Catherine grieves when she must rule in
her husband's absence and does walk with Sir Owain,
she resists his blandishments, and, indeed, kills him

when he tries to seize the ship from Sir Roger. In the framing device the present ruler explains to the captain that for generations young knights sought for Earth as often as they sought the Holy Grail until "the quest petered out." There is irony, too, as when the ruler exclaims, "God be praised, they've finally learned to build spaceships on Old Earth" (191)—for the conquerors never mastered technology. Their feudal kingdom survived because when the Wersgorix, like Rome, fell, the English offered stability in a social and political vacuum.

In a sense the other pole of these imaginary wars is marked by Fritz Leiber's *The Big Time*, which won a Hugo in 1958 after appearing in *Galaxy*, although it did not see book publication until 1961. Widely praised because it reflects Leiber's interest in the theater—its single action occurs in one setting during a sequence of hours—it may be read as a morality play condemning militarism. In *The Big Time* Leiber gave his most sustained presentation of the concept of the "Change War," a background to which he returned repeatedly in shorter fictions, the most important being collected in *The Change War* (1978). He adapts the familiar SF premise that something outside of humanity controls its actions and destiny by positing a seemingly endless (meaningless?) conflict between the Spiders and the Snakes, each side capable of time travel so that it may enter history at any point—past or future—to change events in order to assure its own triumph. Since each manipulation is countered by the enemy, the war goes on. The identity of the Spiders and the Snakes remains unclear. At one point the Spiders are labeled "The West" and the Snakes, "Communists" (16); at another, the narrator wonders if both sides could be manifestations of the Nazi *Schutzstaffel*, the SS Black Shirts (82). To obtain soldiers for their raids, both sides offer to "resurrect" persons dead or about to die. One character in *The Big Time*—Lili—recalls dying both in New York in 1929 and in Nazi-occupied London in 1955 (118).

Between missions the soldiers are given brief respite at special centers. The setting of the novel is one such "Spider" Place—outside time and space. The first-person narrator, Greta Forzane, calls herself an "Entertainer," who amuses and nurses the soldiers. Two aliens and four soldiers enter the Place. The aliens have little importance other than extending the scope of the conflict a billion years into the past (the octopoid from the moon) and a billion years into the future (the Venusian satyr). Similarly, Mark, the Roman legionnaire, and Kabysia Labrys, a woman warrior from ancient Crete, remain largely decorative. Bruce Marchant, a young British poet who would have died at Passenchendale in 1917, and Erich Friedrich von Hohenwald, a Nazi officer, take center stage in a debate growing from Lili's assertion that in three lifetimes she has loved Bruce, actually going to France as a nurse to meet him in 1917. The plot, when Leiber gets to it, is incidental, the quick and casual disarming of a tactical atom bomb.

Of greater importance, for a time they all believe that they are isolated from time and space in the Place. For Leiber wants his characters to talk.

A dissatisfied Bruce questions the methods and aims of the Spiders as he wonders about the nature of reality and the effects of change. Erich listens quietly until Bruce suggests that time travel be used "for healing . . . to bring a peace message" (88); then Erich accuses him of mutiny and ridicules his infatuation with Lili. When Bruce asks his companions to take a stand, they reject him. A truce ensues until Lili speaks. When she suggests that it may well be too late for a peace message, that perhaps "all doomed universes" cast off seeds like this Place, and that perhaps they can have children and begin again (127–28), Erich explodes:

'Can't you see that the Change World is the natural and proper end of evolution?—a period of enjoyment and measuring, an ultimate working out of things, which women call destruction—

'. . . Have you thought what this life will be like without a Door to go out to find freedom and adventure, to measure your courage and keenness? . . . A proliferation of *Kinder*, *Kirche*, *Kuche*—

'Women!—how I hate their bright eyes. . . . I never knew one who didn't want to cripple a man if you gave her a chance' (130–31).

CUL-DE-SAC

When Erich tells Bruce that the young poet is "really not on their side," Bruce knocks him down. The legionnaire remarks, *"Omnia vincit amor,"* while Greta reflects, " . . . us women have our little victories—until the legions come or the Little Corporal draws up his artillery or the Panzers roar down the road" (133). And any mutiny abruptly ends.

In a flurry of action Erich correctly accuses Lili of having deliberately cut the Place off from the cosmos, the door is reopened, and the bomb deactivated. The "Emperor Spider" again assumes command of human affairs. Silently, Lili dances the black bottom at a final party. Erich and Bruce are again *kamerads* as the soldiers prepare to depart, with the bomb, on their next mission. Greta decides that Bruce always wanted "soldierly cavorting and poetic drunks" instead of Lili and "barroom epics" instead of mutiny (165). Then, to end the narrative, Leiber tacks on an SF convention; the alien octopoid explains to Greta that the Change War is not the "blind destruction" that it seems but rather the next step in evolution, producing fourth-order beings who are "possibility-binders" uniting the "mental with the material . . . throughout the whole cosmos" (169). Nor does it help when nearly twenty years later Justin Leiber, Fritz Leiber's son, seizes upon the final passage to explain that *The Big Time* is "the mind, . . . a constructed reality" which may be driven to madness by the interference of the Spiders and the Snakes, although his suggestion that "The Place is like a ghostly theatre in which

characters from different plays meet"[2] is highly pro-
vocative.

The Big Time dramatizes a state of mind during the
late 1950s. At its most limited it provides an emotional
outburst for Leiber himself; its flaws occur, as in the
ending, when he tries to contain that reaction within the
conventions of magazine SF. At its best it uses the stage
props of SF as background for a morality play which not
only condemns militarism but searches for meaningful
identity in an existential universe whose constant
changes are beyond individual comprehension. One
hopes that it is not merely the perspective of the 1980s
which finds the most telling encounter to be between
Lili and Erich. Bruce himself cannot be the main
speaker, for from World War I through Korea and the
Cold War, the "peace message" had proved ineffective.
Lili must become the voice of a continuing humanity.
And at mid-century only the Nazi officer, through his
cynical asides and final diatribe, can give, unwittingly,
effective denunciation to those forces tearing the twentieth century apart. That the denouement remains dissat-
isfying may not only indicate the impact of the issues
but may also explain why Leiber returned again and
again to the central image of the Change War. Nor
should one overlook the insight the novel gives into the
troubled state of the American mind, for there is irony
in the fact that fandom voted Hugos to *The Big Time*
(1958) and *Starship Troopers* (1959) in successive years.

What a reader must notice, at least in passing, is

CUL-DE-SAC

that the Spider versus Snake backdrop of *The Big Time* reminds one of the central conflict of "Doc" Smith's lensmen series. Although the shift in focus anticipates the reactions of the 1960s and later, one must not forget that professional soldiering has continued to shape much of SF, including some of its series of novels. Although in one of Poul Anderson's Nicholas van Rijn collections, *Trader to the Stars* (1964), a character remarks that throughout the galaxy there has not been "much war" because it is "too destructive, with small chance for either side to escape ruin," (53), Anderson had created Dominic Flandry as early as 1951 and featured him in *Agent for the Terran Empire* (1965) and *Ensign Flandry* (1966), two of the earliest books of his adventures as a naval intelligence officer "working in the twilight of a corrupt galactic empire."[3] Similarly, from *Envoy at Large* (1963) to *Reward for Retief* (1989), Keith Laumer's hero, Retief of the Corps Diplomatique Terrestrienne, has kept "full control of the galaxy," albeit with humor and frequent satirical jabs at bureaucracy.

Of particular interest because of its pervasive idealism and its influence on fandom is Gordon R. Dickson's as-yet-incomplete twelve-volume "Childe Cycle." Dickson will trace the development of the human race during a millennium, showing the emergence of Ethical-Responsible Man. This evolution will be effected by the achievements of strong individuals, "Prime Characters," beginning with the "result of the actions of a mercenary soldier named Sir John Hawkwood upon the fab-

SCIENCE FICTION: EARLY 1960s

ric" of the early fourteenth century.[4] Three kinds of men will contribute: the Men of War (Dors), the Men of Philosophy (Exotics), and the Men of Faith (Friendlies), whose interaction will produce a mature race. Also essential are the scientists of Newton and Venus and their technology, epitomized by the Final Computer, a complex artifact so large that when finished it will become a satellite of Earth and will contain all knowledge accumulated up to the twenty-fourth century. Each of the early novels contributes to the whole—*The Genetic General* (1959, retitled *Dorsai*, 1975); *Necromancer* (1962); *Soldier, Ask Not* (1967); and *Tactics of Mistake* (1971)—but the Dorsai, mercenary warriors named for their material-poor plant, remain Dickson's most widely influential contribution to the field. In the person of Donald Graeme, their leader, a youth who must undergo loneliness and initiation into the adult world before he gains his individuality and becomes a superman, the Dorsai have given fandom a kind of role model or peer group with which to identify. The Dorsai appear at most SF conventions in greater numbers than do the "Trekkies," the devotees of *Star Trek*.

In terms of nuclear warfare, Walter M. Miller, Jr., captured the idea of holocaust more effectively than did any of his contemporaries in *A Canticle for Leibowitz* (1960).[5] He dramatizes a future cycle of history which reenacts what he sees as the fate of Western society. He opens the narrative some six hundred years after the "Flame Deluge" with the story of Brother Francis Ger-

CUL-DE-SAC

ard of Utah, who finds in the ruins of a fallout shelter relics of I. E. Leibowitz, for whom his abbey is named; after fifteen years his faith and effort are rewarded when he takes the relics to Rome and hears Pope Leo XXI elevate an "obscure technician" to sainthood. In the second narrative two petty kingdoms—Texarkana and Laredo—go to war; the learned Thon Taddeo discovers that ancient knowledge has somehow been preserved at a monastery and takes it into the secular world. Atomic war has just broken out as the third narrative begins; the action centers on Abbot Dom Zerchi, who cries out: "Are we doomed to do it again and again and again? Have we no choice but to play the Phoenix in an unending sequence of rise and fall?" (271). As "the visage of Lucifer" mushrooms, "engulfing a third of the heavens," a single spaceship bearing monks and children rises into space. With wit and anger Miller fused together his rigorous Catholicism, established conventions of SF, and a grim reading of history into a rich amalgam that remains one of the major achievements in the field.

So wide has been its acclaim that the merits of several other novels published in the same year have been somewhat obscured. If *A Canticle for Leibowitz* succeeds in large part because of its finely imagined world, then John Hersey's *The Child Buyer* (1960) succeeds because both in form and content it intrudes a single horrible premise into familiar daily life. The narrative is presented as a transcript of the hearings of the State Senate

Standing Committee on Education, Welfare, and Public Morality the last week in October, 19—. In this way, although Hersey flays the American public in general, he focuses his satirical attack on education and government, perhaps the two fundamental building blocks in American thought. The Committee investigates the allegation that Mr. Wissey Jones has undertaken the purchase of a "boy child," ten-year-old Barry Rudd, of the town of Pequot. Jones acknowledges that he buys "brains," while the chairman of the Board of Education praises his "innovation in human engineering." Jones proceeds on the assumption that everyone has a price; before the end of the hearing even Barry's mother and favorite teacher have sold out. The young genius is only one "specimen" whom Jones wants to use as a participant in a secret, fifty-year-long national defense project carried out by United Lymphomilloid to enable men to leave the Earth. Initially Barry would be taken to a "Forgetting Chamber," where his five senses would be tied off so that, with the aid of drugs, his brainpower would soar without distractions from the physical world. Barry finally agrees to take part because "a life dedicated to U. Lympho would at least be *interesting*" (256–57), although he wonders what will happen when his memories—pictures, as he calls them—go out. Initial criticism praised the force of Hersey's satire of education, with its emphasis on the gifted child, but did not fully appreciate the darkness of his landscape.

Both Barry's interest in memory and the defense

CUL-DE-SAC

project link *The Child Buyer* to Algis Budrys's *Rogue Moon* (1960), which affords another example of an author's successful use of SF hardware to implement a metaphor exploring the human condition. Neither Faust nor an antihero, Edward Hawks, Doctor of Science, supervises investigation of a half-million-year-old alien artifact on the moon. In the absence of space flight and in the fear that Russia will somehow gain some advantage from the monolith, Hawks undertook a crash program with Continental Electronics and developed a matter transmitter enabling him to send a man to the moon. At that point Budrys introduces the first complication, although the reader does not have immediate knowledge of it. During transmission the machine replaces the original volunteer with two duplicates, each having all the knowledge and memories of the original: one duplicate on the moon (M) and one in the laboratory (L), linked telepathically to share experience. Then the second complication: although man can enter the mazelike interior of the artifact, he cannot turn back; within minutes the experience kills him. So terrible is the disorientation and death—"so beyond the comprehension of human senses"[6]—that the duplicate on Earth has always gone mad. With the aid of a colleague Hawks recruits a soldier of fortune/athletic hero, Al Barker, whose Earthbound duplicate (Barker L) can withstand the shock of death.

The story line develops on two levels: Hawks repeatedly sends Barker M to the lunar site; each time M progresses farther into the maze. Secondly, Hawks falls in love with Elizabeth Cummings. James Blish judged the characters to be "madmen" and essentially dismissed the love story,[7] while Peter Nicholls felt that the image of death permeates the novel, calling the artifact itself a "death machine."[8] Both views distort the manner in which Budrys managed the narrative in order to voice his concerns not only about death but also about identity, intelligence, and memory. Throughout the narrative he confronts an existential universe. The final entry of both Hawks M and Barker M into the maze, with only Hawks knowing that they cannot return to Earth but must die even if they make it through the puzzle, dramatizes vividly humanity's encounter with a seemingly incomprehensible universe; the love story allows Hawks to talk about the philosophical quandary he finds himself in. The ideas of personal death and entropy have always bothered him. Even though "the Universe is dying," even though the "Universe kills our bodies," what has importance is the human mind: "There's the precious thing; there's the phenomenon that has nothing to do with time and space except to use them; to describe to itself the lives our bodies live in the physical Universe." (110). When he tells Elizabeth of a memory that he has held since childhood and asks what will happen to it when his body dies, she replies that it will live in her "mind, a little." Through the love story Hawks arrives at a stoic affirmation before he joins Barker on the moon.

One of his passing remarks to Elizabeth—that as a young boy he could not understand why women had intelligence if their only role was "the continuance of the race" (105)—anticipates Theodore Sturgeon's *Venus Plus X* (1960). Although an erotic tradition carried over from the nineteenth century into modern SF and fantasy, as illustrated by Weinbaum's *The Black Flame* and Williamson's *Darker than You Think,* there had been no explicit treatment of sexuality in the specialist magazines until the 1950s when both Sturgeon and Philip José Farmer published their short stories, perhaps the most controversial being Sturgeon's sympathetic treatment of alien homosexuals in "The World Well Lost" (1953). Farmer's *A Woman a Day* (1960) gave a deceptive title to a routine power struggle in the Jaijac Union, the totalitarian theocracy whose explication figured heavily in the expansion of "The Lovers" to novel length (1961). The often broad satire of his *Flesh* (1960) introduces ideas akin to those of Robert Graves as Farmer shapes a fertility cult which worships a Great White Mother, the goddess Columbia, and rules Deecee, a remnant of the United States in a world turned mostly to desert by pollution and such natural disasters as a brief stripping away of the ozone layer. To this Earth returns a starship absent for eight hundred years; its commander, Peter Stagg, becomes the Sunhero, the Horned King of Deecee, quite literally the Father of His Country as the ceremonial orgy moves from town to town northward from Deecee and Baltimore to Poughkeepsie and Vassar.

Amid these sexual gyrations Theodore Sturgeon undertook an examination of gender roles in American society. One gains a sense of the reception given *Venus Plus X* by the reaction of Alfred Bester, the book reviewer for *F&SF*, who asserted that Sturgeon "has permitted himself to blunder into the trap that undoes many lesser American authors, . . . a deadly and stultifying seriousness about sex" (Jan. 1961: 95). Sturgeon structured the novel as a classic utopia; Charlie Johns, seemingly an American aviator who has survived a crash, is guided through the kingdom of Ledom by the historian Philos, who asks Johns to judge the society. From the outset the only mystery remains the sexual identity of its inhabitants until Johns sees two of them pregnant; Philos and others allow him to infer that he has somehow revived in a future time when humanity has mutated so that it is hermaphroditic. Although this makes him uncomfortable, he accepts it and learns that an all-encompassing love, particularly for their children, governs the lives of the Ledom.

Against this unfolding but essentially static background Sturgeon inserts a series of sharply satirical vignettes focusing primarily on Herb and Jeannette Raile and their two preschool children in order to attack the hypocrisy and inconsistencies in the prescribed sex roles characteristic of mid-century, suburban American society. In addition to referring to a wide variety of sources including Ruth Benedict, Margaret Mead, Erich Fromm, and G. Rattray Taylor (*Sex in History*, 1954),

Sturgeon drew heavily on Philip Wylie's *The Disappearance* (1951), which separates the sexes for four years in parallel worlds so that Wylie can condemn masculine domination and misjudgment. Sturgeon follows Wylie in denouncing humanity's virtual loss of the ability to love and man's breeding women to be submissive. He concludes that throughout history the father-dominated religious orders have been a key element in the Western refusal to adopt "a charitic religion and a culture to harmonize with it" (131). Although *Venus Plus X* retains historical importance because it precedes the women's movement, it remains effective primarily when Sturgeon allowed the vignettes to speak for themselves. His most telling point is the episode in which Jeanette Raile thinks herself "rotten clear through" because she feels sexual desire (101).

In the pastoral utopia Charlie Johns finally learns the secret of the Ledom from Philos. He is not in the future, nor has there been a mutation. Ledom results from conscious social engineering; its inhabitants are "biological 'constructs'" (156). Four generations earlier in an effort to escape Western obsession with gender, unidentified parents hid their children in a cave opening onto an otherwise inaccessible valley. Now almost eight hundred Ledom live in an environment roofed over by an A-field," camouflaged not only for secrecy but also for protection from fall-out because the original experiment was undertaken partly in the certainty that humanity would destroy itself in an atomic holocaust.

The first difficulty arises when Johns asks Philos how long the Ledom will keep themselves "bottled up" in their refuge. He is told that the Ledom regard themselves only as a transitional form, but they will remain separate until humanity has cleansed itself of its deeply ingrained biases and will not destroy the Ledom simply because they are "different." Johns praises them as "most remarkable" until he learns that their babies are born normal—that is, of either gender. There are strong implications that female babies do not survive (142–43, 147–50). Male babies are altered during their "incubation" at the medical center in that an artificial uterus is grafted into each one. Ideally, lovers will impregnate one another. Explosively, Johns denounces "Men marrying men. Incest, perversion," insisting that humanity would "exterminate them down to the last queer kid" (152). Only then does the reader learn that the American pilot died in the crash, but his mind—Charlie Johns—was given to Quesbu, the "Control Natural," a natural child kept asleep and used by the physicians as a means of checking their work. At a post-hypnotic suggestion Charlie Johns again becomes Quesbu, while Philos in a final scene watches the flashes of atomic explosions. This unexpected open ending proves most effective only if Charlie Johns/Quesbu's reaction becomes symbolic of how deeply society's prejudices are ingrained.

Just as Bester did not appreciate Sturgeon's efforts in *Venus Plus X*, so, too, he took exception to Heinlein's craftsmanship in *Stranger in a Strange Land* (1961), al-

CUL-DE-SAC

though it took Hugo the following year and became both a best-seller and a cult book during the 1960s. Bester accepted and praised the basic premise of the story line—the return to Earth of youthful Valentine Michael Smith, whom Martians raised from infancy so that, culturally, he is a Martian. After Smith escapes from those who would control him, according to Bester in *F&SF*, "the novel degenerates into a mishmash of erotic incidents. . . . Most of the second half of the book is dedicated to sex and salvation, with Smith turned into a Messianic figure" (Jan. 1961: 78). In sharp contrast stands James Blish's assertion, dated October 1961, that "Heinlein's treatment of sex is confessedly, designedly, specifically reverent—and this very reverence has produced the most forthright and far-out treatment in the whole history of science fiction." Blish came to the conclusion that the novel "is religious," with Heinlein exploring "eclectic religion [which] is a fascinating potpourri, amazingly complicated to have come from a single brain." [9]

The thrust of the narrative follows the pattern of Heinlein's novels aimed at a juvenile audience in that it concerns itself with initiation into adulthood. After the narrative rids itself of the necessary exposition and initial plot action, it follows Smith's education and career. Child of an adulterous affair and sole survivor of the first Martian expedition, Valentine Michael Smith inherits the income from the space drive invented by his mother as well as the fortunes of the entire crew. As the expedition's heir, through a court ruling upholding ownership by right of occupation, he also owns the planet Mars. Because he has not yet adapted to such new physical conditions as the increased gravity, the World Federation government hospitalizes him as soon as he returns to Earth but keeps him under protective custody in order to control his finances. On the advice of a newsman who loves her, Jill Boardman, a nurse at the hospital, smuggles Smith out to the estate of Jubal Harshaw in the Poconos, where his education begins. Desultory efforts are made to capture him and arrest Harshaw, but Heinlein abruptly terminates that action with a conference when Harshaw announces that Smith wants to appoint the Secretary General of the World Federation his attorney-in-fact with full power to handle all business affairs.

Although Harshaw has instructed Smith widely since his initial appearance at the estate, three other factors shape Smith's actions and attitudes. As a Martian, he can control his metabolism and heartbeat, for example, and "discorporate" (die) if he chooses; moreover, he can use this same ability to destroy things and people. As a Martian, Smith must "grok" everything and everybody. That is, he must know, comprehend: but the term implies—with almost telepathic overtones—an understanding simultaneously emotional, intellectual, and spiritual. It is both holistic and empathic. Repeatedly the narrative declares that grokking involves a sharing or coming together which brings with it a wisdom unattainable for most humans. (In the 1960s "to grok" became one of the catchwords among many elements of the youth culture.) Thirdly, as a Martian, Smith has no awareness of human sexuality, for—with a phrasing that recalls Sturgeon—the "man-woman polarity which controlled human lives could not exist on Mars" (91). All Martian adults are male so that the closest relationship one may form in the communal nest is sharing water with a brother.

From Valentine Smith's first meeting with Jill in the hospital—"her hobby was men" (21)—he expresses a keen interest in women. After his arrival at Harshaw's, he includes Jill and the older man's three beautiful secretaries among his "water brothers"; they cluster around him, remarking once that "Mike gives a kiss his whole attention" (174). For most of the novel Smith approaches sex with the undying enthusiasm of a titillated adolescent, as when he and Jill, together in Las Vegas, indulge in and discuss exhibitionism, voyeurism, and "naughty pictures" (285–90). During the first half of the novel, with the exception of Jill's casual kisses and a brief incident when Harshaw orders Smith to kiss Dorcas—quite agreeable, she faints during the embrace—sexuality is simply talked about.

Throughout the narrative both religion and sexuality have a major importance as Heinlein weaves them together into a central theme. That he must find a unifying principle seems implicit in the early assertion that "random chance was not a sufficient explanation of the

Universe" (135). Even before Smith's troubles with the government are ended, a messenger brings him a special invitation from Bishop Denby to attend services at Archangel Foster Tabernacle of the New Revelation. The Fosterites become the focal point of Heinlein's satire of contemporary religion, for Jubal Harshaw explains that, morally, "Fosterism is the Freudian ethic sugarcoated for people who can't take psychology straight"; yet Foster did tap "the Zeitgeist. Fear and guilt and loss of faith" (246). The basic doctrine exhorts members of the True Church to be happy by loving one another, and this they do literally, as exemplified by the conduct of the church hierarchy.

Although Smith wallows in the emotion of the service, he groks *"wrongness"* in the carnival atmosphere of the church, with its slot machines, and does not grok anything from the confidences of Bishop Denby. Bewildered, he retreats to his room and puts himself in a trance. Almost paradoxically because of the previous emphasis on his Martian background, during this trance Smith "burst out and ceased to be a nestling. The solitary loneliness of predestined free will was then his. . . . Self integrity was and is and ever had been" (249–50). Much earlier he had acknowledged that "God groks," but after meditating over Harshaw's words and what he had been taught as a nestling, he emerges from this experience saying, "Thou are God." Only then does the narrative allow Smith to have sex onstage with an unnamed "water brother" (by implication Dorcas, although Jill remains his favorite and becomes his primary companion). In keeping with Heinlein's treatment of sexuality, the incident is presented almost exclusively through dialogue. In short, they talk their way through the act. Smith murmurs, "Thou art God," and apparently in ecstasy, his partner assures him, *"Oh! Thou* art God!" (252). They "grok God."

This communion transforms Valentine Michael Smith. From an almost neurotic docility, Harshaw decides, Smith has become "self-confident" (255): "From his first change from docility to dominance he had grown steadily in strength and sureness" (263). After this key sequence Smith emerges as the messiah of the Church of All Worlds, Inc. It also underscores the irreparable flaw of the novel. Although Valentine Michael Smith may be the titular protagonist of *Stranger in a Strange Land*, he seldom takes center stage; he is talked about by Jubal Harshaw and his companions, as are many things, but the dominant voice remains that of Harshaw. One might assemble a catalogue of his pithy sayings, many of them reflecting Heinlein's own views.

Smith and Mill leave the Poconos to travel the United States, including Las Vegas. Although Jill refuses to marry him—it would be unfair to Dorcas and the others—one infers that somehow his companionship with her completes his maturation, for only after their skimmed-over travels does he declare that he groks "people" and "love" itself (295). Only then does he ask how to be ordained. When needed, Smith is

summoned on stage to carry through the symbolic
stages in the growth of a messiah: his church will be
burned and he will be jailed (355–56); the mob will stone
him to death, but he will be resurrected (398–401, 402);
Harshaw and his friends will cannibalize his body in a
final act of communion (404). But granting the few
spurts of growth on the way to his destiny, Valentine
Michael Smith serves as an essentially static figure
whose ideas may be speculated about as well as being
illustrated by the actions of others, like Mrs. Patricia
(Patty) Paiwonski, who shifts easily from being a devoted Fosterite to becoming a priestess of Smith's "Inner Nest," ultimately bedding down Jubal Harshaw
himself (380). Ben Caxton, an uneasy water brother because he has "no stomach for group orgies" (339), nevertheless becomes a member of the nest and reports
Smith's activities to Harshaw, who pronounces Smith
"the ultimate anarchist. . . . Freedom of self—and utter
responsibility for self" (367). Smith takes his place
among the pantheon of supermen who can help humanity, for he declares that he and his friends offer
"not faith but truth—Truth for the here-and-now" (325).
Regarding Smith's actions Harshaw insists that "Bac-
chanalia, unashamed swapping, communal living, and
anarchistic code" are all moral if innocents like Valentine Smith (and Jill) "can show us a better way to run
this fouled-up planet" (341, 345). For all his grokking,
however, Smith cuts something of a macho figure because as soon as he ceases to be a nestling, he "accepted

CUL-DE-SAC

homage from the girls as if a natural right" (255). Small wonder that with the example of Valentine Michael Smith and the authoritative voice of Jubal Harshaw, *Stranger in a Strange Land* became a cult book during a period whose restless youth demanded change.

Throughout the remainder of his career Heinlein pondered in his own fashion the question of sexuality and sex roles. The first-person narrator of *Glory Road* (1963), who identifies himself as a discontented engineering student though not a member of the beat generation, becomes the "champion" of the beautiful Star in an alternate universe; the novel becomes a parody of sword-and-sorcery fantasy. Although he marries Star, the Empress of Twenty Universes, multiple sex partners are the standard pattern. Once his mission is completed, he becomes restless as a mere consort—"a gigolo"—to a reigning queen; they separate, he returning to Earth. But amid a final discussion of sexuality, after he decides that his "complaints are against the whole [American] culture with no individual sharing more than a speck of blame" (276), he seeks out the glory road of adventuring, though not necessarily Star herself.

In *Farnham's Freehold* (1964) a group survives nuclear warfare and its aftermath. Its protagonist, Hubert (Hugh) Farnham declares that conflict and survival "will improve the breed" (29). As the radio warns of an imminent attack, the family plays bridge in an underground shelter near the isolated village of Mountain Springs until the concussion of a near-miss shuttles them into the far future, perhaps so they may have a broader stage than the shelter itself. Given a choice among a young black, a brother, and a father, Farnham's pregnant, college-aged daughter insists that she would prefer to marry "Daddy" (93–94). Even before the shift in time, during the tension in the shelter, Farnham has sex with his daughter's schoolmate, Barbara, and then proposes marriage to her when his alcoholic wife decides to leave the shelter (33, 123). His daughter dies in childbirth, but Barbara has twins. Returned to the present, Farnham, Barbara, and the twins live through missiles, bombs, epidemics, and the long disorder after the end of combat. A brief interlude in the society of the future adds little, but does give the princely ruler opportunity to remark about the difficulty of translating ancient texts because of the "lack of cultural context" (144). One must sympathize with James Blish's view that increasingly in Heinlein's novels, particularly *Farnham's Freehold*, editorializing became "blatant . . . to the near-extinction of the story."[10]

His last major novel of the decade, *The Moon Is a Harsh Mistress* (1966), makes a lunar revolution against the Federated Nations of Earth directly analogous to the American Revolution, even using the dates 2075–2076. The Loonies, as they are called, even write a Declaration of Independence, and they must fight off invasion. Potentially the most intriguing aspect of the narrative—the relationship between man and machine—is relegated to the background. The first-person narrator, Manuel (Mannie) Gospodin, is a cyborg, having twelve prosthetic left arms, each for a special task, but he becomes a leader of the rebels and briefly an emissary seeking justice on Earth. The one being who grows is Mike, the HOLMES FOUR computer, capable of human judgment. At one point its gender is questioned, but Mike serves as the mastermind of the revolution. Like Valentine Smith, he is called up when needed. Not only does he assume the role of Adam Selen as the rebel's spokesman, but he devises the weapon which brings about an armistice: a rock-filled missile which strikes the Earth like a meteor. Although most of the speculation concerns politics, because of the comparative lack of women on the moon, Heinlein gives attention to a variety of marriage arrangements that have been worked out. Mannie is involved in a century-old "line marriage" involving "twenty-one links," so that the newest wife is the granddaughter of the elder husband and his first wife (31). No one raises the issue of consanguinity. Except for the collection of the early "future history" stories, *The Past Through Tomorrow* (1967), Heinlein published no further major fiction during the remainder of the decade.

Just as Heinlein introduced Valentine Michael Smith with his Martian acculturation in order to gain a fresh perspective in *Stranger in a Strange Land*, so Philip K. Dick pictured an alternate world in order to make more vivid his most probing inquiry into the fragile nature of reality in *The Man in the High Castle* (1962). Unlike Heinlein, who hoped to make a major affirmative statement, Dick was concerned with the existence of evil as a force within the universe. He structured a many-layered puzzle having no final solution. There is no single flow of action in one authoritative voice. In the world of *The Man in the High Castle*, Germany and Japan "barely managed to win" World War II (27). The Nazis occupy most of the United States, while Japan retains the Pacific coastal states, seeming to colonize them through its business interests instead of simply occupying them militarily. Between the allies, in a kind of buffer zone, the United States exists in the high desert and the mountain states.

To understand more readily the thematic tensions within the novel, one should be aware that in Dick's "paradoxical, unresolved novels . . . there cannot be one, single, objective reality"; also, in one of his last interviews he asserted that "the greatest menace of the twentieth century is the totalitarian state."[11] To show the complexity of that central dilemma he sets up an ideological tension among a triumphant Germany; such characters as Nobusuke Tagomi—a devout Buddhist— who rely on the *I Ching (Book of Changes)* as their oracle; and a work of science fiction—*The Grasshopper Lies Heavy*—which portrays still another alternate world. Of greatest importance to the development of his central theme is Dick's portrait of Nazi Germany, for out of the triumphant Reich spreads the pervasive dilemma.

CUL-DE-SAC

From the outset Dick contrasts Japan and Germany. Although a victorious nation, Japan has bogged down in South America, burning off the Brazilian rain forest and building "clay apartment houses for ex-headhunters" (16). He does create a certain sympathy for his Japanese characters, primarily through their interest in obtaining authentic artifacts from prewar American popular culture—their "ever-growing craze for Americana" (31). On the other hand, he vilifies the Nazi Party. One narrative strategy guides the reader's response: Dick dramatizes the loss of faith of Mr. Tagomi, so essential to the narrative, while he simply reports, piece-meal through a number of characters, the activities of the Nazis. Secure in "Festung Europa," Germany seems able to "remold the world by magic" (28).

Their technology gives the Nazis monopolies in such areas as plastics and polyesters; through the use of atomic power they have completed Project Farmland, sealing off and draining the Mediterranean basin; their interplanetary rockets have reached the moon and Mars, with colonists to follow; they are "busy bustling enormous robot construction systems across space" (16); and the High Command of the Wehrmacht plans to carry out "Operation Dandelion"—a surprise nuclear attack on Japan (175–77). Through a cataloguing of the "frenzied and demented" activities of "the mad creatures in Berlin, . . . automatons, building and toiling away" (42, 18, 16), Germany reminds one of the ants in Simak's *City*.

Unlike the ants, however, the Nazi Party is driven by complex motives most obviously manifested in their racism. Their latest "experiment" has left "a billion chemical heaps in Africa that [are] now not even corpses" (18). Although the American Robert Childan deals in prewar artifacts with the Japanese, he admires the Nazis, even though they "simply let their enthusiasm get away with them" in handling the "African Problem" (28–29). His contempt for "Yellow people" and his praise for "what can be done where whites have conquered" underscore the inevitability of the destruction of Japan, if only to provide the Nazis with more land to incorporate into the Reich. Amid numerous denunciations that of Baynes, the cover name of the German naval intelligence officer planning to meet with Japanese representatives to avert a disaster, most exactly places the Nazi Party in Dick's thematic landscape. As Baynes denounces the "psychotic world we live in" and the "madmen . . . in power," he declares that for them "the abstract is real, the actual is invisible to them":

'They see through the here, the now, into the vast black deep beyond, the unchanging. And that is fatal to life. Because eventually there will be no life . . .

'They identify with God's power and believe they are godlike. That is their basic madness' (42–43).

Only then does he say, "What they do not comprehend is man's *helplessness.*" In this assertion Baynes provides the key to the theme of the novel.

This is another of Dick's visions of entropy. In it one may infer a societal death wish; more importantly, it reveals the Nazi fixation upon a single, materialistic reality. Whatever its apparent accomplishments, the Nazi Party becomes emblematic of brutality and evil. It has no regard for, nor comprehension of, either the individual person or humanity as a whole. At one point even Baynes insists that he and the representatives of the Japanese "reflect solely on reality, on actual power. Not on ethical intentions" (177). Dick emphasizes this concern for power. A syphilitic, insane Hitler has been confined in an asylum. Chancellor Bormann rules until he dies, and that death brings about a struggle between Party factions until the mob sweeps Dr. Goebbels into office. "Period after death of Leader," explains a minor character, "critical in totalitarian society" (103). Impersonal power motivates the dominant reality in the psychotic world where Germany and Japan have won.

Both popular and academic critics have made much of the *I Ching* on which many characters rely. In Taoism reality "is a web of time and change, a seamless net of unbroken movement. . . . Motion is ceaseless; consequently nothing is permanent."[12] With its ever-differing mixture of yin and yang—"the interplay of the two primal forces"—"there is always renewal. It is that which keeps it all from wearing down. The universe will never

be extinguished" (105). Thus, Taoist reality is antithetical to that of the Nazis. Instead of an impersonal (entro-
pic) stasis, it suggests a dynamic and creative flux. Yet
its adherents have no absolute control—no more than
the Nazis have over entropy; they ride with the ebb and
flow, attempting to understand intuitively, as do
Tagomi and Juliana Frink. The hexagrams of the *I Ching*
externalize the characters' efforts to decipher the web
linking the individual consciousness and the apparently
objective external world. The Taoist "single, indivisible"
unity governed by cosmic law"[13] is not more compre-
hensible than the black depth of unchanging chaos.

Often writers have been content to set up this an-
tithesis between a creative Eastern subjectivity and an
impersonal Western objectivity. To complicate further
his unending concern with reality, Dick introduces a
third element: an almost legendary figure Hawthorn
Abendsen, has written an underground, "forbidden"
novel, *The Grasshopper Lies Heavy*, which proposes that
the Allies defeated Germany and Japan. Its world differs from that of the reader in that Rexford Tugwell
replaced Roosevelt as President in 1940 and continued
policies that kept Germany from aiding Japan. Setting
out to meet the reclusive Abendsen, who lives in what
he calls "the High Castle," Juliana Frink travels with and
kills an SD man sent to assassinate Abendsen. Before
she faces the writer and tells him what she has done,
just after she has finished reading the book, Juliana is
certain that only she understands *Grasshopper* (242).

CUL-DE-SAC

All other action takes place in Japanese-occupied San Francisco. In the story line centering on the selling of prewar artifacts and Frank Frink's innovative jewelry, much is made of forgery and authenticity, an issue undoubtedly representing Dick's views on art; it also reinforces his concern regarding the perception of reality, especially when a walk-on character reprimands Robert Childan because the dealer *"cannot distinguish the forgeries from the real"* (56). In San Francisco, Tagomi brings together Baynes and General Tedeki, former Imperial Chief of Staff. When Baynes suggests that Japan help General Heydrich gain the Chancellorship because he opposes the nuclear strike, although he commands the brutal SS, Tagomi cannot accept the "dilemma" of aiding evil to gain power: "That man should have to act in such moral ambiguity. There is no Way in this; all is muddled" (177). Yet he gives at least lip service to General Tedeki and Baynes's agreement that they must be "realists" and consider only power, not "ethical intentions."

His spiritual trauma intensifies when he, a Buddhist to whom all life is holy, must shoot two intruding gunmen who, he assumes, are SS assassins, although identification suggests they are only hold-up men. Tagomi feels that "no human intelligence" can decipher the situation (186). Both General Tedeki and Baynes comment on his "despair" and "perplexity." But his loss of faith is complete: "There is no answer. No understanding. Even in the oracle" (207). So shaken is he that his reality dissolves as he gazes at one of Frank Frink's jewels; somehow he enters briefly into the reader's world, where he is angrily dismissed, "Watch it, Tojo" (216). Returned to his own time and space, he phones a minor Nazi consul, denouncing Germany's descent "into greater vileness than ever" and calling on the consul in the name of "Goodman C. Mather" to "Repent!" (221). When the reader last sees Tagomi, he has suffered a heart attack, ending his career, perhaps bringing him death but not understanding.

As Baynes returns to Berlin, he reflects that the bombing of Japan will destroy "another major section of the planet . . . for a deranged, fanatic ideal." The Nazis may well be seeking a Gotterdammerung, "a final holocaust for everyone," which will make Earth "a dead planet, by our own hands" (225). Desperately he hopes that other worlds beyond human perception exist, but he echoes Tagomi's "terrible dilemma": "Whatever happens, it is evil beyond compare. . . . Why choose? If all the alternatives are the same . . ." (227). Humanity faces only "obscure admixtures" and has "no proper tool by which to untangle the components." Just before he is arrested, his thought that "by making a choice at each step . . . we can only hope. And try" seems more pathetic than stoic. Moreover, whether Goebbels retains power or Dandelion is carried out, evil prevails wherever "the blackshirts, the Partei, the schemes" may decide.

In contrast to this nihilistic view, the final encounter between Juliana and Abendsen remains enigmatic. When she asks why he lives in Cheyenne rather than the isolated hilltop fortress, as his book suggests, he jests with her until she matter-of-factly tells him that she has killed the SD assassin; then he replies, "They can get you . . . if they want to" (235). Initially he denies that he consulted the *I Ching* while writing the novel, but his wife reveals that his every choice was guided by the oracle. When Juliana wonders why the oracle should write *The Grasshopper Lies Heavy*, Abendsen objects to the insinuation that he was nothing more than a typist.

Until Juliana questions the *I Ching* directly, inquiring why it wrote the novel, Abendsen seems almost too casual. The scene is tied directly to that in which Tagomi suffered the heart attack. In both the hexagram is "Inner Truth." Juliana asserts that she knows the novel's meaning, but Abendsen first wonders if the hexagram means that his book is "true," and then in reply to her simple affirmation, "with anger" he asks if Germany and Japan did lose the war. Then he remarks, "I am not sure of anything" (237). To see in this reaction Dick's concern with the role of the artist and possibly his unwillingness to find a single meaning in any book seems possible, but it also illustrates his contention that all realities—perhaps especially those stories in which a writer immerses himself so completely that they seem real—are fictions.[14]

As Tagomi himself acknowledges, the space and time "creations of our own psyches" falter (217). In response to his wife's judgment that Juliana's activities have been "terribly disruptive," Abendsen says, "So is reality" (238). Earlier Juliana had told him that, apparently as a result of her finishing *The Grasshopper Lies Heavy* just that evening, Abendsen has done a lot for her: " . . . there's nothing to be afraid of, nothing to want or hate or avoid, here, or run from. Or pursue" (234). Certain parallels between Tagomi and Juliana offer themselves. Throughout the novel he has been calm, reasonable. Juliana has been excited, almost panicky, several times considering suicide. Tagomi went into deep depression after he killed the two intruders spontaneously, without thought. Almost ill, thinking of resisting physically when her companion demands that they leave Denver to visit Abendsen that same night, once Juliana guesses that he is an SD man she plans to kill him and, still upset, almost nonchalantly slashes his throat. Then quite calmly she goes to Abendsen. Tagomi's reality collapses as he enters the reader's world. Juliana's questioning reveals that the world of *The Grasshopper Lies Deep* is the "real" world. Tagomi calls on the Nazi consul to "repent"; she tells Abendsen to "believe." (He shakes his head negatively.) Tagomi suffers a heart attack, perhaps dying. Juliana walks alone into the night. She survives the anxieties which she has known since the beginning of the novel, whereas the stability which Tagomi once knew is destroyed. So, one infers, is that of Abendsen. Only Juliana does not seriously question the order of things; only she retains her faith—her illusions?—despite the events of *The Man in the High Castle*. Only she escapes the collapse of reality. One must wonder whether or not in her seeming naïveté Dick has captured the single character to escape the existential helplessness which Baynes attributed to mankind, for only Juliana seems impervious to the evil of the Nazis.

Like *Stranger in a Strange Land*, *The Man in the High Castle* gained a Hugo Award as best novel of the year. Perhaps Dick's fine texturing of his alternate universe provided the deciding factor, for his dark pessimism stands in contrast to the quasi-mysticism of Heinlein. Yet at the heart of all Dick's work lie his troubled religious concerns, becoming ever more apparent as his career continued. The strength of *The Man in the High Castle* rests in the skill with which Dick at least partially masked (objectified) his deepest personal anxieties with the emblematic world dominated by the Nazi Party.

In contrast, Dick himself repeatedly told a single anecdote revealing how intensely subjective was the origin of his next major novel, *The Three Stigmata of Palmer Eldritch* (1965), which lays bare his anguish. Yet because Dick continued to explicate the basic incident ten to fifteen years after the fact, one cannot but suspect some of its elaborations, for one infers that as fame and notoriety came to Dick, he dramatized his mental and spiritual plight. The mythologizing of Philip K. Dick that led to a cult began somewhat later. In a review of *The Three Stigmata of Palmer Eldritch* for *F&SF*, Judith

Merril—a pivotal figure in the changes occurring within the field in the 1960s—praised him for his attention to "virtually every current crucial issue" but judged the novel "a riotous profusion of ideas, enough for a dozen novels, or one really good one; but the stuff is unsorted, frequently incompleted, seldom even clearly stated" (June 1965: 75).

Early in 1963 Dick was confirmed in St. Columba's Episcopal Church at Point Reyes, California, where he and his wife Anne then lived. In a headnote written in 1980 for a reprint of the short story "The Days of Perky Pat," originally published in 1963, he explained that while he walked to an isolated shack where he did his writing, he had a vision; in the sky he saw "a vast visage of perfect evil. It was immense; it filled a quarter of the sky. It had empty slots for eyes—it was metal and cruel and, worst of all, it was God."[15] One still cannot be sure whether the "actual mystical experience" occurred before or after he became "a convert to the Anglo-Catholic Church" and took "the rite of unction." It persisted for "almost a month." Apparently he sought aid from the priest at St. Columba's, but neither the church nor psychiatry helped. He attempted to exorcise the vision by writing the novel in the spring of 1963; the visage became that of Palmer Eldritch. Almost immediately he "wandered away from the Church" because "their teachings do not include that of a real, active, evil power who has control—or near control—of the earth we live on."[16]

CUL-DE-SAC

Because hallucinations and the use of drugs inform the story line, *The Three Stigmata* has generally been called his LSD novel—"a runaway book" capturing "the essence of a psychedelic trip with uncanny accuracy"[17]—although at the time he relied only on amphetamines regularly to maintain his rigorous writing schedule, while LSD had not yet become fashionable. Yet Dick called the vision "a true trip" and suggested that his first experience with LSD "confirmed my vision of Palmer Eldritch."[18] His subsequent critics of the 1970s emphasized his participation in the drug culture and his interest in Eastern mysticism, as illustrated by *The Man in the High Castle,* but by and large they seemed to overlook his continuing concern with Christian theology, as exemplified by his "lengthy discussion with Bishop James Pike" in the late 1960s.[19] At this point one can only speculate as to whether or not the tumult in American Protestant theology during the early 1960s, originating with Gabriel Vahanian's *The Death of God* (1961), affected Dick's intellectual and emotional obsession with religious matters. As the controversy of the early 1960s involved Dietrich Bonhoeffer, with his concern for the downfall of the church in Germany during the 1930s, one sees a possible source for Dick's fascination with the Nazis and Germany as a symbol of evil.

Briefly in *The Three Stigmata of Palmer Eldritch* he sketches Dr. Willy Denkmal, who operates an E Therapy clinic in Eichenwald. His treatment speeds up evolution, causing a growth of the cortex area of the brain so that his patients become hydrocephalic—"bubble-heads," as they are popularly known. With a passing reference to the controversies of Erasmus and Luther, Denkmal speaks of the "new and exciting concepts . . . especially of a religious nature" which his patients experience (79). He also makes an ambiguous comparison between transubstantiation and the effect of Can-D, one of the illegal hallucinogenic drugs figuring in the novel. But the protagonist, Leo Bulero, dismisses him as "a little pseudoquack," although wishing that his own treatment could evolve "the human brain to entire new orders of conception" (83). The incidental character Anne Hawthorne belongs to the reformed branch of the Neo-American Church, which claims apostolic succession; she is dismissed by a Martian colonist as a member of a church "with all the sacraments and the rituals, all that old outdated junk" (174).

The main thrust of the novel shifts back and forth between a confusing assortment of altered states of consciousness and alternate realities. On an Earth increasingly damaged by the greenhouse effect, the United States conscripts citizens for colonies in the hostile environments of Venus, Mars, and Ganymede, hoping through this project to save some remnant of the human race. Only the use of Can-D, the hallucinogenic drug, makes the lives of the colonists tolerable, for it allows them to "translate"; that is, to assume the identities of dolls in the Perky Pat Layouts—miniaturized constructs emulating supposedly idealized mid-twentieth-century

CUL-DE-SAC

American settings (Dick said frequently that he got the idea from watching his daughters with their Barbie dolls). The psyches of the colonists can fuse together to share these experiences. Early in the novel Leo Bulero pronounces Can-D "the religion of the colonists" (27). To complicate this already dystopian future, Palmer Eldritch returns from the Proxima Centauri system, bringing with him another hallucinogenic drug, Chew-Z, which he immediately makes available to the colonists. What might well be no more than another struggle between monopolistic corporations for domination of the solar system moves through a maze of hallucinations to a cosmic level as one learns first that all the fantasy worlds which Chew-Z produces are products of Eldritch's mind and that he himself is not a human, but a god capable of assimilating everyone and everything into his own identity. Leo finally attributes to Eldritch "the evil, negative trinity of alienation, blurred reality, and despair" which through Eldritch fills the cosmos (276). Ambiguously, Leo seems to equate him with *the original ancient blight* (277). Even though Dick wanted the reader to see Leo's prefatory remark that "we can make it" as something of an affirmation, it is not convincing. *The Three Stigmata of Palmer Eldritch* marks the depths of Dick's despair.

The early 1960s produced one other cult book, Frank Herbert's *Dune* (1965, serialized in *Analog* as "Dune World," 1963–64, and "Prophet of Dune," 1965). Like *Stranger in a Strange Land*, it did not become an underground favorite until later in the decade, although it subsequently grew into a best-selling tetralogy and led Willis E. McNelly to issue *The Dune Encyclopedia* (1984). While the story line does bring together familiar motifs, the vividness with which he pictures the desert environment and feudal culture of the planet Arrakis—Dune—brings to mind the thoroughness of Hal Clement and Poul Anderson. Herbert's uniqueness lies in the completeness he gives to the necessary social and religious background of the Fremen, a warrior society calling up romantic images of traditional bedouins. One of the first writers to emphasize ecology throughout his fiction, he expanded his definition of that science beyond physical ecosystems to include social ecology in order to stress the need for an understanding of the consequences of actions. Such understanding provides a key to the development of *Dune*.

A barren world, Dune has importance to the Galactic Imperium as the one source in the known universe of "melange," an addictive drug which is the spermicide of the Shai-Hulud, the monstrous sandworms indigenous only to Dune. The drug is invaluable because it can affect an individual's longevity and prescience. Political intrigue and legend combine to shape the narrative's course of action. In order to maintain a precarious balance of power, the Emperor of the Imperium allows the ruling families of the scattered planets to fight among themselves as long as they do not use atomic weapons or other machines of war. Thus when Duke Leto, head of the family of Atreides, is summoned to rule the planet Dune, he is killed by a hated rival, but his wife Jessica and son Paul flee into the desert, where they find refuge among the deeply religious Fremen society. Jessica is an adept, a member of the Bene Gesserit, a society of women who have for centuries been conducting a project in genetic engineering by breeding with the aristocratic families and determining the sex of their offspring in an effort to produce the Kwisatz Haderach, the first man to have full access to the memories of all his ancestors. For them he will be a means to political power in the empire which they have been denied because of their sex. From the beginning the fifteen-year-old Paul has a heightened awareness and visionary dreams.

Despite the SF trappings this is the stuff of heroic fantasy, particularly when played out on the primitive stage of Dune. While the daily ingestion of melange makes the Fremen the finest warriors in the universe, ever-increasing doses of the addictive spice drug increase Paul's psychic powers. The drama grows as much from his heightened consciousness as from his survival in the violence of the desert. His visions agonize him, for he sees the consequences of his action, a terrible jihad which will destroy the Imperium. Yet he becomes Paul Muad'Dib, the Mahdi of the Fremen, who see in him the one to bring about the longed-for flowering of the barren world. A new religion sweeps him to power. He accepts the role imposed on him by the Bene

Gesserit, although as his powers have grown, he has seen beyond their attempts to manipulate and control the genetic fluctuations of the race. He hopes that he can guide the turmoil he foresees to a better end. The tension of the narrative grows out of Paul's private anguish about the demands placed on him as the Messiah of the new religion. *Dune* was the first novel to win both the Hugo Award and the new Nebula Award given by the Science Fiction Writers of America (SFWA).

Although Judith Merril praised Herbert in *F&SF* for the "delicacy and precision" of his skill in portraying the Fremen and the ecology of Arrakis, she decried the "odd hodgepodge of concepts in the novel," especially the treatment of the wise, self-disciplined Bene Gesserit women who "allow themselves to become hopelessly involved in court intrigues on the pattern of the Borgias' Italy, dealing wholesale in assassinations and assignations" in order to bring about the Kwisatz Haderach. Merril revealed something of her beliefs when she insisted that "beyond a certain level of civilization, there *are no esoteric mysteries*" (Mar. 1966: 51–53). As for Herbert himself, in a 1979 interview he declared that "cult leaders have feet of clay, if not worse. . . . They lead their followers into the Coliseum where they get to be eaten by lions. . . . The bottom line of the *Dune* trilogy is: beware of heroes. Much better rely on your own judgment, and your own mistakes."[20] In addition to echoing something of Heinlein's emphasis on the individual, this retrospective appraisal underscores the reversals in the saga of Paul Atreides. In *Dune Messiah* (1969) the effects of the jihad have irreparably damaged the Fremen culture, while the fervor of the new religion has hardened into ritual entirely dependent on the omniscience of Muad'Dib. Blinded during one of the palace conspiracies to depose him, he renounces his mission to shape and control the future and wanders into the desert to die. *Children of Dune* (1976), according to John Clute, "is a deeply and convincingly pessimistic novel about the impossible cost of attempting to master the universe" (*F&SF*, Feb. 1977: 52).

Paradoxically, these novels—from Miller and Sturgeon to Heinlein and Herbert—not only represent the cutting edge of SF in the early 1960s but also reveal the cul-de-sac the field found itself in. Topical interest—primarily the emotional impact of Hiroshima—had summoned science fiction from the specialist magazines to the book stalls at mid-century. Criticism of various elements in American society—the fascination with the possibility of a dystopian future—colored and sustained the main thrust of the field as it responded to its wider audience.

Almost at once the science fiction community as a whole became increasingly self-conscious. An indication of what was to come surfaced when Lloyd Arthur Eshbach, founder of Fantasy Press, published *Of Worlds Beyond: A Symposium* (1947), the first book to explore "The Science of Science Fiction Writing." In presenting it as "a practical guide, a handbook," the seven contributors discussed the nature and function of SF. John W. Campbell reiterated his basic premise that "an honest effort at prophetic extrapolation of the known be made" and stressed the need "to forecast the *development of a science* of sociology" since the areas of sociology, psychology, and parapsychology were still "not true sciences" (91). (The essay helps to fix a date showing the mind-set which led to his interest in Dianetics and psionics.) The sleeper of the symposium proved to be Heinlein's mention of a kind of story not usually included in SF; namely, "the story of people dealing with contemporary science and technology" (16). He labeled it "the speculative science fiction story," thereby introducing a term which was to lie fallow until the 1960s.

Reginald Bretnor's *Modern Science Fiction: Its Meaning and Future* (1953) sought to address a wider audience. The most important contribution, because it broke new ground so far as the general reader was concerned, came from Anthony Boucher (the pseudonym of William Anthony Parker White), coeditor of *F&SF* and long-time writer and editor of mystery fiction. In "The Publishing of Science Fiction" he observed that the splitting up of fiction "by critics and publishers alike, into a series of specialized categories: the serious novel, the mystery, the historical novel, the western . . . with the latest being the science-fiction story" had not occurred until after World War I. By implication he saw this concentration on a single type of fiction by both writer and reader as an effect of the mass market, but he also blamed "a new school of criticism, dominating our critical quarterlies and our Departments of English, which insists upon seeing a sharp distinction between commercial appeal and literary quality" (25). This specialization also had economic consequences for the publisher; in principle it assured a minimal market for each kind of novel. He might have added, as subsequent analysts did, that this often gave the marketing department authority over the editorial department in selection of titles. "Ghettoization"—the use of publishers' labels in marketing—rankled the writers in particular, as the 1960s would show. While Boucher predicted that a larger number of original SF paperbacks would be published, he lamented the field's emphasis on anthologies since "an anthology is not necessarily a selection of the best work available" (36). Again, he might have emphasized even more the often "wildly capricious" packaging of magazine fiction, whether serials or stories, in book form, for even as the 1960s began, with the exception of a very few titles often not published as SF, most SF books were "fix ups" (Peter Nicholls's term) of novelettes, serials, or related short stories.

A year earlier, in one of the so-called "fanzines" circulated among devotees of the field, writing under the pseudonym William Atheling, James Blish had begun a series of often caustic appraisals of the fiction in current magazines. He dismissed out-of-hand mere adventure stories, like those of Burroughs and A. Merritt, and called upon his colleagues to bring higher standards to their work. A scholar who was to be for a time one of the editors of *Kalki*, the journal of the James Branch Cabell Society, Blish sincerely wanted the writers to try to achieve the quality of such of his favorite authors as Joyce, Shaw, and Pound. He sought the "technical critic" who could help both writer and reader, the former in terms of craftsmanship and the latter in the manner of the formalist criticism of the mid-century. Not surprisingly, he was among the first to say that the writing of science fiction should not be "divorced by the critic from the mainstream of fiction writing, or from artistic creation as a whole."[21] Many of his pieces written primarily in the 1950s were collected in *The Issue at Hand* (1964) and *More Issues at Hand* (1970).

Blish's friend and early collaborator, Damon Knight, had established his reputation early with a scathing attack, "Destiny's Child" (1945), on the extravagances of A. E. van Vogt's works, particularly the serialized version of *The World of Null-A* (1945), which van Vogt revised before book publication (1948). Occasional editor and witty storyteller, Knight reviewed for a variety of amateur and professional magazines, most notably *Infinity* and *F&SF*. During the early 1950s his was the second voice asking that SF be judged on the same criteria as all fiction. The Chicago-based publishers Advent gathered a selection of those reviews together as their first title. Knight's *In Search of Wonder*

CUL-DE-SAC

(1956) won him a Hugo. Blish and Knight were the tip of the iceberg of activity among the professional writers. Ted Cogswell, a member of the English Department at Ball State University, circulated *Proceedings of the Institute for Twenty-First Century Studies* among writers and editors so that they might discuss literary and scientific matters.

In 1956 Knight, Blish, and Judith Merril organized the initial Milford Science Fiction Writers' Conference, held annually at Knight's home in Milford, Pennsylvania, well into the 1960s. Participants were invited to join in a workshop that blended together informal yet rigorous critical discussions of unpublished manuscripts and consideration of such professional matters as contractual agreements, including the selling of reprint and international rights. Significantly, from the beginning writers new to the field were invited to attend so that there were always fresh perspectives. The Milford Conferences led to the formation of the Science Fiction Writers of America in 1965, with Knight as its first president and Robert Silverberg—who had gained a Hugo as the most promising new writer in the same year Knight won his as a reviewer—as the second president. So influential did the group with its ever-changing membership become that anecdotes about the "Milford Mafia" are still recalled at conventions. Especially, through Knight and his wife, Kate Wilhelm, Milford contributed to the formation of the Clarion Science Fiction Writers'

SCIENCE FICTION: EARLY 1960s

Workshop for beginning writers, held first at Clarion College (Pennsylvania) in 1968 and directed by Robin Scott Wilson.

By the beginning of the 1960s one could sense a growing restlessness in the field. Even before Bretnor's *Modern Science Fiction* had circulated widely, Boucher's point on ghettoization had been reinforced when in 1953 Doubleday fulfilled his shrewd guess that a major publisher would form a Science Fiction Book Club. Although his prediction that novels would one day replace the anthology as the chief vehicle of SF had begun to be realized, almost without exception any book published drew on fiction from the magazines. The Hugos were awarded by popular vote of the fans attending the conventions, but before 1959 the nominations in the various categories came from the convention committees so that there was talk of publishers, agents, and small groups of friends influencing the nominations. Even in 1964 after the nominating ballot had been introduced, only 164 members responded, with none of the five novels nominated to the final ballot receiving more than twenty votes; Clifford D. Simak's *Way Station* won with sixty-three votes.[22] For eleven years, from 1955 through 1965, either *Astounding* or *F&SF* was named the best professional magazine, with *Galaxy* always an also-ran. In 1960 at a regional conference in Pittsburgh, Blish asked that when the fans next voted a Hugo to a best novel, they ask but a single question: *"Is it about anything?"*[23]

CUL-DE-SAC

Throughout the 1950s Campbell had undertaken a sales campaign; by selling SF to a wider audience through articles in such journals as *The Saturday Review* and *Writer*, he hoped to gain support for the scientific community itself. He began toying with the *Astounding* title in February 1960, stabilizing it as *Analog Science Fiction-Science Fact* in April 1965. In December 1961 Frederik Pohl replaced Horace Gold as editor of *Galaxy*. Between 1953 and 1959 he had edited six annual volumes of *Star Science Fiction Stories*, the first anthology series asking for original fiction. At *F&SF* after Boucher's retirement in 1958 three editors followed him until Edward L. Ferman assumed the position in April 1965. Between May 1956 and January 1964 an occasional filler in *F&SF* became a featured series as sixty-eight vignettes entitled "Through Time and Space with Ferdinand Feghoot" parodied the shopworn plot situations and characters of SF by turning each episode into an outrageous pun. Reginald Bretnor wrote them under the name Grendel Briarton.

Perhaps the state of affairs in the field can best be illustrated by starting with a judgment Judith Merril made some six months after she had attended the Worldcon in London in 1965. In the same issue of *F&SF* that she found Herbert's *Dune* "a bit pretentious," she went on to say that Simak's *All Flesh Is Grass* "will probably be my personal nomination for the best science fiction novel of 1965. . . . A book both meaningful and eminently readable" (Mar. 1966: 54). From the early

1960s on, Simak found himself a central theme and through variations on a peaceful setting gained a reputation as the outstanding pastoralist in SF. Drawing on his youth in the valley of the Wisconsin River, he returned again and again to the emblematic town of Millville. One could also say that in his most memorable fiction he worked with variations on a single plot: the encounter between sympathetic, often lonely humans with aliens who are their equal or superior. In a sense he brought the inhabitants of the universe to Earth in order to give substance to a vision of all sentient creatures, however diverse their forms, as part of a single community which in itself gives purpose and meaning to the universe. In his Hugo-winning novelette, "The Big Front Yard" (1958), aliens warp space so that the house of the protagonist opens into an endless number of parallel worlds; aliens appear, wanting to trade and exchange ideas. The persecution of mutants who have the parapsychic ability to escape the individual isolation and the confines of Earth in *Time Is the Simplest Thing* (1961) may be a commentary on racial matters, but the protagonist's meetings with beings of many worlds provide the thematic core. Such meetings make him feel that he is "brother to everything that ever existed or ever will exist" (69). Earth itself is a *Way Station* (1963) for aliens as they traverse the galaxy; Earth is admitted into the federation of worlds. The alien intelligence of *All Flesh Is Grass* (1965) has an outward appearance of flowers but possesses a communal mind; it offers humanity a partnership spreading across many worlds. Simak would move toward fantasy and a quest theme in many of his later works, but in *A Choice of Gods* (1972) he reached the heights of *City*. Throughout his fiction he expresses an affirmation absent from many of his contemporaries. A popular author and an excellent storyteller, he was a safe choice for Merril, but *All Flesh Is Grass* did nothing new technically or thematically.

A few other examples from the American SF of the early 1960s may suffice. In H. Beam Piper's *Little Fuzzy* (1962) a gemstone having a thermofluorescent quality causing it to glow brilliantly when worn as a jewel is unique to the planet Zarathustra. For twenty-five years a chartered corporation has owned the Class III planet and maintains a monopoly until the prospector Jack Halloway discovers a hitherto unknown "cuddly," two-foot, teddy bear alien sufficiently intelligent to classify as a "sapient being." The ensuing investigation and legal battle, complete with trial, pit "Pappy Jack" Halloway and his friends against the director of the corporation and his scientific staff, who must be reminded not to treat Fuzzy as a laboratory animal. Early in the novel the point is made that "Sapience is the result of evolution by natural selection" (53) and is characterized by "conscious thought, by ability to think in logical sequence and by the ability to think in terms other than mere sense data" (166). The psychology is Freudian, and the highest qualities of mind are the imagination and the skill to use symbols. The suicide of the corporation chief of Scientific Study and Research and the testimony of Lieutenant j.g. Ruth Ortheris, a naval intelligence officer who had worked within the corporation, ensure the court decision in favor of Fuzzy. Piper published a second novel, *The Other Human Race* (1964, retitled *Fuzzy Sapiens* when reprinted), which resumes the action immediately after the decision against the corporation and concerns primarily an attempt to gain control of the gemstones.

James H. Schmitz also dealt extensively with alien cultures in his fiction, but his first novel, *The Universe Against Her* (1964), shows clearly the difficulties arising from patching together short stories to make a novel. The unifying thread is the "emerging promise of brilliance" of fifteen-year-old Telzey Amberdon as she grows increasingly aware of her psi powers. Initially she and her pet Tick Tock go on vacation to the planet Jontarou, where her ability as a xenotelepathist enables her to communicate with the indigenous Baluit crest cats who prove to be as "rational" as humans. Tick Tock, a partially grown Baluit cat, provides the necessary link. After a treaty between the Federation of the Hub and the new Affiliated Species of Jontarou is signed, that action is forgotten as Telzey becomes involved in thwarting the efforts of the guardians of a school chum, Gonvil Lodis, to kill that young woman so that she will not assume control of her share of stock in a major family corporation. Having come under surveillance by the psionic machines of the Psychology Service, Telzey understands that one day she will become a secret agent. Her further adventures were not gathered into book form until the 1970s.

Much has been made of the close relationship between the detective story and science fiction in that both present a problem to be solved. Because of the interest in dystopia and social criticism by so many critics, what seems to have been shortchanged in any overview of contemporary SF is the legion of protagonists who act as secret agents. While they are not identical to James Bond, particularly in that by and large they do not share his sexual proclivities, they undoubtedly grow out of essentially the same tensions that made the novel of espionage so popular after World War II. Moreover, as the films based on Agent 007 emphasize, they do share a fascination for advanced technological hardware. In SF they range from the independent young woman Telzey Amberdon to the protagonist of *Supermind* (1963) by Mark Phillips (the pseudonym of collaborators Randall Garrett and Laurence M. Janifer); Kenneth J. Malone, an agent of the FBI, involves himself with Russian spies, psionics, and the Psychical Research Society as he discovers that telepaths are systematically trying to improve society, although on one occasion they must kill a governor who has the potentialities of being a Hitler and sees himself as President.

Supermind represents one of Garrett's more pedestrian efforts when contrasted with the accomplishments of his Lord Darcy stories, which reached a high point in his novel *Too Many Magicians* (1967). As chief investigator for the Duke of Normandy in a twentieth-century alternate world deriving from the Anglo-French empire founded by Richard the Lionhearted, Lord Darcy works in a world where magic and science coexist. Not only does Garrett combine elements of fantasy, SF, and the detective story, but he parodies all three areas of literature. Granting the differences in tone, his interest in the medieval parallels that of Andre Norton, one of the most distinguished of all contemporary fantasists. In *Witch World* (1963), the first of a series of five novels completed by 1967, Norton created an alternate universe drawing in part on her "on-going and in-depth research" concerning "the Norman holdings in medieval Outremer."[24] As a point of departure she allows her protagonist, Simon Tregarth, to escape pursuit in the present-day world by using the Siege Perilous to catapult him into the mysterious kingdom of Estcarp, where he immediately rescues a witch from pursuit. Although the power of magic resides with the "matriachate of Estcarp" instead of with individual men, Norton's narrative deals with sword and sorcery as much as anything by Robert E. Howard. The emotional core of the novel focuses on the growing love between Tregarth and the witch Jaelithe, although the action centers on the conflict with the scientific "offworlders," the Kolder. Norton weaves an intricate tapestry as she follows the

adventures of Tregarth and Jaelithe and their three children (triplets)—Kyllan, the warrior; Kemoc, the seer/
warlock; and Kaththea, the witch—in the five novels
that make up the earliest of her four fantasy series.

In sharp contrast to the world of fantasy, the central
action of Ward Moore and Avram Davidson's collabora-
tive *Joyleg* (1962) takes a congressional committee to the
Tennessee mountains to investigate a veteran who has
been drawing a pension as long as records have been
kept. Isachar Joyleg served in the Revolutionary War
and seems to have discovered immortality by means of
a certain kind of moonshine. Eventually a Russian dele-
gation gets involved, but the narrative exists primarily
to let Joyleg present a sometimes slightly ribald revision
of early American history.

Similarly, when a bolt of lightning hits a still aboard
the 89-foot yawl *Alice*—supposedly intended to investigate countermeasures against submarines—Ensign
Joseph Rate and his crew find themselves aboard G. C.
Edmondson's *The Ship That Sailed the Time Stream* (1965).
Encountering first a Viking ship fleeing from the rule
of Olaf Tryggvasson—from which they rescue a Spanish
damsel, Raquel—they fail to regain 1965 until after episodes with a Moorish slave trader, a volcanic Aegean
island, and a Roman galley, with a side trip to Piraeus
for one sailor, Howard McGrath, who has both religious
and sexual hang-ups. They meet several accidental time
travelers—a Glastonbury monk and a Chicago madam
from the 1920s, the latter complete with a crib of blonde

Syrian girls from Tyre. Science is replaced by historical detail and a casual sexuality supposedly appropriate to tales of American sailors, although both Raquel and Ensign Rate retain their virtue. Indeed, her disappearance during the last transition—a brief jump from 1942 to 1965—reinforces his desire to resume his travels.

Although the publication of the short story collection *The Mile Long Spaceship* (1961) indicated that Kate Wilhelm would develop into one of the fine SF writers, her collaboration with Theodore L. Thomas in *The Clone* (1965) exemplifies those narratives relying entirely on horror for their impact. It is an intriguing variation of the Frankenstein theme; its authors take as their premise the idea that the array of chemical wastes in Chicago's sewer system can generate life spontaneously and that the resultant mindless organism will keep growing initially until it fills every conduit, air line, and pipe under the metropolitan area. They tell the story well, maintaining a tension by emphasizing the hour-by-hour growth of the tissue and alternating among the reactions of a variety of characters as the monster erupts onto the surface, consuming everything that can provide it with immediate nutrition. It is, of course, a classic problem story as well as a catastrophe novel. The ever-present danger is that the creature will reach Lake Michigan, the Great Lakes, and all the cities around them. The protagonist, Mark Kenniston, learns that an iodine solution will irritate it. Aerial spraying contains the one-hundred-square-mile thing, but the collabora-

CUL-DE-SAC

tors leave open the idea that such a phenomenon can occur again.

Random as these examples may seem, they give several insights into the development of contemporary science fiction. One must remember that with the exception of *Supermind*, all of these novels were nominated for either the Hugo or the Nebula. Perhaps the most important thing to note is that despite the insistence of subsequent academic critics especially, there was no simplistic separation between science fiction and fantasy; the writers mixed elements of the two as they pleased in an individual work, sometimes playing them off against one another, as in the case of Andre Norton. Secondly, without exception action remained more important than in-depth character study. These narratives were stories told for their own sake; entertainment seems the goal. One may judge the magazine format and audience responsible for this emphasis. What becomes most important, even with the mix of fantasy and SF, is that neither technically nor thematically did these novels show anything new—unless one notices, as in Randall Garrett, a tendency to parody the conventions of the field.

The main thrust of the 1950s, which gave new vitality to the field, had exchanged the optimistic view governing SF from the turn of the century until mid-century for a dystopian vision of the future. The continued progress brought about by an elite of scientists and technicians—the cornerstone, at least, of Campbell's early years as editor of *Astounding*—had been set aside in favor of the rebel or the outcast. The landscape of a post-nuclear holocaust readily established itself as a popular narrative framework. Psionics—the parapsychological development of humanity, whether as individuals or a society—became another given. In the absence of assured leadership, despair set the tone by the end of the 1950s. Daniel Galouye's *Dark Universe* (1961) examines the subterranean world inhabited by the descendants of a shattered bomb shelter, U.S. Survival Complex Eleven; but the young lovers, Jared Fenton and Della Anselm, reach the surface, where for a generation survivors of Complex Seven have begun to renew the vast "Original World." For all its imagery of light and dark and rebirth, *Dark Universe* remains an adventure story.

Coming from a Mars which has long quarantined the Earth, the protagonist of Lester del Rey's *The Eleventh Commandment* (1962, revised 1970)—Boyd Jensen—learns that almost two centuries after nuclear war destroyed society in 1993, the American Catholic Eclectic Church rules with totalitarian strictness. Slowly he comes to understand that because genetic mutation still threatens to destroy humanity, enforcement of that newest edict—"Be fruitful and multiply and replenish the Earth"—means that unrestricted population growth holds the only hope that some day in the future even the invisible genetic weaknesses will be eliminated so that "a new race of men" may reach toward the stars. Again, for all the novelty of the newest invention of Dr.

CUL-DE-SAC

Felix Hoennikker, "one of the so-called 'Fathers' of the first atomic bomb," and the warnings of the new religion growing out of the teachings of Bokonon, Kurt Vonnegut's *Cat's Cradle* (1963) adds nothing but fresh icing to the dark vision of *The Sirens of Titan*. As in the cases of those writers who told their stories for the sake of the action, one may say that those who meditated on the dystopian view in the SF of the early 1960s rearranged the furniture but added nothing that was new.

Two books from these years stand out as notable innovations: Zenna Henderson's *Pilgrimage: The Book of the People* (1961) and Edgar Pangborn's *Davy* (1964). Henderson linked a series of six stories published earlier with a narrative frame centering on a depressed, suicidal young woman, Lea Holmes. On a bus somewhere in the desert of the Southwest she meets an older woman—named simply Karen—who speaks of healing and takes her to the People. From the outset the reader suspects that Karen is unusual. At the initial "Gathering" she becomes the first-person narrator of a story that echoes the theme of the frame. Valancy Carmody comes to Cougar Canyon as a new teacher. Somewhat reserved, calling herself an "outsider" when she rejects a marriage proposal, she seems only mildly surprised when a pupil levitates, but when she and a group of children face a brush fire in the mountains, she calls down a violent rainstorm to extinguish the fire. Her action identifies her as one of the People, and she is accepted by them as the daughter of a couple supposedly lost when they came to Earth in the late nineteenth century to escape the destruction of their home world. Physically indistinguishable from humans, they are aliens possessing "Gifts, Designs, and Persuasions, . . . landmarks on a road as yet untraveled by humanity," as Sandra Miesel says of them in the introduction. A long-time elementary teacher in Arizona, Henderson relies heavily on children and teachers as each of the stories—told in the first person by different narrators—reveals individuals in personal, sometimes spiritual crisis whom the People aid. These are aliens with psi powers, but the language and incidents typical of that SF motif are muted by the examination of the closely knit community. Nor should one overlook the many biblical ties as Henderson evokes the image of their quest for a promised land. A second collection, *The People: No Different Flesh* (1967), reinforces that theme by sketching more of the history of the People's exodus from their deluged world.

In *A Mirror for Observers* (1954), which won the International Fantasy Award, Edgar Pangborn had introduced Martians who have moved among humans for some thirty-one thousand years after fleeing their dying world, but the effect is quite different from that of *Pilgrimage*. His Martians have become students of human culture, hoping for an ethical revolution that will allow the two peoples to merge. The narrative is the report of Elmis to a superior. It concentrates first on the struggle between him and the Martian Namir, who hates humans, to guide the young boy Angelo Pontevecchio, a potential leader, a messiah. However, as though reflecting Pangborn's reaction to the McCarthy era, the second half of the narrative concentrates on the efforts of Joseph Max—specifically compared to Hitler—and his Organic Unity Party to gain control of the United States by preaching a doctrine of racial purity and world domination. Irresponsible biochemical research unleashes an epidemic killing forty-two million Americans. The inference that Pangborn surrendered to his anger is reinforced by Namir's declaration that he influenced what happened because he wanted to "annihilate" the "greedy little ape" who has so polluted the world and profaned human potential. Pangborn's personal reactions may surface again as Elmis responds, saying that "all citizens . . . are responsible" for letting the world be as it is (214–15). As Elmis sails from Honolulu, melancholy grips him, for the plague has spread worldwide and a Russo-Chinese war continues in Asia.

The same melancholy cloaks much of *Davy*. The nuclear holocaust narrative frame is there. More than three centuries earlier an "abortive idiotic nuclear war" and plagues brought on "the Years of Confusion," following a cultural decline which, among other things, involved "a dithering refusal to let ethics catch up with science" (50). Now after a "sort of religious frenzy" gave the Holy Merucan Church its power, it dictates the life style throughout wilderness areas that are scarcely more than fiefdoms—Vairmant, Penn, Nuin, Katskil—hud-

dling on the transformed Atlantic coast. This SF furniture is shopworn, but Pangborn gives it new vitality
through his narrative strategies. On the Atlantic aboard
the *Morning Star*, Davy writes an account of his life,
addressing it to whatever Europeans may survive. He
reflects on what has happened to him; he does not
dramatize his wanderings as a member of Rumley's
Ramblers, his participation in several border wars, his
heresy, or the effort of him and his friends to bring
about reform. The process of his recollections garbles
chronology. The effect lies somewhere between a historical romance and *Bildungsroman*. Initially one does
not see how his reminiscences of his affairs with numerous "delicious" girls—explicitly presented—develop his
central theme. The core of his story, as befits a novel
having a medieval flavor, dwells on his love for the
woman he marries, the aristocratic Rickie. Throughout,
his flashbacks return to the island Neoarcheos, where
the crew of the *Morning Star* winter during Rickie's first
pregnancy. He breaks off the narrative with an account
of the time he met her; she was disguised as a young
cavalier who admitted him to the Society of Heretics.
In a final chapter, written six years later, he tells of her
death after long labor giving premature birth to a "mue"
(mutant). By the wish of his dearest friend, Dion of
Nuin, he fathers a child with Dion's wife. That, too, is
a "mue"; he knows then he carries "an evil that Old
Time set adrift, that came down through the generations" (265). On the eve of his departure for the main-

land of Europe, Davy asks the sea "whether the generations could some day restore the good of Old Time without the evil, and the ocean that was a voice in [his] mind suggested: Maybe soon, maybe only another thousand years." Perhaps no novel dealing with nuclear holocaust in the 1950s and 1960s found such an effective narrator or symbolic action.

Ironically, *Davy* lost the Hugo that year to Fritz Leiber's *The Wanderer*, perhaps the most puzzling novel to emerge from the early 1960s. One critic sees in it "the conviction that the universe may be intrinsically hostile to beings" like humans.[25] When one rereads it, particularly when one compares it to Leiber's *The Big Time* or anticipates the humor of his *A Specter Is Haunting Texas* (1969), one gains the impression that *The Wanderer* parodies both science fiction itself and some of its most devoted adherents. The basic narrative frame involves a worldwide catastrophe which "starkly affected every human being on Earth [and] opened deep fissures in the human mind" (9). As a lunar eclipse begins, the Wanderer, a ship the size of Earth, materializes from hyperspace to capture the moon gravitationally and devastate the Earth with tidal floods and volcanic action. As the moon breaks up, the ship collects its fragments, and the reader eventually learns that the sole reason for the ship's visit is to refuel its matter converters (193). To capture the panorama of destruction, Leiber develops a number of story lines, following a wide variety of characters, individually or in groups, through cycles of vignettes. Three lines of action seem particularly important. Don Merriam, U.S. Space Program, is caught at Moonbase. Margo Gelborn, his fiancée—with her cat Miaow—joins Paul Hagbolt, a mutual friend and publicist for the Moon Project, to head toward the project base, Vandenberg Two, to see the eclipse, but they encounter the members of a Flying Saucer Symposium meeting on the Pacific beach. Near Miami, Barbara Katz, "self-styled Girl Adventurer and long-time science-fiction fan" (21) goes to the home of Knolls Kelsey Kettering III (KKK)—who has been spying on her with his telescope—to see the eclipse. There are innumerable minor characters, one of them dying of a heart attack when he first sees the Wanderer. Essentially the characters remain two-dimensional, showing only superficial changes as a result of violence or of their sexual antics.

Throughout the novel, even before the appearance of the Wanderer, Leiber refers to SF matters. As they bicker over the presence of Miaow, Margo Gelborn tells Hagbolt, "Even your great god Heinlein" acknowledges that cats are "second-class citizens" (11). As the moon first cracks apart, Merriam speeds through the narrow split, just as Burroughs's John Carter once flew through a narrow shaft on Barsoom. Barbara Katz and KKK share an enthusiasm for "Doc" Smith in particular. He tells her that they are "fellow lensmen," while the bone-plastic splice in his hip reminds her of "the old soldiers that run the space academies in the Heinlein and E.E. Smith stories" (37). In short, Leiber keeps the reader constantly aware of the heroics of space opera. In one of his first vignettes, an "English novelist" declares that "science fiction is as trivial as all artistic forms that deal with phenomena rather than people" (14). Leiber proceeds to tell a story dealing with phenomena involving "terror and the supernormal" (9) instead of in-depth studies of character.

When a tidal wave threatens the symposium, a flying saucer carries Hagbolt and Miaow to the Wanderer, where they meet the cheetah-like Tigerishka, who initially prefers Miaow, dismissing Hagbolt as an "ape" (138–41). Although Margo Gelborn readily becomes the lover of a professor of sociology among the saucer students, not until she has killed a man does her lover tell her that she resembles a "vestal Valkyrie" who seems "vibrantly alive" (202, 204). As they struggle with more fleeing refugees, the sociologist watches police and youths battle and exclaims, "It's a war. . . . It's the Day of the Children" (226). In Florida, Barbara Katz thinks of old KKK as "her own private millionaire, to preserve and to cherish" (88), while he gladly substitutes her for his Barbie doll (153). Together with his black servants they flee inland before the rising water. Only his being a member of the KKK saves them from belligerent "crackers"; when he dies from exhaustion, Barbara and his servants escape by boat. Meanwhile, Merriam is picked up by the Wanderer.

When Hagbolt condemns the Wanderer for the destruction it has caused and accuses Tigerishka and her people of fleeing from something they fear, Tigerishka angrily denies the charge but later admits that they are fugitives. At length she explains that the universe is filled with intelligent life, that all of the planets at the center of the galaxy are artificial, that "its engineers" burn untold amounts of matter because they want "more form, more structure, more mind." The psionic immortals who govern the universe, making it a smaller place than the solar system, have as their aim the conservation of "intelligence until the cosmos ends . . . until mind is maximized." Soon the "wild" planets on the rim, like the Earth, will be seized. Her people are "the Wild Ones—the younger races, races . . . which grew from solitary killers, which have lived closer to death and valued style more than security, freedom more than safety." Her people dream of exploration and expansion, "bursting from this cosmos as from a chrysalis, no matter if this cosmos be destroyed." For a century since the Wild Ones were to be put on trial, they have fled a government "which values every frightened mouse and falling sparrow as equal to a tiger burning bright" (256–59). That night they make love; when Tigerishka tells him that he must leave, he asks to remain, "even as your pet." She claws Hagbolt and seizes Miaow (305–306). Even as Merriam conveniently begins their return to Earth, a "Stranger"—another planet—appears, and the two worlds fight as humanity watches; "Like the Lensmen battles," exclaims one character

(307). Abruptly first the Wanderer and then the other world vanish.

One can imagine the impact of Margo's rhetoric in the mid-1960s. Yet none of those ideas is new; they crystallize concepts that have echoed through space opera since its beginning. When people glimpse the pilot of the ship which rescues Hagbolt and Miaow from the tidal wave, one of them thinks, "My God, the second Buck Rogers Sunday page! The Tiger Men of Mars!" (128). When one speaks of "a benign Galactic Federation," another replies, "Cosmic Welfare State" (106). What the reader notices—almost suddenly—is the counterbalance in the names Barbara Katz and Tigerishka. Even more importantly, a number of explicit references call up the images of Gully Foyle and *The Stars My Destination*. One cannot readily dismiss the inference that *The Wanderer* parodied the SF that had given the field new vitality in the 1950s as well as the heroic images of the earlier space opera. In this way *The Wanderer* epitomizes the restlessness of the SF community and the need for new direction in the early 1960s.

Notes

1. Under the pseudonym Peter Bryant, Peter George's novel, *Two Hours to Doom* (1958), published as *Red Alert* in the United States,

SCIENCE FICTION: EARLY 1960s

was a story of preventive war, inaugurated by a general, leading to "worldwide HOLOCAUST." A novelization of *Dr. Strangelove* was issued under the name Peter George in 1963. Nicholls 250.

2. Justin Leiber, "Fritz Leiber & Eyes," *Starship: The Magazine about Science Fiction* 16 (Summer 1979): 13–14.

3. Gunn 210.

4. Gordon R. Dickson, introduction, *Three to Dorsai! Three Novels from the Childe Cycle* (Garden City, NY: Doubleday, 1975) ix.

5. *A Canticle for Leibowitz* was published in 1960, although the copyright date appears as 1959. The difference causes some inconsistencies in dating the novel. The stories were first published in *F&SF* between 1955 and 1957.

6. Algis Budrys, *Rogue Moon* (Garden City, NY: Doubleday, 1960) 11.

7. William Atheling (the pseudonym of James Blish), *More Issues at Hand* (Chicago: Advent, 1970) 64–65.

8. Bleiler 309.

9. William Atheling (the pseudonym of James Blish), *The Issue at Hand* (Chicago: Advent, 1964) 63–64.

10. Atheling (Blish), *More Issues* 57.

11. Charles Platt, *Dream Makers* (New York: Berkley, 1980) 146,149.

12. Patricia Warrick, *Mind in Motion: The Fiction of Philip K. Dick* (Carbondale, IL: Southern Illinois University Press, 1987) 44.

13. Warrick 45.

14. Paul Williams, introduction, *The Man in the High Castle* (Boston: Gregg, 1979) xxix.

15. Cited in Warrick 95–96. Dick's commentary occurs in William F. Nolan and Martin Greenberg, eds., *Science Fiction Origins* (New York: Fawcett, 1980) 98–101.

16. A letter dated 8 June 1969 from Dick to Bruce Gillespie, editor of *SF Commentary*, is included by Williams as an appendix to his introduction to *The Three Stigmata of Palmer Eldritch* (Boston: Gregg, 1978) xix.

CUL-DE-SAC

17. Williams vi.

18. Williams vi.

19. Warrick 134.

20. Platt 191.

21. Atheling (Blish), *More Issues* 12.

22. Donald Franson and Howard DeVore, *A History of the Hugo, Nebula and International Fantasy Awards* (Dearborn Heights, MI: Misfit Press, 1981) 25.

23. Atheling (Blish), *Issue at Hand* (129–30).

24. Roger C. Schlobin, "The Witch Series," *Survey of Modern Fantasy*, ed. Frank Magill (Englewood Cliffs, NJ: Salem Press, 1983) 5:2140.

25. Bleiler 423.

CHAPTER FOUR

The Late 1960s: Revolt and Innovation

What became a shouting match that split the American science fiction community by 1968 began quietly in London when Michael Moorcock succeeded E. J. "Ted" Carnell as editor of *New Worlds* with the May-June 1964 issue. Beginning in 1946 Carnell had "provided a stable domestic market for the leading British writers,"[1] although he lost some of them, particularly Arthur C. Clarke, to the American magazines. Carnell had serialized Philip K. Dick's *Time Out of Joint* (1959–60) and Theodore Sturgeon's *Venus Plus X* (1961), the only magazine appearance of Sturgeon's last major novel published during his lifetime. Carnell had helped the careers of both Brian Aldiss, who has acknowledged that under his editorship "anything experimental or new got in with the hack work,"[2] and J. G. Ballard, whose fiction became a focal point of the ensuing controversy, although it was virtually ignored by the American critics before 1965. (Berkley Books, however, issued seven of his titles between 1962 and 1964.)

That Moorcock intended something different from

REVOLT AND INNOVATION

Carnell's offerings became immediately apparent in his initial editorial, "A New Literature for the Space Age," in that May-June issue when he extolled William Burroughs both technically and philosophically. In that same issue the first installment of Ballard's "Equinox" accompanied his own article praising Burroughs's *The Naked Lunch* (1959). Except for a single review the American SF establishment disregarded Burroughs; indeed, several of the basic SF reference books now available do not have an entry for him.[3]

One finds that the "New Wave"—the sobriquet given the literary movement by Judith Merril—referred to the *nouvelle vague*, the French experimental films associated with such producers as Jean-Luc Godard and François Truffaut. Aldiss and Ballard took center stage quickly, to be joined by John Brunner, who had published even more widely than Aldiss in the American magazines during the late 1950s. Kingsley Amis, however, did not mention any of them in his brief *New Maps of Hell* (1960). Different as the three were from one another, what unites them on first impression was their shared concern with style and narrative technique. No one ever really spoke for all three of them, but soon comparisons between science fiction and poetry and talk of the surreal qualities of both content and form grew common. The manner in which a character's state of mind and setting interlocked became a trademark of Ballard's fiction. One cannot be certain when he first used the term "inner space," but in *F&SF* Judith Merril passed on his definition: "that area where the outer world of reality and the inner world of the psyche meet and fuse. Only in this area can one find the true subject matter of mature science fiction" (July 1965: 80). While both British and American writers subsequently disliked being lumped together, often disavowing that there was such a movement as a single New Wave, one of the terms that became a catchword was "inner space." After the Worldcon met in London in 1965, Merril did a comprehensive report on the British scene for *F&SF* (Jan. 1966: 39–45). Although she did not introduce the label New Wave at that time, the importance of the British scene in shaping contemporary SF undoubtedly stems from that convention and that article. Despite the nonliterary tensions of that period, however much the New Wave became a battle of critics and ideologies, it had its foundations in the fiction of a new generation of writers seeking to find their own idiom and manner. In December of that year Berkley Books published the first novel *The Genocides* (1965)—indeed, the first book— of Thomas Disch, the American expatriate most closely associated with *New Worlds*. When Judith Merril published her anthology, *11th Annual the Year's Best S-F* (1966), taking up the term used initially by Robert Heinlein, she advised her readers that as of then the *S* in her title stood not for science but for "speculative" fiction. Thereby she gave the SF community its second catchword. (She made her last public sales pitch for the New Wave with the anthology *England Swings* in 1968.)

Although James Blish later suggested that she did so because she "knew as little about the sciences as she did about the arts, and indeed never has felt comfortable with them," he quickly noted that there had been "a large number of writers and fans waiting in the wings who were as uncomfortable with, or actively resentful of, the sciences as Miss Merril." Indeed, in the same speech he asserted that Ballard, at one time a medical student, "has a most imperfect grasp of the sciences."[4] Unwittingly he may have spoken to a more profound discord which began, at least, with the exclusion of Rider Haggard and the "lost race" motif from the field and with the heated discussions of Gernsback's handling of "gadgets": namely, the place of the "hard" sciences in the field. One infers that the writers contributing to *New Worlds*, like their contemporaries in the United States, attempted in their own ways to accomplish a goal set by every writer, a goal that Blish himself had set up: "The science-fiction writer chooses, to symbolize *his* real world, the trappings of science and technology. . . . Instead of Main Street—in itself only a symbol—we are given Mars, the future." In writing of the choice of a set of symbols—"the religion of their age"—like C. P. Snow he addressed the old problem of two cultures when he asserted that "most humanists are *still* [twenty years after Hiroshima] stoppering their ears and looking the other way, and hence hardly dare to think that science fiction can be anything more cogent than a Disney fairy tale—amusing now and then, perhaps, but not 'real.'"[5] It may well be that for Blish, Merril, Ballard, and innumerable other writers, science fiction may provide the bridge between the two cultures.

Concentration just on Moorcock and those writers associated with *New Worlds* gives a distorted view of the science fiction scene. Although he and Judith Merril, who was then editor of a series of annual anthologies as well as reviewer for *F&SF*, may have reached an increasingly wide audience, theirs were not the only voices, the only efforts. Damon Knight had begun editing anthologies as early as *A Century of Science Fiction* (1962). In 1966 he released *Orbit 1*, the first of a series running through the 1970s; with the exception of Pohl's effort in the 1950s, *Orbit* was the most successful anthology publishing original fiction. In a brief introduction Knight expressed a credo that showed his ties with Blish but at the same time captured the essence of the change writers were trying for. "These are stories by master craftsmen," he wrote. "They are *about* something; they are not the sort of stories you forget as soon as you have read them. . . . Every one is a voyage of discovery into strange places of the universe and of the human psyche" (vii). Beyond its overall quality and the discovery over the next decade of many top quality writers, *Orbit* has extreme historical importance in that, together with its numerous imitators during the 1960s and early 1970s, it broke the monopoly that the magazines had had as the only market for original short science fiction.

REVOLT AND INNOVATION

In the autumn of 1965 in response to an offhand challenge from an old friend, Robert Silverberg, who had ostensibly left SF at the end of the 1950s, Harlan Ellison approached Doubleday through its SF editor, Larry Ashmead, proposing an anthology of original stories. In his introduction to the resultant *Dangerous Visions* (1967), he insisted that his "'new thing' in speculative fiction" had nothing to do with either Moorcock or Merril (xxiv). He said that the book "was intended as a canvas for new writing styles, bold departures, unpopular thoughts" (xxvii). Shaped by the fiery imagination of a young man whose talent spilled over into screenplays, television scripts, mystery fiction, and newspaper columns and reviews of science fiction, *Dangerous Visions* had a major influence on the American scene. It marks a turning point. It dominated the nominations for both the Hugo and Nebula in the short fiction categories, showing the adaptability of established writers like Philip José Farmer ("Riders of the Purple Wage") and Fritz Leiber ("Gonna Roll the Bones"), while recognizing a young writer who had not published in the magazines, Samuel R. Delany ("Aye, and Gommorah"). Leiber and Delany swept both awards, while Farmer tied with Anne McCaffrey ("Weyr Search") for the Nebula. Ellison himself gained a special Hugo as editor of *Dangerous Visions*. (In 1965 he had received both awards for his short story, "Repent, Harlequin! Said the Ticktockman.")

In one of two introductions to Ellison's volume,

Asimov, who was to publish no new major work of fiction during the 1960s, spoke of "The Second Revolution"—the first having been instigated when Campbell assumed editorship of *Astounding*. After chatting about Campbell's writers, he invited readers to explore the field at its "most daring and experimental" in *Dangerous Visions*, although he mentioned in passing "a science-fictional revolution" which had taken place at *Galaxy* in the early 1960s under Frederik Pohl. Subsequently Aldiss recognized Ellison's intention "to challenge long-established taboos (mostly sexual, it seems) . . . and to write subversive material"; then he went on to note "how uncontroversial most of [that fiction] was set against writers like Henry Miller, William Burroughs, and D. H. Lawrence, and how stylistically limited it was by comparison to writers like Herman Melville, James Joyce, B. S. Johnson, and William Golding."[6] He excepted Farmer's novella, which has frequently been compared to Joyce. One must realize how central in terms of language and narrative strategy Joyce was to Aldiss and Ballard. Again, John Brunner has openly acknowledged that in his prize-winning *Stand on Zanzibar* (1968) he deliberately emulated the narrative technique of Dos Passos. In terms of their writing, Lester del Rey identified the New Wave as being "avant-garde," while Donald Wollheim accused New Wave "pioneering" of reverting "back to antiquated experimental styles of the twenties and thirties without acknowledging it," suggesting that its "material smacks of Dadaism."[7] Both

REVOLT AND INNOVATION

men, especially del Rey, questioned the comprehensibility of the resulting narratives, particularly those of Ballard.

Although Wollheim identified Ellison with the New Wave in terms of content, he immediately praised Ellison for having found "ultramodern ways of narration." Charles Platt calls Ellison's style "direct, reaching out to accost the reader, and its rhythms are conversational, so that each piece is like a stand-up monologue."[8] In view of Ellison's breadth of writing, although he frequently scourged television, as in *The Glass Teat* (1969), one senses that he got his language and his narrative manner from the popular media. Just as he attacked TV and many of the social issues of the period, so did he attack the limitations of magazine science fiction, damning it as an unwanted publishers' marketing device and finally refusing to have his books identified with the category. Beginning with such stories as "Repent, Harlequin! Said the Ticktockman," his fiction played down the typical scenes and moved "toward dark, personal fantasies" which center on "an elemental confrontation between man and the forces that animate his universe, . . . a world that is not only indifferent but openly hostile to his existence."[9] Aldiss said of those stories that they "did much to unsettle that part of the genre which was still preoccupied with hardware and problems in engineering and hyperspatial mechanics,"[10] while more recently Terry Dowling has concluded that "Ellison's fiction is frequently a tool for biting social commentary and the expression of rage, as well as a showcase for humor, exuberance, and compassion."[11] In these judgments, paradoxically, lie the factors that both unite and separate Ellison—and many of --the American writers whom *Dangerous Visions* influenced or introduced—from their British contemporaries.

Harlan Ellison has always sincerely committed himself to causes he thought were just: civil rights, the antiwar movement of the 1960s, gun control. Some angered fans apparently said that he should not "politicize" science fiction. For whatever reasons, they had forgotten that during the 1960s SF, like the entire nation, was sharply politicized. In the June 1968 issue of *Galaxy*, for example, appeared two full-page advertisements: the first listed the names of those writers who believed that "the United States must remain in Vietnam to fulfill its responsibilities to the people of that country"; the other, the names of those who opposed the war. They split almost evenly. Science fiction, as noted, has always been topical, responding to the immediate scene, as do all the media of popular culture.

In an introduction to an anthology which Norman Spinrad dedicated to Philip K. Dick, *Modern Science Fiction* (1974), Spinrad struck out at SF as "a commercial genre with its own strange history and an attendant subculture," suggesting that the Golden Age "existed primarily in the minds of the aging fans of the 1950s and 1960s."[12] With the exception of those few novels which became part of the canon of the younger writers—Be-

REVOLT AND INNOVATION

ster's *The Demolished Man,* Sturgeon's *More Than Human,*
Dick's *The Man in the High Castle,* and Arthur C. Clarke's
Childhood's End—during the 1950s "the rash of new
magazines was filled with pretty dreadful stuff."[13] Because most of the SF editors and publishers were "commercial pragmatists" dealing with packaged materials
for fixed markets "instead of literary values and thematic content," not until the young writers "marooned
in this disaster area rapidly lost their youthful naivete"
did any real change occur: "This being the 1960s, when
consciousness changes were impelling young people
everywhere to fight against the constrictions of moribund social constructs, the result was not the bitter and
cynical resignation of the 1950s, but nascent revolutionary awareness." Unlike Ellison in *Dangerous Visions,* he
acknowledged Ballard as a "key figure" and saluted
Moorcock as "the most influential editor the field had
seen since John Campbell."[14] Among the notable British
writers not identified with the field, he added the
names of the fantasists Mervyn Peake and Anthony
Burgess.[15] In arguing that "originally, all fiction was
speculative fiction" and that "'realistic,' here-and-now,
single-reality fiction" was a product of the nineteenth
century, Spinrad did make a telling point about the
mind-set of the generation of writers coming to maturity
in the 1960s when he declared:

Today, after Einstein, Freud, psychedelics, quantum
mechanics, McLuhan, cybernetics, the Heisenberg Un-

certainty Principle, systems analysis, and a few hundred other little vision-expanders, we're back where we were before the Victorians defined reality as a rigid Tinker Toy construct (4–5).

Already renowned as the author of *Bug Jack Barron* (1969), Spinrad could speak with the authority of a writer who had helped to shape the field, but possibly he himself did not realize at that date the full impact that the exponential development of science would have on American society and the responsive SF writers, both young and old.

One thinks of such earlier writers as Emerson—with his call for an American poet—Wordsworth, Whitman, Amy Lowell, Yeats, and Eliot, who declared that their national literature had grown stale with convention and needed innovation in form and language and extension of content in order to gain a new vitality. The artist demands to be allowed to speak in a fresh idiom; the artist demands to be allowed to deal freely with the subject matter mirroring new concerns. The writers who endorsed literary reform within science fiction, whether British or American, issued such a manifesto. That fact united them, even when, like Ellison, they spoke as individuals.

But one should not think of them as isolated Young Turks in a commercial field of popular literature. In an article, "Freud and Fantasy in Contemporary Fiction" (1965), Edwin B. Burgum took as his point of departure

REVOLT AND INNOVATION

the premise that the "rise of the novel of fantasy is the most noteworthy innovation in present-day fiction throughout the Western world." The introduction of fantasy undercut the "predominant tradition" shaping modern fiction since the eighteenth century; that is, the acceptance of "the objective existence of society as a common point of reference" between writer and reader—whether the writer emphasized the external world, as did Sinclair Lewis, Steinbeck, and Hemingway, or the internal world—"inner space"—as did Joyce, Woolf, and Faulkner.

Two recent patterns had emerged. On the one hand, writers used "the preposterous" to convey "a tenable interpretation of the social reality external to the subjectivity of the individual." On the other hand, some writers abandoned all "social referent," thereby blurring the "distinction between the real and the plausible and the distorted and implausible to leave the reader in a troubled state of ambiguity about fact and fantasy whatever his concept of reality may be."[16] Burgum did not explicitly mention science fiction. He concentrated on Joseph Heller's *Catch-22* (1961) and Kafka's *The Trial* and *Metamorphosis*. He might have included John Barth's *Giles Goat Boy* (1966), which blends together traditional myth and a vision of a computerized future, where the world is a university dominated by WESCAC, a computer. Or he might have chosen Anthony Burgess's visions of a nightmarish near-future Britain, *A Clockwork Orange* (1962) and *The Wanting Seed* (1962).

In December 1968, making an appearance at the annual Modern Language Association (MLA) Seminar on Science Fiction,[17] Samuel R. Delany, whose every work of fiction seemed to gain him additional recognition, echoed Burgum when he spoke of the "subjunctivity" of literature. He emphasized that the new awareness of the young writers was literary in nature when he suggested that "any serious discussion of speculative fiction must first get away from the distracting concept of SF content and examine precisely what sort of word-beast sits before us.[18] At that same meeting he laid the groundwork for his later admonition that academic critics in particular not consider science fiction on simply a utopian-dystopian axis. Referring to W. H. Auden, he suggested that Western society had created four rather than two myths: New Jerusalem; its opposite, Brave New World; Arcadia; its opposite, the Land of Flies. He noted that any combination of the four could coexist within a single fiction, using Bester's *The Stars My Destination* as his primary example. He also agreed with Ballard's judgment that the "bulk" of science fiction, basically "a romantic and affirmative literature," had been "rendered trivial by its naïvely boundless optimism."[19]

In that judgment he touched the nerve center which divided the SF community into warring factions. Two days later a crowd of some five hundred listened to an MLA forum, "Science Fiction: The New Mythology," as its participants discussed the function and nature of the field.[20] Only when discussion from the floor began did the tensions within the field make themselves apparent. From as many views as there were discussants certain patterns surfaced: first, much of what the panelists had said about such matters as SF as a means of prediction were irrelevant to any consideration of the field as literature or as a possible source for metaphors concerning the human condition in the twentieth century; secondly, unlike other fiction, SF had an intellectual instead of emotional appeal; third, SF sought to create "forward looking" myths; and finally, the new writers were violating the spirit of the field, introducing literary naturalism into a field where it has no place.

In *The World of Science Fiction* (1980) Lester del Rey began a denunciation of the philosophy behind the New Wave for its "distrust of both science and mankind. . . . And mankind was essentially contemptible, or at least of no importance. There was an underlying theme of failure throughout. . . . Futility was a strong keynote":

There had been an earlier interest in social consciousness, but that had largely involved adapting large hunks of anthropology into the backgrounds of the stories. This time, there was the self-conscious self-consciousness of the writing of the twenties and thirties, with its dedication to showing the ugliness of society, the sad plight of the helpless and lost people who became such fiction's leading characters, etc.[21]

Donald Wollheim agreed with del Rey. But at the heart of Wollheim's *The Universe Makers* lies the vision—shared with such individual writers as del Rey himself, the early Heinlein, and Arthur C. Clarke throughout his career, as well as the thousands of men and women who have worked with and supported NASA or its worldwide counterparts—of humanity moving outward to the stars. One has only to turn to current journalism to see how that dream cuts across cultural and national boundaries. Although Wollheim acknowledged that the New Wave brought "an awareness of stylistic possibilities" which strengthened "some of the more talented writers," he said that its proponents—and he focused essentially on the British writers—accused science fiction of being dead "because the future was no longer credible. The crises of the twentieth century—the Bomb, overpopulation, pollution—were obviously insurmountable. We would never make it into the twenty-first century." He was most eloquent and firm in his final judgment: "The New Wave represents a departure from the science-fiction directives for mankind, and its most devoted advocates have ceased to be universe makers."[22]

To understand what happened in American science fiction during the 1960s, one must keep in mind the unrelieved public and private anguish and anger of the decade, which affected SF as it did every other element of society. Whatever else may be said about the literary text, one sees it as the product of its immediate culture,

REVOLT AND INNOVATION

its immediate period. Moreover, however much escapism may be found in such areas of fiction as the Western and the Romance—to say nothing of television and cinema—the main thrust of American fiction throughout the twentieth century has remained critical of society, though the particular focus may shift from the small town and Main Street to the "proletariat" emphasis of the 1930s and the later attack on Madison Avenue and the urban scene.

With these general matters in mind, turning to science fiction specifically one finds that several questions seem not to have been asked. First, remembering that the primary group of readers—the audience aimed at— between the late 1940s and the 1960s was the same as surveys show it to be now—men and women under the age of thirty-five—how long can a generation be bludgeoned with pessimistic assumptions before those assumptions are accepted and reacted to as fact? One can, of course, ask the same question of the fiction of social realism as well as the other media. But when an area such as science fiction pictures the future, the effect can be even more powerful, particularly upon the young. Perhaps at this time adequate research cannot be done to reach a firm conclusion, but one wonders to what extent SF itself fed and shaped the temper of the 1960s. Speculation goes beyond the knowledge that such books as *Stranger in a Strange Land* and *Dune* became underground best-sellers. Certainly they led readers to other SF titles. Perhaps the critic can never be certain of the impact of one of SF's basic givens: from the late 1940s onward, however they dealt with the premise in an individual work of fiction, the writers accepted as inevitable the ravaging of the earth by nuclear holocaust.

In the context of the development of contemporary science fiction, the more pragmatic question asks whether or not the response of American and British writers to the world scene was philosophically identical. Harlan Ellison, for example, remarked in at least one interview that his own "perceptions of the world seem minuscule by comparison with the work of any of the really, really great writers like Isaac Bashevis Singer or Tom Disch."[23] Lester del Rey did not like Disch's first novel, *The Genocides,* which he named specifically when he called Disch "the most consistently cynical of all the writers" of the New Wave.[24]

Earth has withstood the invasion of aliens since Robert Potter's *The Germ Growers* (1892) and Wells's *The War of the Worlds* (1898). The aliens themselves are never seen in *The Genocides,* only the effects of their work. In 1972 they seed the entire earth with a plant that grows to a height of six hundred feet. Anarchy and famine engulf the world, but Disch localizes the action to the area of a religiously conservative farming town, Tassel, Minnesota, to which his protagonist has managed to return. The outcome is never in doubt from the moment that the remains of the last bull and the protagonist's brother are found among twelve ash heaps of cattle mysteriously burned. Disch underscores the insignificance of both humanity and Earth itself with two directives setting up the time schedule—4 July 1979 to 2 February 1980—for the incineration of "the remaining artifacts" and, specifically, the "artifact . . . 'Duluth-Superior'" as well as the two or three hundred "large mammals"—humans—which somehow escaped into the nearby fields ([1], 31–32). Jeremiah Orville, the one man with scientific knowledge, explains that "Survival is a matter of ecology" (53), but he turns into an ax-wielding brute seeking revenge because the townspeople cannibalized his wife. Incinerated as pests or burrowing like termites amid the roots which grow together to make the plant a single entity, humanity sinks through terror toward madness even before the harvest and sowing of a second crop. With that seeding Disch announces, "Nature is prodigal. Of a hundred seedlings only one or two would survive; of a hundred species, only one or two. Not, however, man" (143).

His second novel, *Camp Concentration*, serialized in *New Worlds* (1967) and first published in book form in England (1968), focuses almost entirely within the consciousness of Louis Sacchetti as revealed through daily entries in his journal. A poet and lapsed Catholic, he has been imprisoned in 1975 as a conscientious objector because he refused to fight in an ongoing war. Transferred to an underground establishment near Telluride, Colorado, apparently supervised by a private corporation working for the military, he learns that he and all the inmates are being injected with a mutant form of the syphilis bacterium which will greatly enhance their intelligence before it kills them in nine months time. The project originated as a result of work of the Armed Services, "the most active researcher into the little world of the spirochete," after discovery that one mutation enhanced the intelligence of rats (60–61). Through Sacchetti's poetic and religious sensibility the novel reeexamines the Faustus theme, reinforcing the symbolism in the second part of the novel with the introduction of the scientist Skilliman, who happily accepts death if he can first solve the problem of developing a superbomb. The political dimension of the theme is intensified because as the inmates rehearse a performance of *Dr. Faustus*, Sacchetti undertakes his first original play, "Auschwitz: A Comedy."

His friend, a black prisoner, Mordecai Washington, who plays Mephistopheles in *Dr. Faustus*, dies of an embolism during the rehearsal after telling Sacchetti that all who take the injections are condemned to death. The enhancement of intelligence is, of course, a motif common to contemporary SF. Through Mordecai, somewhat conveniently, Disch obtains a second tie. As Skilliman insists that Sacchetti be shot, he himself is killed by the general who heads the project. Only then does Sacchetti learn that the talk of alchemy early in the novel was a code devised by the prisoners to disguise their research to produce a "mind reciprocator" enabling them to transfer themselves to their guards' bodies. Sacchetti finds himself alive and transformed; Mordecai has long inhabited the body of the general, though he has maintained the authoritarian personality in order to conceal the plan. It is all too convenient. It transforms Sacchetti's joy at the approach of death to a spiritual emptiness. Yet *Camp Concentration* remains the finely textured literary achievement of the New Wave, showing how the conventions of SF can be expanded to encompass all circumstances.

Walter Tevis's *The Man Who Fell to Earth* differs sharply from Disch's work, but among American novels it is the only one to evoke a final reaction in a reader akin to that of *The Genocides*, although for very different reasons. The author of *The Hustler* (1959) and a professor of English at Ohio University, Tevis produced a memorable inversion of the first-contact motif. After studying television signals from Earth and being trained for some fifteen years for his role as a human, in 1972 Thomas Jerome Newman comes to Earth in a one-man craft from the planet Anthea in order to save his dying world. Those critics who explain his failure because of Earth's xenophobia oversimplify a noteworthy confrontation. From a base in Kentucky, Newman takes advantage of Anthea's advanced technology to obtain patents and launch business projects ranging from oil refineries and 3-D television to a client whose corporation experiments with chemical warfare. As World Enterprises he amasses a fortune.

Yet even before he had landed, he knew that he

would be "sick with worry" and a sense of crisis. As he looks in a mirror, "his own body stared back at him; but he could not recognize it as his own. It was alien, and frightening" (78). Long before his success he had begun living with Betty Lou, who had taught him to drink gin. Fascinated by a new kind of film, a scientist from a midwestern school, Nathan Bryce, seeks him out. They converse; Bryce takes an x-ray photo that reveals "an impossible bone structure in an impossible body" (90). When they converse again, Newman reveals not only that Anthea has "almost no water, no fuel, no natural resources" but also that less than three hundred Antheans "barely survive . . . after five wars fought with radioactive weapons" (101, 103). As an advance scout he is building a ship that will be guided to Anthea; his people will return, dispersing around the world.

Whether the result of the Anthean immigration will be manipulation or guidance, when Bryce asks if the Antheans intend "just to help," Newman replies that they came to Earth to save themselves: "we do not want the Indians burning up our reservation after we have settled on it" (106). Bryce agrees not to reveal his plan, but the government already knows. The CIA arrests him as an illegal alien but releases him; then the FBI takes its turn, blinding him with x-rays to get a photo of his retinas and occipital ridges. After a two-months' detention and another year during which he becomes an alcoholic, he and Bryce talk again. He knew when he first arrived that he would never be able to return to

Anthea. As he admits having been "afraid of all manner of things," he asks Nathan to imagine living and dying "with insects . . . with busy, mindless ants." Yes, he loves some humans; indeed, he may be more human than Anthean because humanity has been his "field of research" (141–42). As Bryce and a bartender watch him cry, they agree that, like humanity, he needs help. One contrasts him at once with the indifferent aliens of *Genocide*, who did not deign to communicate with the builders of the tiny artifacts they incinerated. Both writers dispensed with all but the minimum of SF furniture, but like Pangborn in *Davy*, Tevis created a character who raises questions and whose anguish is accessible.

Within more conventional SF formats the dystopian emphasis continued. Harry Harrison pictured the dehumanizing poverty of a New York having a population of thirty-five million in *Make Room, Make Room* (1966, retitled *Soylent Green* after the film made from it). In *Slaughterhouse-Five or The Children's Crusade* (1969) Kurt Vonnegut finally was able to dwell openly upon his painful memories of Dresden, as a flying saucer takes Billy Pilgrim in 1967 to a zoo on Tralfamadore, where "he was mated . . . with a former Earthling movie star named Montana Wildhack" (22). Although Billy becomes "unstuck in time," Dresden holds center stage. If *The Sirens of Titan* voices the essence of Vonnegut's despair, then *Slaughterhouse-Five* provides the symbolic action in his recollection of Dresden. One must nevertheless agree with Aldiss when he remarks that time travel and other SF "apparatus seem intrusive, fascinating though they are,"[25] a judgment echoed by Scholes and Rabkin, who believe that Vonnegut "casually incorporated materials from his science fiction past" in a novel "based on real experiences."[26]

After two conventional space operas, *The Solarians* (1966) and *Agent of Chaos* (1967), and the sadism of *The Men in the Jungle* (1967), with its violent overthrow of the Brotherhood of Pain on the planet Sangre, Norman Spinrad finished his first major novel, *Bug Jack Barron* (1969). Serialized in *New Worlds* (1967–68), it gained immediate notoriety for its language and explicit sex. Spinrad was denounced in the House of Commons, while W. H. Smith, the largest British distributor and retail outlet, dropped *New Worlds*. The sexuality receives most attention early, before the plot gains momentum. In contrast to his earlier novels, *Bug Jack Barron* employs a minimal but essential SF framework as it uses a power struggle between two men as a means of commenting on the political scene projected into the 1980s. But as in Pangborn's *Davy* and Tevis's *The Man Who Fell to Earth*, the novel gains its strength from Spinrad's study of his protagonist, Jack Barron, the charismatic and egotistical host of a TV talk show. He dominates the novel because much of the narrative emphasizes either the shows themselves or Barron's interior monologues. The format of his programs employs "vidphones" instead of a live audience. Individuals call in (they "bug" Jack Barron), and he then interrogates appropriate national figures. The story line involves cryogenics, opening as Benedict Howards, the millionaire head of the Foundation for Human Immortality, tries to get a Freezer Utility Bill through Congress to give the Foundation a monopoly.

As the two men confront and manipulate one another, Spinrad works from the premise that every man has his price. Whatever else, the novel is a male power fantasy. Howard represents the oppressive establishment. Passionately fearing death and cursing everything liberal as a dupe of the Reds, he and the president that he elects will decide who gains immortality. Although a former Berkeley radical and a self-proclaimed champion of the people, Barron—and his estranged wife, Sara—accepts Howards's offer of immortality, actually taking the treatment. But Sara kills herself when they learn that the Foundation buys black children, irradiates their glands to achieve a homeostatic endocrine balance, and then kills the children as needed, transplanting their glands into the chosen few. Only after Sara's death does Barron undertake the successful exposure and destruction of Howards, who goes insane with anger and fear. Barron's investigation takes him to Evers, Mississippi, where an old Berkeley friend, Lucas Greene, has become the first black governor of the state. After Barron's redemption and victory, he and Greene become the presidential slate of an alliance between a moribund Republican Party and the liberal Social Justice

Coalition—which Barron had helped to found during his student days—to oust the Democratic Party. Although critics have agreed that Spinrad captured a vivid image of the world of TV at the time, they disagree in their final estimate of the macho Jack Barron as a credible hero. Yet *Bug Jack Barron* did have "a liberating and shocking effect" on the SF community. [27]

In contrast to Spinrad's extrapolation into a familiar near future, among the novels of the late 1960s the most elaborate dystopian paraphernalia occurs in Philip K. Dick's *Do Androids Dream of Electric Sheep?* (1968, retitled *Blade Runner* after the successful film in 1982). Although Dick projects only to 2021, he pictures a dying world after "World War Terminus" so befouled the world with radioactive dust that the sun can no longer be seen and virtually all animal life is extinct. The lonely remnant of humanity is obsessed with the purchase of simulated electric animals fully programmed to seem real, while the possession of a live animal sets one apart. Innumerable "specials"—persons suffering brain damage as a result of radiation—clutter the decimated population. During the war governments developed androids— Dick refers to them early as "humanoid robots"—to serve as synthetic freedom fighters; afterward the androids were adapted to live on alien planets so that they became "the mobile donkey engine of the colonization program" (13). The point of departure for the story line is the return to Earth of a group of androids after they kill their masters on Mars. They are the latest model,

REVOLT AND INNOVATION

Nexus-6, virtually indistinguishable from humans. The plot develops along two lines: John R. Isidore, a "chickenhead"—slang for a retarded person affected genetically by the radiation—shelters some of the androids, including Pris Stratton, while Rick Deckard, a police inspector in San Francisco whose task is killing ("retiring") androids who infiltrate Earth, hunts them down.

Because of the emphasis on androids, the central issue of the novel could well explore the question of what it means to be human, a theme in keeping with Dick's concern for identity. But Dick's personal obsession with the problem of evil interferes with his effective development of theme or story. Individuals typified by Deckard's depressed wife, Iran, can rely on the Penfield mood organ to saturate themselves with electronic tranquilizers, or they can use an "empathy box" to fuse with the consciousness of Wilbur Mercer, a tottering old man who continually ascends a hill while he is being stoned. Obviously Dick's adaptation of the myth of Sisyphus, Mercer is haunted by an "absolute" but unidentified evil pervading the universe. If he somehow symbolizes the human condition, Isidore undercuts him by suggesting that he is not "a human being; he evidently is an archetypal entity from the stars, superimposed on our culture by a cosmic template" (61). Whether hallucination or vision, both Isidore and Deckard converse with him. He tells Deckard, *"There is no salvation,"* and that everyone "will be required to do wrong ... to violate your own identity" (156). Although Deckard tells Iran that Mercer is "just an old man climbing a hill to his death" (157), he later declares that Mercer is real "unless all reality is a fake" (207). Opposed to Mercer is a TV comic, "Buster Friendly and His Friendly Friends," who denounces the empathy box. Isidore declares that Mercer and Friendly "are fighting for control of our psychic souls" (67). Buster Friendly exposes Mercer as a prewar, drunken bit actor (183–84), while one of the Nexus-6 androids announces Friendly as an android.

One cannot agree completely when Warrick argues that Dick resolves his theme through the use of doubles, effecting a reconciliation through the spiritual union of Isidore and Deckard after their experiences with android women.[28] Although Deckard must go to Isidore's isolated apartment to kill the last three androids, the two lines of the story do not fully mesh, primarily because both Isidore and Deckard remain essentially static figures who gain no deeper insight. However much the philosophical confusion may have spoken to the readers of the late 1960s, in the long run the narrative suffers because there is no in-depth focus on the consciousness of any of the characters. They get lost in Deckard's relentless elimination of the androids, although he finally judges himself as "a scourge, like famine or plague" (199).

Deckard lives with his role as executioner by rationalizing that empathy exists "only within the human community" and that "like any other machine," androids have "no ability to appreciate the existence of another" (26, 37). Early in the narrative through the use of the Voigt-Kampff Empathy Test, he deduces that Rachel Rosen is an android, and a representative of Rosen Associates tells him that that information was withheld from her program. He and Rachel are attracted to one another. Uptight, even though he has talked with Mercer (hallucinated?) and bought a live black Nubian goat, he calls her to come to San Francisco to help him against the three remaining androids. Perhaps at the suggestion of another bounty hunter (125–26) he goes to bed with her despite laws forbidding a man to copulate with an android. Her confession that she has the "illusion" of being a person and that she identifies with Pris Stratton, an android woman Deckard hunts, implies that she has the power of empathy, while Deckard abruptly realizes that she is the prototype for the Nexus-6 females and that there are a legion of her, including Pris, whom he must "retire." In bed, confessing that she loves him, Rachel remarks that Androids can't bear children and wonders if that is a loss (165–70).

Dick blurs any emphasis on their mutual humanity by turning to his obsession with the impersonal (evil) manipulation of humanity. Rachel bluntly tells Deckard that at the instruction of the Rosen Association she has gained information from him so that they can adapt the Nexus-7 model to avoid detection by the Voigt Test and that she has involved him sexually so that he can no longer kill androids. (He is one of nine—"here and in Russia"—that she has bedded.) In his anger he threatens to kill her, but does not. She tells him that he loves the Nubian goat more than he loves her or his wife (171–78). They part. Perfunctorily he kills the three androids; indeed, he meets Isidore before he kills them, and the two do not grieve over Pris. Again Dick shifts unexpectedly. He emphasizes the humanity of Rachel by reporting that she killed Deckard's goat (201–2), but he does not allow her back on stage. In the final sequence Deckard finds a toad that he is certain is a real animal, but his wife immediately exposes it as a simulation. As Deckard sleeps, exhausted, Iran orders electric flies for his electric toad to which he is "devoted" (216). In short, rather than exploring fully what it means to be human, Dick reduces all of his characters to distraught things in an incomprehensible universe.

Perhaps Dick could have more fully developed his theme had he presented the consciousness of a single character, as Alexei Panshin did in *Rite of Passage* (1968), winner of the Nebula Award the year that *Do Androids Dream of Electric Sheep?* was published. Whereas Dick paid almost no attention to a vivid setting once he had sketched it,[29] Panshin gave a fresh perspective to life aboard the familiar "multigeneration spaceship" created by Heinlein in "Universe" (1948) simply by shifting the first-person narrative of the young woman Mia Havero as she reflects on events seven years earlier. Panshin chose his protagonist and narrative strategy in reaction against Heinlein's fifteen-year-old heroine, *Podkayne of Mars* (1963), who romps through her journal account

REVOLT AND INNOVATION

of a series of interplanetary intrigues with her uncle and a younger brother. (Panshin makes no mention of the superficiality of Schmitz's telepathic schoolgirl, Telzey Amberdon.) With attention to such matters as soccer, her tutor, her family, and a new school, Mia Havero presents a convincingly realistic portrayal of early adolescence. Throughout the novel both her growing insight and the workings of the closed society abroad the ship are more important than plot action. Early in the twenty-third century she lives aboard one of seven great ships which survived the destruction of Earth in 2041 after a series of wars caused basically by the pressures of overpopulation. The seven travel freely throughout the star systems, trading when necessary with any one of a hundred and twelve worlds colonized by humanity. They exchange a minimum of scientific and technological information for needed natural resources, and they consider themselves an elite, far superior to the descendants of the farmers and pioneers—"the mudeaters"—that the seven of them carried to the stars as colonists. Late in the narrative Mia herself declares that "people who live on planets *can't* be people" because they do not have the advantages and knowledge that persons aboard the ships do. Besides, they are "free-birthers." If any idea controls the memories of Earth and the structure of the shipboard societies, it is the threat of overpopulation. A woman who has a fifth pregnancy without the permission of the ship's eugenicist, is sentenced to live on the nearest colony planet; during that woman's trial Mia realizes that "we are a tiny precarious island floating in a hostile sea" and must follow "the ways of living that observed exactly allow us to survive" (115).

The story line focuses on that issue. The narrative follows Mia and her classmates as they are trained to undergo the ritual ceremony through which each must pass to become a member of adult society. When a group reaches the age of fourteen, they face the Trial; each one is dropped separately on the nearest colony world for a thirty-day survival test. Mia and her companions are dropped on Tintera. Problems of style aside,[30] the flaw of the novel occurs in those chapters involving Mia's adventures on a world which reminds her of "the Western-cowboy stories I used to read" (213), complete with warrants, bad men, and a jail break, although the enslavement of the Losels, an indigenous alien, adds an unexpected dimension. When twelve of the twenty-nine youths fail to return from Tintera, the ship's adult society votes after open debate to destroy the planet. In an epilogue dated five years later, Mia judges the ship's society in a manner that echoes the angry young men in the fiction of Panshin's contemporaries but sets her, and Panshin, distinctly apart from them:

It is easy now to see the relevance of the religious wars of the past, to see that capitalism in itself is not evil, to see that honor is most often a silly thing to kill a man for, to see that national patriotism should have meant nothing in the twenty-first century. . . . It is harder to assess as critically the insanities of your own time. . . . If you want to accept life, you have to accept the whole bloody universe. The universe is filled with *people*, and there is not a single solitary spear carried among them (241–42, 252).

Thus does Mia Havero reject the intellectual snobbery not only of the ship's society but also of many of her SF predecessors. Elitism would never vanish from the field, and the ruthless wars of space opera would continue, but Mia Havero turned a thematic corner. Perhaps less dramatically because of the lack of action but more convincingly because the reader knows her so well, Mia recalls the protagonists of Simak's fictions with their concern for a community of life.

In like manner Daniel Keyes revitalized the myth of Frankenstein by introducing a fresh narrative perspective in *Flowers for Algernon* (1966). Originally a Hugo-winning short story (1959), the novel shared both the Hugo and the Nebula with Samuel R. Delany's *Babel-17*. As a short story it concentrated on the experiment of Dr. Nemur and Dr. Strauss to enhance the intelligence of moronic Charlie Gordon from an IQ of 68 to 200. The meteoric success of their neurosurgery fails when Charlie returns to a moronic level. The pathos of the situation rises from Keyes's reliance on a personal journal to capture Charlie's full, changing awareness of what has happened to him. (The title comes from the white mouse whose response to surgery led to the initial experiment on a human.) Presented as first-person narrative, the novel necessarily becomes a psychological portrait of Charlie.

In many ways *Flowers for Algernon* is antipodal to Anderson's *Brain Wave* because of Charlie's regression; in another, its artistry combines Mary Shelley's nameless creature and the crazed scientist into the single figure of Charlie. That makes possible the development of Keyes's double-edged theme: the unthinking brutality with which society treats the mentally retarded and the terrible isolation of soaring intellect. As a laborer in a bakery Charlie is the butt of the endless jokes of the other workers; for Nemur and Strauss he is simply a specimen whose sister must give her permission before they can operate. Suddenly an intellect far in advance of his colleagues, he is as uncaring as any of them, finding his "storehouse of general knowledge" a challenge and condemning the experts who evade him as specialists "afraid to reveal the narrowness of their knowledge" (89, 113). Although he knows that Nemur is jealous of his new ability, he cannot understand the feelings of Alice Kinnian, his teacher at an adult education center who first suggested him as a subject for the experiment. At one point she vents her frustration by telling him that in his intellectual hunger he has ignored her: "I wanted to help you and share with you—and now you've shut me out of your life" (112). The laughter of a young neighbor who tells Charlie how "confused and silly" he became when he was drunk (173)—thereby underscoring that Dr. Charles Gordon knows how thin the façade of his intelligence is—leads into the most poignant scene of the novel. In the bewildered antics of a busboy who has dropped a tray of dishes in a diner and is angrily berated by customers and boss, Charles Gordon senses "something familiar" and denounces the manner in which "people of honest feelings and sensibility . . . think nothing of abusing a man born with low intelligence" (175–77). For a moment he had forgotten. As he slips back into the abyss of his former self, knowing that his intelligence will kill him, in his last note he unwittingly underscores Keyes's theme: "Its easy to have frends if you let pepul laff at you." And then he asks a favor: "please if you get a chanse put some flowrs on Algernons grave" (274). In the film *Charly* (1968) Cliff Robertson won an Oscar for his portrayal of Charlie Gordon.

Although Keyes chose an SF frame to address a problem so close to everyday society, because of his choice of narrative perspective *Flowers for Algernon* remains unique in the science fiction pantheon.

Despite the social criticism which has allowed some of SF to retain a savagely dystopian tone, and despite an emphasis on character study which has enriched the field, by the 1960s the main thrust of American SF took still another road. Because nothing is ever lost, that decision only added to the permutations which diversify the contemporary field. Most simply, in the manner of such an early writer as Jack Vance, the American writers turned increasingly to the creation of imaginary worlds that have little or no relationship to present-day or future planet Earth. This development anticipates the later admonishments of Samuel R. Delany, partly because he was one of the young writers who brought this most telling revolution within the field into being. But to discover the events which brought it about, one must turn to Frederik Pohl as editor of *Galaxy* and *Worlds of If* during the 1960s. Ironically, too, despite the seeming conservatism of Donald Wollheim's assessment of the New Wave, as editor of Ace Books he published the novels of many of the innovators perhaps before they realized fully the impact of what they were doing. Increasingly he issued books that had not seen magazine publication. He published, for example, the earliest novels of Samuel R. Delany, Roger Zelazny, R. A. Lafferty, and Joanna Russ, to name only writers who began their careers in the 1960s. Late in the decade Terry Carr edited the Ace Special line, but the initiative had been Wollheim's.

It would be conveniently oversimplistic to suggest that Pohl began the process by issuing the stories of the innovators. He did publish Jack Vance, Cordwainer Smith, Lafferty, Zelazny, Dick, and Ellison—and one title by J. G. Ballard, "The Time Tombs" (*Worlds of If*, Mar. 1963). Throughout the decade he did have an agreement with Robert Silverberg to publish anything that Silverberg submitted to him, so that many of his finest stories and novels appeared initially in *Galaxy* or *Worlds of If*. (To John Campbell's credit, however, he continued to attract new writers such as Anne McCaffrey.) Pohl's influence showed itself in the editorial policy that he initiated as soon as he replaced Gold in 1961. Perhaps the basic premise of the policy was most clearly enunciated in an editorial, "The Day after Tomorrow" (Oct. 1965). Not surprisingly in view of his close relationship with Gold, he enlarged on principles formulated by his mentor—principles which Delany in his subsequent criticism seems to assign exclusively to Gold. Pohl wrote of three important steps in the development of contemporary American science fiction. Campbell had taken the first when he repeatedly urged his writers to domesticate the future, to write as though they dealt with a scene in the twenty-second century familiar to their readers. Gold had wanted stories emphasizing the impact of science and technology on society and human individuals instead of following the exploits of heroic engineers. His idiosyncrasies had led to satire. Now Pohl elaborated on another of Gold's premises, although he cited such writers as Vance and Smith in developing the point. Readers should see the "people of the world of the future operating on their own terms" because those people and that future will be different. It will not be "a mere extension of the present" (*Galaxy* Oct. 1965: 6–7).

Numerous writers of the 1960s, among them Robert

Silverberg and Norman Spinrad, found the prototype of these worlds in such early works as Jack Vance's *The Dying Earth* (1950), a sequence of six tales having both a common setting in the far-distant future and several characters who reappear in the different episodes. Magicians compete for power and knowledge. During an apprenticeship to the magician Pandelume in the land of Emboyon,[31] Turjan of Muir learns the "master matrix" needed to create intelligent life from the "vat"—in this case the beautiful woman Floriel, who is wantonly killed, and T'Sain, who loves him. Spinrad spoke of the "baroque tapestry" created by Vance's style and content, while Silverberg called the novel "a covert fantasy of the medieval" bristling "with artifacts of the fourteenth century; ... a continuation of the work of Scheherazade, ... a *Thousand Nights and a Night* romance of never-never land. To Vance, the dying Earth is only a metaphor for decline, loss, decay, and, paradoxical though it may sound, also a return to a lost golden age ... of absolute values and a clash of right and wrong."[32] All critics regard it as fantasy, Richard Tiedman tying the work to a tradition going back through *Weird Tales* and Clark Ashton Smith to A. Merritt and E. R. Eddison.[33] "The milieu," writes one critic, "is that of fairy tale: magical duels and heroic quests in a decaying world of ruined cities and monster-haunted forests under the red light of a dying sun."[34] Vance returned to that same future in *The Eyes of the Overworld* (1966), building the narrative around a single protagonist, Cugel the Clever, featured in a series of novellas first published in *F&SF*. At Ace, Wollheim published the book. Although one may argue that the texture of Vance's narrative is more elaborate, one is reminded of the medieval romance even more than the fairy tale.

A simple story line, a medieval flavor, societies that have evolved to meet the exigencies of life on a particular planet, and increasingly a hero capable of freeing his people—these became the trademarks of Vance's fiction as it developed through the 1950s and 1960s. In *The Big Planet* (1957, already referred to, although it was not published in its entirety until 1977), Claude Glystra starts the survivors of a shipwreck on a forty-thousand-mile trek so that the reader may encounter a variety of cultures made up of dissidents who long ago fled Earth. Perhaps the most interesting is the city of Kirstendale, founded by a syndicate of millionaires who wished to escape the tax laws.

The Languages of Pao (1958) explores the linguistic premise identified with Benjamin Lee Whorf that the way a people think of themselves is shaped by the way their language structures experiences. Because Pao is a richly fertile world, its passive multitude has developed a language without verbs, while it is governed by an increasingly insane ruler of the planet Breakness, a harshly inclement world whose people have had to compete fiercely to survive. That language has no first person. Furthermore, the ruler attempts to maintain control of Pao by having each social class—warriors, industrialists, and scholars—speak a different language. Concerned with political intrigue, the story line can move toward resolution only when the rightful heir regains power and starts to reunite Pao by having all of its people speak a new language, "Pastiche," which in twenty years will change their world view and thus enable them to deal with outsiders.

Blish refers to Vance's "timeless medieval world" when he calls *The Dragon Masters* (1963) another "fantasy of the far future."[35] The short novel exemplifies sword and sorcery with a minimal SF background. Twelve generations earlier exiles from the War of the Ten Stars fled to the isolated world Aerlith at the edge of the universe when the human empire apparently broke up. Since then, for no given reason, two family clans have continually fought. Now the two leaders, Joaz Banbeck and Ervis Corcolo, try unsuccessfully to come to some agreement in order to resist a raid by reptilian aliens, the Basics, whose attack eleven generations ago Corcola treats as legend, although their ancestors took twenty-three prisoners from which they bred dragon-mounts. After the attack of the Basics interrupts the clans' fighting, they learn that the Basics have bred twelve-foot-tall warriors, although no explicit reference is made to genetic engineering. When the ambitious Corcola and the scientific Banbeck are not fighting, they talk of a mythic Eden, at least once identified as Earth, and wonder whether they are the last remnant of humanity in the universe. A second humanoid culture, the

REVOLT AND INNOVATION

Sacerdotals—withdrawn pacifists about whom little is known—complicate the scene; they remain aloof to all threats, but the attack of the Basics destroys a spaceship they have been building for more than eight hundred years.

In *The Blue World* (1966) descendants of a ship of convicts fleeing Earth long ago dwell on the floats, giant lily pads of a worldwide ocean; civil war with a priestly class erupts when the protagonist, Sklar Hast, undertakes a successful campaign to kill the sea monster, King Kragen. Warfare also shapes *The Last Castle* (1967) when humanoid slaves, the Meks, rebel against the decadent, clannish society settled on Old Earth; the conflict ends when the Meks repair the old spaceships and return to their own planets. The changes, particularly the abandonment of slavery, suggest a possible new future for human society, for all of the old castles have been destroyed. While the fighting limits the potential of all the brief novels, the fascination with Vance's cultures has drawn a following. Repeatedly he emphasizes the difficulties separate cultures have in communicating with one another.

Although both *The Dragon Masters* and *The Last Castle* were prize-winners, perhaps Vance's best novel of the period is *Emphyrio* (1969), praised by Joanna Russ in *F&SF* as a *Bildungsroman* (Jan. 1970: 41). The narrative follows young Ghyl Tavrock as he overthrows the stagnant welfare state governing the city of Ambroy on the distant planet Halma. Tavrock gives the novel an unex-

pected depth because he takes as his personal model the
ancient hero Emphyrio, who saved his own world from
monsters. Although Tavrock must go briefly to Earth to
uncover Halma's basic history, he learns that since humanity arrived on Halma, aliens have established a ruling class of lords to manipulate and restrain the humans
through the oppressive welfare rolls and guild structures stifling Ambroy. As he brings about the downfall
of the system, he fulfills the legend of Emphyrio. The
story gains "a satisfying mythic resonance. . . . [The use
of the legend] makes for Vance's most complexly structured work, the only one in which he has satisfactorily
progressed beyond simple quest or rebellion plots."[36]
The final strength of Vance's fiction as a whole relies
on its portrayal of "a universe of infinite variety";[37] it
has helped to free both writers and readers from the
restrictions imposed by earlier conventions of the field.

Writing under the pseudonym Cordwainer Smith,
Paul Myron Anthony Linebarger, the distinguished professor of Asiatic politics at Johns Hopkins University,
served science fiction in much the same way. Although
he published as early as the 1940s,[38] unlike the prolific
Vance, Cordwainer Smith wrote stories falling within a
single framework called "The Instrumentality of Mankind" spanning fifteen thousand years during which a
universal utopian government comes to rule thousands
of worlds. His first published story, "Scanners Live in
Vain" (1950) was voted into the Science Fiction Hall of
Fame in 1965. It deals with a guild of sixty-eight men

who surrender their humanity to become the cyborgs
who guide the early ships through space. The denouement introduces a discovery which allows them to resume their humanity. Early on, the guild acknowledges
that they are Agents of the Instrumentality; at the end
they are admitted to its bureaucracy.

To emphasize any single story at the expense of the
others, however, distorts Cordwainer Smith's accomplishment. Unlike Heinlein, Asimov, Anderson, or
even Vance, he had no intention of providing a system-
atic history of the future. Nor did he need to explain
how a planet became isolated. The empire never fell.
Over a span of fifteen thousand years, humanity and its
technology had conquered external and human nature.
That in itself was no accomplishment to be celebrated;
he accepted it as a given—complete with robots, computers, any advanced gimmick needed at the moment
in a story, and perhaps most important of all, the underpeople—those animals who through surgery and genetic engineering had evolved into human simulacra.
In the novel first published in two parts as *The Planet
Buyer* (1964) and *The Underpeople* (1968)—subsequently
united as *Norstrilia* (1975)—two worlds are given importance: Old Earth, apparently content in its hedonism,
and Old North Australia (Norstrilia), the sole supplier
to the universe of the "santaclara drug," stroon, ob-
tained from sick sheep, which prolongs human life in-
definitely—made enjoyable with periodic rejuvenation.
One must not overlook Smith's satire of Norstrilia,

which despite its monopoly and wealth has taxed itself back into the simplicity of the rural culture which long ago it brought from Earth, has rejected technology as known on other worlds, but has multiplied its defenses against anyone seeking to steal the drug. An additional complexity of Smith's concerns reveals itself when the protagonist's computer tells him that it "cannot share your human, animal side of life" (70).

Norstrilia is also the home world of Rod McBan, the hundred and fifty-first heir to the sheep farm Station Doom. An unlikely SF protagonist in the 1960s, he is neither warrior nor rebel. Indeed, because of his telepathic deafness—he can neither "hier" nor "spiek"—he has been cycled through the three allowable childhoods in an effort to master that power, as behooves a farmer and a landowner. The law of the Commonwealth says that anyone who tests substandard at age sixteen must be done away with—but easily and quickly by drugs, the "giggle" death. Faced by a death sentence, Rod is granted his life at a public trial, but a public official, the Onseck (Honorable Secretary), an unpleasant man who dislikes everyone because he is a "short-lifer," wants to see McBan dead. Hard-pressed, McBan instructs—or is persuaded by—his ancient, "all mechanical" computer to gamble on stroon futures; he wins a fortune large enough to buy Old Earth and flees there, where his companion is the voluptuous cat woman, the "girlygirl," C'mell. So ends the first volume.

To see the plight of *The Underpeople* as one of

REVOLT AND INNOVATION

Smith's concerns is undoubtedly correct, but to see it as an "inescapable ... analogy to blacks in America" may oversimplify, just as the suggestion that "religious overtones are too prominent for their own good, interfering with reader enjoyment" may be a highly subjective reaction.[39]

The imposition of any limited theme ignores how cosmopolitan was Smith's background. Because his father had served as a legal adviser to Sun Yat Sen, he had grown up and was educated in China as well as Hawaii and Germany; he studied at the University of Nanking before he took a degree at Georgetown. He had a broader background than did any of his American SF contemporaries; his concern seems to be the whole of humanity. For example, he was one of the earliest writers of the period to suggest that "civilization is the creation of women," although that view was not new with him nor with this century. But it may help to explain why C'mell remains one of his most noteworthy characters, for she "makes incandescent the union of animal, human, and spiritual" that Smith sought for throughout his fiction.[40]

What does surprise one is that, with the possible exception of the early "Scanners Live in Vain," critics have shied away from Cordwainer Smith. Of the collections of his stories in the 1960s, only *The Planet Buyer* was reviewed widely among even the specialist magazines. Although Judith Merril conceded in *F&SF* that his was perhaps "the most exciting new 'name' in s-f this

decade" (Mar. 1965: 57), she added nothing of substance, abandoning him for Ballard and the New Wave.
A decade later when Algis Budrys praised him in *F&SF*
for being "so new, so much not like anything else" (Feb.
1976: 52), he referred to Smith's having "too much impact on the field" and fostering "too many legends to
be lost from sight." Mixing whimsy and satire, writing
in a conversational manner that sometimes directly addressed the reader, Smith was the first American SF
writer to follow the injunctions of all three editors—
Campbell, Gold, and Pohl. What came out—perhaps
because of his background more than his having been a
reader of SF since his youth—was something new. Instead of concerning himself with the exactness of his
scientific data or the plausibility of his ideas, instead of
belaboring a philosophical view of humanity and the
universe, instead of taking up some topical issue, he
concentrated on the interplay of character, assuming
that his readers accepted the world he wrote about,
often alluding to events in other stories, some of which
did not exist. He was not a historian of the future; he
was a fabulist who created an "exotic, poetic, and myth-
filled future."[41]

Increasingly, each in an individual manner, the
writers of the 1960s found their way to Cordwainer
Smith's "universe . . . of myth and legend."[42] Joneny, a
doctoral candidate in the field of galactic anthropology,
the protagonist of Samuel R. Delany's early novel,
draws the assignment of making a complete historical

analysis of a folk song in *The Ballad of Beta-2* (1965). Much against his will, because he thinks it the folktale of a culture involving the remnant of some multigenerational starships, he undertakes the *explication de texte* only to find that it masks the first contact between beleaguered humans and a transcendent alien whose progeny born of Leela RT-857, the captain of the *Beta-2* and the subject of the ballad, is a son capable of cloning and sharing the consciousness of his father and brothers. Apparently the entity is immortal and can live outside the crumbling ships. Log books and tapes reveal such familiar motifs as the authoritarian state which attempts to maintain the "norm," but for the first time the puzzle to be solved is linguistic.

Delany's interest in linguistics led to the Nebula-winning *Babel-17* (1966), in which the galactically known poet and captain of the ship *Rimbaud*, Rydra Wong, not only demonstrates the truth of the Whorf-Sapir hypothesis regarding language and perception but breaks through a character's programmed conditioning so that Rydra Wong teaches him to think in terms of the first- and second-person pronouns. This accomplishment, in turn, leads to her cracking the code Babel-17, thereby bringing to an end the war between the Alliance and Invader coalitions. In portraying her descent into Transport town to select a crew, Delany captured one of the sequences of action and setting for which he was to become famous; the crew must be able to mesh psychically, but some have to be cyborgs because certain tasks aboard ships cannot be performed by humans. In her final suggestion that she may write about her experience, Rydra Wong anticipates Mouse, a musician, and Katin, a would-be novelist, in *Nova* (1968). The discussion of the book Katin wants to write about the struggle for economic power between Lord Von Ray and Prince Red holds the foreground of the novel, although the story line follows the life-long rivals to their deaths in a sun going nova. Many critics have judged the novel to be the equal of Bester's *The Stars My Destination*. It can also be seen as a "re-casting of the Prometheus myth,"[43] although Delany also incorporates "Grail and Tarot lore," as he acknowledges.

His most complex use of myth occurs in *The Einstein Intersection* (1967). Extracts from his personal journals during the autumn and winter of 1965–66, when he traveled from Venice to Istanbul, underscore his interest in Greek myth, and critics have identified his characters with a wide range of mythic figures, ranging from Orpheus and Theseus to Hollywood stars and rock musicians. The narrative develops at three levels but remains ambiguous at best. Summoned by Kid Death, a young musician, Lo Lobey, who has helped round up a herd of dragons and is paid off, journeys forth from a village to the city of Branning-on-sea to find Friza, the girl he loved, and bring her back from the dead. He is one of a race of beings who, far in the future, have taken over a deserted Earth abandoned by humans capable of "interstellar commerce" who went to "no world in this continuum"; the new people took over "their bodies, their souls, both husks abandoned here for any wanderer's taking." As the world and humanity began to change, the new people were "drawn slowly here . . . from the other side of the universe" (117). Repeatedly the idea of genetic flux, with countless mutations, is referred to as the change continues in the new people. Behind the disappearance and change lies a tension between the concept of Einstein's Theory of Relativity as it expressed mathematically "just how far the condition of the observer influences the thing he perceives" and Goedel's "mathematically precise statement" about the infinity of possibilities which cannot "be deduced [from] any closed mathematical system" (116–17). By implication humanity gained some knowledge or insight which made them abandon the world they had known. The new people have inherited that world, with its complex cultures. As they gain more knowledge, the more things change, even the vast mazes beneath the surface of the world. They find "myths always lie in the most difficult places to ignore" (120). Moreover, each person carries numerous mythic identities. As Lobey plays music at Kid Death's command, one infers that only originality in art has meaning. Lobey does not find Friza, but as the novel ends, he contemplates a journey to the stars. In complex, ambiguous fashion Delany has combined both a generic quest and a desire for "a Goedelian . . . answer" to the nature of myth (118) to symbolize humanity's/the artist's journey through an unknowable life. Yet as with music or poetry, no schema can reduce his theme to a single statement. *The Einstein Intersection* gained Delany his second Nebula; he was the only writer to win it for a novel two years in a row. He dedicated this novel to Don Wollheim, his first publisher.

Brian Aldiss is one of those who has pointed out that "a common use of myth as an underpinning" links the fiction of Delany and Roger Zelazny,[44] both of whom gained wide popular reputations in the mid-1960s, although Aldiss has reservations about both. Whereas Delany's concern for myth focused on art and the artist, Zelazny used it to give new vitality to what must be regarded as power fantasies. Winning a Hugo in 1965 in its magazine appearance as "And Call Me Conrad" (1965), *This Immortal* (1966) introduces a protagonist stereotypical to much of Zelazny's fiction. Conrad Nomikos, an immortal who may be the incarnation of a Greek god, serves as a guide for a Vegan emissary a century after Earth has been devastated by atomic holocaust. Earth serves as a museum and a tourist resort for alien Vegans, seemingly the dominant race in the galaxy. Humans are scattered through many worlds; Nomikos is a leader of the party that wants to restore Earth. As he protects a Vegan emissary against assassination in Greece, where mutated monsters resembling mythic beasts make their appearance, the reader understands that he reenacts many of the labors of Hercules.

REVOLT AND INNOVATION

An earlier novella, *He Who Shapes* (1965), which won a Nebula, was expanded into the novel *The Dream Master* (1966). It studies a psychologist who enters the minds of his patients in order to shape their fantasies in an attempt to cure them. Jungian psychology determines the conflicts here, as it does through many of Zelazny's novels. Because Charles Render himself is a neurotic as a result of his obsessions with death and perfection, when he enters the mind of Eileen Shallott, a blind psychologist who has created an idyllic reality based on Arthurian mythology, the two become locked in a struggle where the myth of Tristan and Isolte and the Grail Quest engage Render's dark visions of Ragnarok. She has the stronger mind; he dies.

Zelazny's next novel, *Lord of Light* (1967) takes place on a far distant world settled by refugees from India. A group of immortals who make use of a high technology—they can transfer bodies, for example—have elevated themselves to gods resembling the Hindu pantheon. They hold the masses in servitude until another immortal, Mahasamatuman, seemingly an incarnation of the Buddha, liberates the people. Zelazny went on during the 1960s to work with Egyptian gods in *The Isle of the Dead* (1969) and *Creatures of Light and Darkness* (1969).

Reviewers, like Judith Merril in *F&SF*, who were caught up in the social and political scene of the 1960s, remain uncertain about the use of mythology. Although she believed that the "as-yet unformulated contemporary mythology is the map modern man must use in the search for his soul," she finds the attempts to "search for viable modern myths ... emerge as imitations, rationalizations, or cosmetic-modernizations of the no longer vital mythotypes of the agrarian and nomadic cultures of the past" (Dec. 1966: 31). James Blish was much more fierce in his denunciation of Delany and Zelazny specifically. Quite simply he could not stomach the award of the Nebulas to Delany because Delany's style and organization of a narrative seemed "self-indulgent and misdirected." As he berates Zelazny's treatment of the Egyptian pantheon, a major point emerges: The reliance on myth attempts to explain any resultant mythic world "in terms of eternal forces which are changeless. The attempt is antithetical to the suppositions of science fiction, which center around the potentialities of continuous change."[45] This judgment exposes the conflict which lay at the heart of the science fiction community throughout its formative period. In a sense Blish and his contemporaries represent C. P. Snow's scientific culture, whatever their individual literary aspirations, for they see science as the means by which the individual and society will advance to a better future. This is the reason that one has heard so often from SF enthusiasts the cry that if technology did indeed get modern society into its present situation, then technology—rather than a retreat to pastoral innocence—will eventually release and cleanse modern society. That debate goes back at least to Wells and his contemporaries and includes the reactions of the great European dystopian writers like Zamiatin, Huxley, and Orwell.

The writers of the 1960s, often from a new generation, could no longer accept the basic contention of Blish's generation—which beyond entertainment and adventure could lead only to a utopian or dystopian vision of the future. From Ballard and Disch of the New Wave to Delany and Zelazny, their interest was at bottom literary rather than ideological, however loud their individual criticism of current affairs. They understood that, whether social realism or fantasy, the task of fiction is to rise from a literal level to a metaphoric level which somehow surmounts the immediate and achieves a more enduring statement about the condition of humanity, individually or collectively. In a sense this was a restatement of the quarrel that Howells, Gissing, and the literary naturalists had had with their predecessors. In a world where science and technology continue to change not only the conditions of everyday life but the concepts of the universe itself, many of the SF writers no longer thought that replication of a "real" world around them was adequate to carry the weight of their metaphors.[46]

And so more of them turned to myth. In *Chthon* (1967) Piers Anthony explored the ramification of the Oedipus myth by examining imagined societies. In *Dragonflight* (1968), the first of a series of novels dealing with the world of Pern, Anne McCaffrey explained that for the descendants of the colonists of Pern memories of old Earth were forgotten, fading through myth and legend to "oblivion'; thus did she free herself entirely to start a new mythos, centering at first on the woman Lessa. McCaffrey examines a society shaped by a continuing ecological battle. The stories that make up her *Ship Who Sang* (1969) center upon a deformed woman who must live as a cyborg—as the brain and nervous system of the "brainship" XH-834. In *Past Master* (1968), the first of the Ace Specials series, R. A. Lafferty brings Sir Thomas More forward in time to examine the distant planet Astrobe, where an advanced technological society catering to everyone's needs is failing; the leaders call upon him because after the failure of Earth and America, Astrobe may be humanity's last chance. It is the first novel in which Lafferty restates traditional Christian values, including an "antipathy to the thought of Teilhard de Chardin." As a result some judge his work as "unfashionable."[47]

Perhaps the best way to understand what happened in American SF during the 1960s is to sketch the career of one of the major writers of the period, Robert Silverberg. In 1956 he received both a BA in comparative literature from Columbia and a Hugo as the Best New Writer of the year. At least part of his honeymoon he spent at the Milford Writers Conference, and within a year to gain "economic security" he decided to turn out 50,000 words a month (at a penny a word that equaled $500 a month). "I was the complete writing machine," he reported later, "turning out stories in all lengths at whatever quality the editor desired, from slambang adventure to cerebral pseudo-philosophy."[48] Between 1957 and 1959, not including collaborations and excluding fiction he did outside the field, he had eleven novels and 220 stories published. In the early 1960s he gave most of his energy to the "lucrative juvenile non-fiction hardcover field," popularizing such topics as *Treasures Under the Sea* (1960) and *Lost Cities and Vanished Civilizations* (1962) as compulsively as he had written SF. In 1966 he edited his first anthology and became seriously ill with a thyroid disorder.

In 1963 "To See the Invisible Man" (*Worlds of If*, April) and "The Pain Peddlers (*Galaxy*, August) mark the beginning of a series of stories and serials that he published with Frederik Pohl. Apparently, according to them both, Pohl agreed to publish anything that Silverberg submitted to him; if he rejected a story, the arrangement was finished. Silverberg has dated his "return to science fiction as a serious artist" from these stories; at once he identified himself with those writers attempting to introduce new materials and new narrative strategies into the field; "a trifle belatedly" he joined the "revolution" to overthrow the conventions that readers more than editors had imposed on American science fiction.[49] Two novels, *Thorns* (1967, never published in a magazine) and *The Man in the Maze* (1969, first serialized in *Galaxy* in 1968) illustrate the darkness of his vision during the mid-1960s. In *Thorns*, Duncan Chalk, who feeds on pain as others feed on bread, shares his sadomasochism with a worldwide TV audience by selling them as star-crossed lovers a man mutilated by aliens so that he is in endless pain and a woman used experimentally as a source of fertile but immature eggs. Given this point of departure, *Thorns* may be regarded as Silverberg's fullest exploration of the redemptive power of pain in a natural, existentialist world. *The Man in the Maze* is Richard Muller, whose mind has been operated on by aliens, fixing him so that "a torrent of raw despair" which he cannot control pours from him (113). Aware that "what he offered was nothing more than an awareness of the punishments the universe devises for its inhabitants" (114), he isolates himself in a ruined city on a distant planet. When he calls himself "the most human being there is, because I'm the only one who can't hide my humanity" (124), a visitor accuses him of "blaming humanity for being human" (150).

While this dark vision never disappears from Silverberg's fiction, atonement and redemption become a more primary theme. Occasionally he relents, somewhat at least, to achieve the humor of *Up the Line* (1969), "a ribald tale of a time-courier who guides sightseers through the Byzantine Empire [and] falls in love with his many-times grandmother."[50] His fullest statement of transcendence occurs in *Nightwings* (1969) and *Downward to the Earth* (1970). In a sense the novels echo one another, for they present two fresh perspectives on a familiar theme. *Nightwings* portrays a decadent Earth

REVOLT AND INNOVATION

during the Third Cycle of civilization ages after humanity has fallen from interstellar heights through the sin of pride. The first-person narrator, as one of the guild of the Watchers, has been trained to project his consciousness far out into space to discover if alien ships approach. He does so because when humans finally encountered humanoid beings on H236, a collecting team brought back specimens to breed in a zoo despite the protestations of the aliens, who threatened that one day they would turn Earth into a compound for its own people. The chance came when, as the final step in creating an earthly paradise, the attempt to control the planetary climate ended in disaster transforming the face of the globe. As the more powerful galactic races took care of Earth, the inhabitants of H236 reimbursed them, asking only that one day they be allowed to collect their investment. The invasion occurs overnight. The Watcher, who had no faith in his mission, becomes an apprentice to the Rememberers, thereby having the chance to find records that prove the aliens' claims. Out of guilt, individually and cumulatively, the narrator becomes a pilgrim to Jorslem, during which he has a vision showing him a Fourth Cycle in which individual isolation will be ended and even the alien invaders will be part of a new spiritual unity. *Nightwings* rises out of disaster to become the most complete statement of affirmation in Silverberg's fiction.

Whereas the Pilgrim participates in a quest that may bring about a spiritually awakened world, in *Down-*

ward to the Earth a remorseful Edmund Gundersen undertakes a private quest on the planet Belzagor, where he once served as a colonial administrator. (Silverberg had visited the great game parks of Africa early in 1969; that experience and his indebtedness to Conrad, especially *Heart of Darkness*—as indicated by the use of the name Kurtz—shape this novel.) Gundersen's trek into the Mist Country parallels Marlow's venture into the interior. Haunted by a sense of sin because humans used the intelligent species of Belzagor—the elephantine nildoror and the seemingly secondary, baboonlike sulidoror—as servants and beasts of burden, Gundersen learns that the two species are complementary in that periodically they are transformed from one form to the other, retaining full knowledge of all previous cycles. Gundersen asks for transformation, and during rebirth experiences a spiritual unity not only with the nildoror and sulidoror, but also with the few humans who have remained on Belzagor. Like *Nightwings,* the ending of *Downward to the Earth* holds forth promise; Gundersen assumes a messianic role, declaring that he must help Kurtz and the others who remain deformed, prisoners of their isolated humanity. There is yet another implication; like Simak, Silverberg suggests the telepathic and spiritual unity of all intelligent life forms.

He turned from private vision to social visionary in *Tower of Glass* (1970), in which he combines the theme of the death of God with a commentary on racial relations. *Tower of Glass* is Silverberg's *Frankenstein*, for the protagonist, Simeon Krug, has created androids from "the vats"; they worship him, but he will not recognize their humanity. Dismissing his creatures as mere artifacts, comparable to robots and computers, the lonely Krug broods upon the reception of radio signals from a planetary nebula NGC 7923 as a sign of intelligent beings, though they would take unimaginable form. As Krug departs in his ship, the world he has brought into being falls apart as the androids riot. One more fully appreciates the texture of Silverberg's work through such devices as the androids' bible, which opens: "In the beginning there was Krug and He said, Let there be Vats, and there were Vats. And Krug looked upon the Vats and found them good."

In *Dying Inside* (1972), Silverberg found his most effective metaphor for the condition of twentieth-century man. The first-person narrator, David Selig, a citizen of present-day New York, tells how he loses the telepathic abilities he was born with as he grows older. His final cry, "Hello, hello, hello, hello . . ." completes the symbolic dramatization of humanity's total isolation in an uncaring universe. In short, beginning as a hack writer in the 1950s, during the late 1960s and early 1970s Silverberg "deliberately experimented, both technically and thematically, in an attempt to discover how much science fiction could be expanded so that, like contemporary social and psychological realism, it could convey metaphorically statements" about humanity and its society.[51]

Cumulatively, the consistency of his accomplishments surpassed that of any of his long-standing contemporaries, but the new writers would match him. In her first novel, *Picnic on Paradise* (1968), Joanna Russ makes use of a familiar device as a point of departure. The Trans-Temporal Authority rescues a woman—Alyx—drowning near ancient Tyre so that they can use her as their agent on the tourist planet Paradise to guide a party of refugees fleeing across glaciers, mountains, and desert to escape a "local war." (It is also labeled a "commercial war," although a lieutenant wonders what the opponents will fight with because no radiation, viruses, or heat may be used since Paradise is "too beautiful" to have anything mar its "landscape or ecological balance" [13].) Armed only with crossbows, the party undertakes its fifty-seven-day trek to the polar station where they will be picked up. A murderer and thief in her own time four millennia ago, Alyx proves to be more than an adequate leader on what becomes a survivalist exercise. She hates Gunnar, "a freak Norseman" (18) who is repeatedly described as an "amateur" adventurer, the most "macho" individual among the group; she also has a brief affair with the youth who calls himself "Machine" before the cowardly Gunnar causes his death. Alyx kills Gunnar. But the details of the story line are less important than the fact that Russ satirizes the stereotype characters as they represent the emphasis on youth, beauty, and drugs in the 1960s. Most importantly, as a murderer and a thief in her own

REVOLT AND INNOVATION

society, Alyx lies outside the concepts of the tradition-
ally feminine woman. Her role as guide dramatizes the
inappropriateness of stereotyped sexual roles.

If Alyx may be called the first radical feminist in
contemporary SF, then in *The Left Hand of Darkness*
(1969) Ursula K. LeGuin questions the whole matter of
gender by having her protagonist, Genly Ai, act as the
first emissary from the galactic confederation to the
planet Gethen, whose humanoids are androgynous.
Seizing upon the crucial issue in American cultural politics—already finding its voice with the formation of
NOW (1966)—she addressed it so effectively that her
effort gained her immediate, deserved attention. But
this acclaim overlooks her principal accomplishment in
terms of the development of American science fiction.
At its simplest level *The Left Hand of Darkness* builds from
the premise of first contact, but with a difference. On
the basis of a report by an early scouting team, the humanoid Genly Ai, representative of the Ekumen
("Household") League, finds himself on a backwater
planet to negotiate a possible trade agreement. Caught
up in complex Gethenian intrigue, he forms a friend-
ship with Estraven, an adviser to a king who soon goes
into exile. As they make the first attempt to cross the
Gobrin Ice in a winter journey, Genly Ai learns that
Gethenians may become either male or female during
estrus, depending upon the situation and the other person involved; thus each adult has probably been both
mother and father. By utilizing such a concept, LeGuin

goes far beyond the matter of sexual roles in order to explore the very nature of the society that would result from this biological arrangement. In short, with Gethen as an alternate model, LeGuin makes the reader ask questions about human society. This is what gave the novel its cutting edge. Effective as *The Left Hand of Darkness* is, it is only one step in LeGuin's major accomplishment, already begun in her earlier novels *Rocannon's World* (1966), *Planet of Exile* (1967), and *City of Illusions* (1967), all concerned with "planetary exploration ... first contact, and human-alien integration."[52] She takes as a basic premise uniting all of her major fiction that an ancient world, Hain, seeded innumerable habitable worlds with humanoid life. The humanity of Earth makes up one such world, but such a premise allows, perhaps insists, that each world develop separately and thus presents a writer with LeGuin's background in anthropology the opportunity to explore a variety of cultures, individually or as they interact. This Hainish empire—with the implication that some of the humanoids may be the result of deliberate experiments by the older, now vanished culture of Hain itself—becomes a metaphorical basis for the exploration of widely varying cultures and therefore an exploration of the potentialities open to human culture. Instead of a simple extrapolation from the present Earth, as Heinlein and his colleagues made in their future histories, LeGuin created a chessboard, so to speak, which opened wide the range of possible worlds. Gethen, whose intrigues

remind one of the Balkan and Middle European kingdoms created in turn-of-the-century popular fiction,
provides only one brilliant example of the potential
LeGuin's plan held for writers. In retrospect, she, Cordwainer Smith, and Robert Silverberg opened the potential of SF more widely than any of their contemporaries.

Accomplished as was the work of their colleagues,
LeGuin, Silverberg, and Smith gave the field a literary
sophistication which brought the formative period to
an end. One should not overlook the fact that all three
had published in widely different areas before they published their finest SF. In a sense the problem for SF has
been one of popular culture and high culture; in another, a matter of definition and belief. When Damon
Knight added his voice to those who had long belabored
"the ghetto world created by publishers like Hugo
Gernsback," he seems to have forgotten that after
World War I, when magazines—whether pulp or slick—
flooded the mass market, they were all specialized. Science fiction was never the only label; indeed, it was the
one that survived the restrictions of World War II and
the sudden shift from magazines to paperback books.
When he went on to say that once again "indications"
suggested that SF might emerge and become part of the
"mainstream," so that in a decade "survivors of our
little group may be rich and famous [but] scattered,"[53]
there is a tension between envy and pride at being one
of a select few. In Britain that specialization had never
occurred, nor at least until the Campbell years was there

the widespread camaraderie characterizing the American group.

An idea more than a market place had produced "science fiction." The impact of the nineteenth-century sciences, fused with a desire for social reform, transformed the Western concept of progress into a vision of utopia; subsumed in that vision of the near or distant future was the American infatuation with the machine. By the time that John W. Campbell began to edit *Astounding*, fed by the dream of space flight, the visionary speculation producing utopia had crystallized into an ideology; the engineer—an emblematic manifestation of the scientist/inventor/technician—would shape a far better world for a worthy people. (In politics the concept of technocracy has never fully disappeared.) Although Frankenstein lurked in the shadows, while catastrophe became a problem to be solved, the creed of Campbell's Golden Age looked forward to "galactic man." That writers and editors shared this central idea reveals itself in the manner in which a number of popular nineteenth-century motifs arising from topical interests in science were denied the status of science fiction, while debate about how science should be used in the fiction has continued in partisan arguments regarding "hard" and "soft" sciences. In short, the emphasis was on ideas, even when L. Sprague deCamp and Willie Ley collaborated on *Lands Beyond* (1952), a delightful and highly informative account—ranging from Atlantis and the Kingdom of Prester John to pre-Columbian America and Symmes "Hole"—of the imaginary lands used as settings by writers past and present.

Idea remained dominant throughout the 1950s, although the vision of the future was blurred by mushroom clouds. The image of the superman fused with that of the rebel against authority. When one turns to the reviewers and critics who emerged from the writers, like Blish and Knight, one finds the major thrust of their work focusing on content rather than technique, although all of them acknowledged such individuals as Sturgeon as stylists beyond compare. All too often the interest in language centered on the science of linguistics—again, an idea. To the degree that the SF of the 1960s reflected the complex new social awareness, it was also a literature of ideas, sometimes of nihilistic proportions. In pursuing this concept of literature as idea, one recalls Blish's admonition to ask what the story is *about* as well as by the knowledge that all fictions—SF, fantasy, social realism, romance—are about something. Any discussion of literature (texts) in this manner remains at the sociological level in that it views the work as a product of, or creator of, a given culture at a given time. In that direction lies a conflict of ideologies.

Whatever the persuasion of the individual, the rebellion that Silverberg joined brought fresh questions to the field. Involving persons too diverse to be placed under a single label, it was a version of the literary revolution which shapes the expression of each generation of writers. This one perhaps proved noisier than most because it came to a comparatively small, certainly specialized field. Just as no ideology comes out of nowhere, so, too, this movement had no single, overnight source. It culminated in a new freedom, a greater diversity, which enriched the field of contemporary science fiction. As noted before, nothing is ever lost. In the same year that LeGuin published *The Left Hand of Darkness*, Michael Crichton's *The Andromeda Strain* (1969), a best-seller, gave an account of a five-day crisis in American science when an unmanned satellite lands in Arizona contaminated with a microorganism which threatens epidemic. Catastrophe—natural or manmade—has gone through many permutations as one of the oldest human myths. Crichton's dedication to "A.C.D., M.D. *who first proposed the problem*" calls to mind Hal Clement's assertion that an SF story is a puzzle to be solved.

Perhaps the landing of Apollo 11 on the moon 20 July 1969 may become emblematic of that exponential flow of events during the twentieth century which leads even TV newscasters to speak of contemporary America as a "science fiction" world. Reinforced by the popularity of *Star Trek* and *Star Wars*, perhaps these events have shaped a wider audience for science fiction. In addition, the idea that the end of the decade marks a turning point in the development of the field gains strength from a change in personnel. After winning three consecutive Hugos between 1966 and 1968 as editor of *Worlds of If*, Frederik Pohl resigned as editor in the spring of 1969. By the spring of 1970 Michael Moorcock had left *New Worlds*. On 11 July 1971 John W. Campbell, editor of *Astounding/Analog* for thirty-four years, died.

During the interval of Campbell's editorship, science fiction reflected the ever-changing, oftentimes contradictory moods of America toward science/technology and the nation itself. It began as a cult literature confined almost exclusively to specialist magazines. To the degree that its writers escaped the conviction that they must draw the blueprints of heaven or hell, they found in SF the literary vehicle which has the greatest freedom to create metaphors that speak of the nature and experience of humanity. Free of the restraints imposed by social and psychological realism, though it may use them as its tools, science fiction is able to create imaginary worlds, to distort time and space, as it seeks to expand humanity's perception of itself.

Notes

1. Nicholls 425.
2. Aldiss 298.
3. L.W. Currey's *Science Fiction and Fantasy Authors: A Bibliography* (Boston: Hall, 1979) skips from Edgar Rice Burroughs to Francis Marion Busby, as does James Gunn's *New Encyclopedia*. Magill includes only *Nova Express* (4: 1566–70), while Nicholls gives him little more than a column (97).
4. Atheling (Blish), *More Issues* 125, 126, 128.
5. Atheling (Blish), *More Issues* 11, 13.

6. Aldiss 297–98.

7. Wollheim 106.

8. Platt 162.

9. Bleiler 358–59.

10. Aldiss 296.

11. Gunn 150.

12. Norman Spinrad, ed., *Modern Science Fiction* (Boston: Gregg, 1976) 1, 13.

13. Spinrad 165.

14. Spinrad 273–74.

15. Anthony Burgess is not included in Aldiss, Bleiler, or Currey. Nicholls includes him, as does Gunn, both giving him little more than a column. Magill has entries for *A Clockwork Orange* (1: 396–401) and *The Wanting Seed* (5:2402–06).

16. Edwin B. Burgum, "Freud and Fantasy in Contemporary Fiction," *Science and Society*, 28 (Spring 1965): 224–31. Discussed in Thomas D. Clareson, "Science Fiction and the Literary Tradition," *Nebula Award Stories 6*, ed. Clifford D. Simak (Garden City, NY: Doubleday, 1971) xi-xiii.

17. Beginning in 1958 MLA sponsored an annual seminar devoted to science fiction which continued into the mid-1970s. Only "English Literature in Transition: 1880–1920" was an older seminar. In 1959 *Extrapolation* became the seminar's newsletter; it is now published as a quarterly devoted to SF and fantasy by Kent State University Press.

18. Samuel R. Delany, "About Five Thousand One Hundred and Seventy Five Words," *Extrapolation* 10 (May 1969): 66. Reprinted in Thomas D. Clareson, ed. *SF: the Other Side of Realism* (Bowling Green, OH: Bowling Green University Popular Press, 1971) 130–46.

19. Samuel R. Delany, "Critical Methods: Speculative Fiction," *Many Futures, Many Worlds* 288.

20. "MLA Forum: Science Fiction: The New Mythology," *Extrapolation* 10 (May 1969): 69–115.

21. Lester del Rey 253, 258–59.

22. Wollheim 103, 105.

23. Platt 165.

24. del Ray 255.

25. Aldiss 328.

26. Scholes and Rabkin 97.

27. Gunn 439.

28. Warrick 23–28.

29. After Dick gives the necessary exposition to establish his near-future setting, he provides no further detailed description. Perhaps the strongest element of the film *Blade Runner* was its portrayal of the congested, smog-cloaked streets of San Francisco. But it must be noted that the film distorted the story line, making Deckard a Hammett/Chandler tough-guy detective and simply eliminating his wife so that the film could have a happy ending. Deckard and Rachel escape the city, whether with marriage in mind or not is never made clear, because they wish to be together for however long the beautiful android has to live. An experimental model, she does not have a set life span.

30. Aldiss 325.

31. Although all critics and reviewers assign a far-future setting to *The Dying Earth*, there is an ambiguity in that both Turjan of Muir and T'sais move easily between the land of Emboyon and Earth. In the first story, "Turjan of Muir," a sage tells Turjan that "where this land [Emboyon] lies, no one knows [but] a spell exists to take one there" (8). He invokes the spell, wonders if "Emboyon is of Earth", and finds himself in that land (11). In the third story, "T'sais," when T'sais tires of Emboyon, the magician Pendelume touches her, telling her she will feel dizzy; she opens her eyes and finds herself on Earth (43–44). Jack Vance, *The Dying Earth* (New York: Pocket Books, 1977). Granted that it is a trivial matter, it nevertheless either emphasizes the magic Vance relies on or implies a parallel world.

32. Tim Underwood and Chuck Miller, eds., *Jack Vance* (New York: Taplinger, 1980), 16, 122.

33. Underwood and Miller 188, 192.

34. *Dictionary of Literary Biography* 8/2: 173.

35. Atheling (Blish), *Issue at Hand* 105, 106.

36. Bleiler 547.

37. Gunn 487.

38. Under the pseudonym Felix X. Forrest he published two novels—*Ria* (1947) and *Carola* (1948). As Charmichael Smith he published *Atomsk* (1949), concerning the sabotage of a Russian nuclear plant.

39. Bleiler 523–24.

40. *Dictionary of Literary Biography* 8/2: 130, 132.

41. Bleiler 523.

42. Gunn 423.

43. Aldiss 292.

44. Aldiss 293.

45. Atheling (Blish), *More Issues* 124, 137.

46. In a chapter entitled "Purveyors of Myth and Magic" in *Yesterday and After: The History of the English Novel*, vol 11 (New York: Barnes & Noble, 1967), Lionel Stevenson reminds his reader that "it is frequently forgotten that the predominance of realism in both the theory and practice of novelists during the early years of the twentieth century did not preclude the active survival of fantasy (111). The point made in "SF: The Other Side of Realism" that both realism and fantasy (science fiction) responded to the scientific thought of the nineteenth century may be extended to include their response to the innovations of twentieth-century scientific thought.

47. Gunn 242.

48. Robert Silverberg, "Sounding Brass, Tinkling Cymbal," *Hell's Cartographers*, eds. Aldiss and Harrison 20, 22.

49. Silverberg, *Hell's Cartographers* 28–29.

50. Clareson, *Silverberg* 34–35.

51. Clareson, *Silverberg* 46.

52. Gunn 276.

53. Damon Knight, *In Search of Wonder* (Chicago: Advent, 1967) 283–84.

BIBLIOGRAPHY

Fiction

The books listed here are those which have been discussed at length in the text. Both the first American edition, whether hardcover or paperback, and the first British edition have been cited. Because the first paperback editions are out of print, one must rely on the reprint editions, primarily from Garland or Gregg, which reissued hardcover editions of books originally published in paper. These are frequently the only editions available in libraries. Citations in the text are either to the original American editions or to the Garland/Gregg reprints, unless otherwise cited.

Anderson, Poul. *Brain Wave*. New York: Ballantine, 1954; London: Heinemann, 1955. In 1954 Walker simultaneously issued a hardcover American edition; that is the edition cited in the text.

———. *The High Crusade*. Garden City, NY: Doubleday, 1960.

———. *War of the Wing-Men*. New York: Ace, 1958; London: Sphere, 1966. Boston: Gregg, 1976.

Asimov, Isaac. *The Caves of Steel*. Garden City, NY: Doubleday, 1954; London: Boardman, 1954. Greenwich, CT: Fawcett Crest, 1972.

Bester, Albert. *The Demolished Man*. Chicago: Shasta, 1953; London: Sidgwick and Jackson, 1953. New York: Garland, 1975.

———. *The Stars My Destination*. New York: New American Library; published as *Tiger, Tiger*, London: Sidgwick and Jackson, 1956. Boston: Gregg, 1975.

Blish, James. *A Case of Conscience*. New York: Ballantine, 1958; London: Faber and Faber, 1959.

BIBLIOGRAPHY

Brackett, Leigh. *The Long Tomorrow*. Garden City, NY: Doubleday, 1955; London: Mayflower, 1962. New York: Ballantine, 1974.

Bradbury, Ray. *Farenheit 451*. New York: Ballantine, 1953; London: Hart-Davis, 1954.

———. *The Illustrated Man*. Garden City, NY: Doubleday, 1951; London: Hart-Davis, 1952. New York: Bantam, 1952.

———. *The Martian Chronicles*. Garden City, NY: Doubleday, 1950; London: Hart-Davis, 1951. New York: Bantam, 1951.

Budrys, Algis. *Rogue Moon*. Greenwich, CT Fawcett, 1960; London: Muller, 1962.

———. *Who?* New York: Pyramid, 1958; London: Gollancz, 1962. Boston: Gregg, 1979.

Clement, Hal. *Mission of Gravity*. Garden City, NY: Doubleday, 1954; Harmondsworth: Penguin, 1963. New York: Pyramid, 1962.

Clifton, Mark, and Frank Riley. *They'd Rather Be Right*. New York: Gnome, 1957; Garden City, NY: Doubleday, 1981.

Cole, Burt. *Subi: The Volcano*. New York: Macmillan, 1957.

Delany, Samuel R. *Babel 17*. New York: Ace, 1966; London: Gollancz, 1967. Boston: Gregg, 1976.

———. *The Ballad of Beta 2*. New York: Ace, 1965; London: Sphere, 1977.

———. *The Einstein Intersection*. New York: Ace, 1967; London: Gollancz, 1968.

Dick, Philip K. *Do Androids Dream of Electric Sheep?* Garden City, NY: Doubleday, 1968; London: Rapp and Whiting, 1969. Boston: Gregg, 1979. In 1982 Ballantine issued the novel as *Blade Runner*, the title of the film adaptation.

———. *The Man in the High Castle*. New York: Putnam, 1962; Harmondsworth: Penguin, 1965. Boston: Gregg, 1979.

BIBLIOGRAPHY

———. *The Three Stigmata of Palmer Eldritch*. Garden City, NY: Doubleday, 1965; London: Cape, 1966. Boston: Gregg, 1979.

Disch, Thomas. *Camp Concentration*. Garden City, NY: Doubleday, 1969; London: Hart-Davis, 1968. New York: Avon, 1971.

———. *The Genocides*. New York: Berkley, 1965; London: Whiting and Wheaton, 1967. Boston: Gregg, 1978.

Heinlein, Robert A. *The Door into Summer*. Garden City, NY: Doubleday, 1957; London: Gollancz, 1967.

———. *Farnham's Freehold*. New York: Putnam, 1964; London: Dobson, 1965. New York: Signet, 1965.

———. *The Moon Is a Harsh Mistress*. New York: Putnam, 1966; London: Dobson, 1967. New York: Berkley, 1968.

———. *The Past Through Tomorrow*. New York: Putnam, 1967; London: New English Library, 1977. New York: Berkley, 1967.

———. *The Puppet Masters*. Garden City, NY: Doubleday, 1951; London: Museum Press, 1953. New York: Signet, 1951.

———. *Starship Troopers*. New York: Putnam, 1959; London: Four Square, 1961. New York: Berkley, 1968.

———. *Stranger in a Strange Land*. New York: Putnam, 1961; London: Four Square, 1965. New York: Avon, 1962.

Herbert, Frank. *Dune*. Philadelphia: Chilton, 1965; London: Gollancz, 1966.

Hersey, John. *The Child Buyer*. New York: Knopf, 1960.

Karp, David. *One*. New York: Vanguard, 1953.

Keyes, Daniel. *Flowers for Algernon*. New York: Harcourt, Brace, 1966.

LeGuin, Ursula K. *The Left Hand of Darkness*. New York: Ace, 1969; London: McDonald, 1969.

BIBLIOGRAPHY

Leiber, Fritz. *The Big Time*. New York: Ace, 1961; London: Four Square, 1965.

————. *The Wanderer*. New York: Ballantine, 1964; London: Dobson, 1967. Boston: Gregg, 1980.

Miller, Walter M., Jr. *A Canticle for Leibowitz*. Philadelphia: Lippincott, 1960; London: Weidenfeld and Nicolson, 1960. New York, Bantam, 1961.

Pangborn, Edgar. *Davy*. New York: St. Martin's, 1964; London: Dobson, 1967. New York: Garland, 1975.

————. *A Mirror for Observors*. Garden City, NY: Doubleday, 1954; London: Muller, 1955. New York: Avon, 1975.

Panshin, Alexei. *Rite of Passage*. New York: Ace, 1969; London: Sidgwick and Jackson, 1969.

Piper, H. Beam. *Little Fuzzy*. New York: Avon, 1962.

Pohl, Frederik, and Cyril M. Kornbluth. *Gladiator-at-Law*. New York: Ballantine, 1955; London: Digit, 1958.

————. *Search the Sky*. New York: Ballantine, 1954; London: Digit, 1960.

————. *The Space Merchants*. New York: Ballantine, 1953; London: Heinemann, 1955.

Russ, Joanna. *Picnic on Paradise*. New York: Ace, 1969; London: Macdonald, 1969.

Silverberg, Robert. *Downward to the Earth*. Garden City, NY: Doubleday, 1970; London: Gollancz, 1977.

————. *Dying Inside*. New York: Scribner, 1972; London: Sidgwick and Jackson, 1975.

————. *The Man in the Maze*. New York: Avon, 1969; London: Tandem, 1971.

————. *Nightwings*. New York: Avon, 1969; London: Sidgwick and Jackson, 1972.

BIBLIOGRAPHY

———. *Tower of Glass*. New York: Scribner, 1970; London: Panther, 1976.

Simak, Clifford D. *City*. New York: Gnome, 1952; London: Weidenfeld and Nicolson, 1954.

———. *The Cosmic Engineers*. New York: Gnome, 1950.

Spinrad, Norman. *Bug Jack Barron*. New York: Avon, 1969; London: Macdonald, 1970. Walker simultaneously published a hardcover edition in the United States in 1969.

———. ed. *Modern Science Fiction*. New York: Doubleday, 1974. Boston: Gregg, 1976.

Sturgeon, Theodore. *More Than Human*. New York: Farrar, Straus, and Young, 1953; London: Gollancz, 1954. New York: Garland, 1975.

———. *Venus Plus X*. New York: Pyramid, 1960; London: Gollancz, 1969. Boston: Gregg, 1976.

Tevis, Walter. *The Man Who Fell to Earth*. New York: Fawcett, 1963; London: Pan 1963. Boston: Gregg, 1978.

Vance, Jack. *The Dying Earth*. New York: Hillman, 1950; London, Mayfair, 1972. New York: Pocket Books, 1977.

Vonnegut, Kurt, Jr. *Player Piano*. New York: Scribner, 1952; London, Macmillan, 1953. New York: Dell, 1974.

———. *The Sirens of Titan*. New York: Dell, 1959; London: Gollancz, 1962.

Reference Works

Aldiss, Brian W. *Trillion Year Spree*. Garden City, NY: Doubleday, 1986.

———and Harry Harrison, eds. *Hell's Cartographers: Some Personal Histories of Science Fiction*. London: Weidenfeld and Nicolson, 1975; New York: Harper, 1975.

BIBLIOGRAPHY

Amis, Kingsley. *New Maps of Hell*. New York: Harcourt, Brace, 1960.

Atheling, William (pseudonym of James Blish). *The Issue at Hand*. Chicago: Advent, 1964.

———. *More Issues at Hand*. Chicago: Advent, 1970.

Barron, Neil, ed. *Anatomy of Wonder: A Critical Guide to Science Fiction*. 3d ed. New York: Bowker, 1987. The first edition (1976) is of interest because of the difference in books included.

Bleiler, E. F., ed. *Science Fiction Writers: Critical Studies of the Major Authors from the Early Nineteenth Century to the Present*. New York: Scribner, 1982.

Blish, James. See Atheling, William.

Bretnor, Reginald, ed. *Modern Science Fiction: Its Meaning and Its Future*. New York: Coward McCann, 1953.

Carter, Paul A. *The Creation of Tomorrow: Fifty Years of Science Fiction*. New York: Columbia University Press, 1977.

Clareson, Thomas D., ed. *Many Futures, Many Worlds: Theme and Form in Science Fiction*. Kent, OH: Kent State University Press, 1977.

———. *Robert Silverberg*. Mercer Island, WA: Starmont House, 1983.

———. *Science Fiction Criticism: An Annotated Bibliography*. Kent, OH: Kent State University Press, 1972.

———. ed. *SF: The Other Side of Realism*. Bowling Green, OH: Bowling Green University Popular Press, 1971.

Coward, David, and Thomas L. Wymer, eds. *Dictionary of Literary Biography*. Vol. 8. *Twentieth Century American Science Fiction Writers*. 2 vols. Detroit: Bruccoli Clark/Gale Research, 1981.

BIBLIOGRAPHY

Currey, L. W. *Science Fiction and Fantasy Writers: A Bibliography of First Editions of Their Writing*. Boston: Hall, 1979.

del Rey, Lester. *The World of Science Fiction: 1926–1976*. New York: Garland, 1980.

Eshbach, Lloyd Arthur, ed. *Of Worlds Beyond: A Symposium*. New York: Fantasy Press, 1947. Chicago: Advent, 1964.

Extrapolation: The Newsletter of the MLA Seminar on Science Fiction: 1959–1969. Boston: Gregg, 1978. Available from Greenwood Press on microfilm. *Extrapolation* is now published as a quarterly by Kent State University Press.

Franson, Donald, and Howard DeVore. *A History of the Hugo, Nebula, and International Fantasy Awards*. Dearborn Heights, MI: Misfit Press, 1981.

Gunn, James, ed. *The New Science Fiction Encyclopedia*. New York: Viking, 1988.

Hall, H. W. *Science Fiction Book Review Index, 1923–1973*. Detroit: Gale Research, 1975.

Hassler, Donald M. *Hal Clement*. Mercer Island, WA: Starmont House, 1982.

Hillegas, Mark R. *The Future as Nightmare: H. G. Wells and the Anti-Utopians*. New York: Oxford University Press, 1967.

Ketterer, David. *New Worlds for Old: The Apocalyptic Imagination, Science Fiction, and American Literature*. Bloomington: Indiana University Press, 1974.

Knight, Damon. *In Search of Wonder*. 2nd ed. Chicago: Advent, 1967.

Mackey, Douglas A. *Philip K. Dick*. Boston: Twayne, 1988.

Magazine of Fantasy and Science Fiction (F&SF). 1949–79.

Magill, Frank N., ed. *Survey of Science Fiction Literature*. 5 vols. Englewood Cliffs, NJ: Salem Press, 1979.

BIBLIOGRAPHY

Moskowitz, Sam. *Explorers of the Infinite: Shapers of Science Fiction*. Cleveland: World, 1963.

Newman, John, and Michael Unworth. *Future War Novels: An Annotated Bibliography of Works in English Since 1946*. Phoenix: Oryx Press, 1984.

Nicholls, Peter, ed. *The Science Fiction Encyclopedia*. Garden City, NY: Doubleday, 1979.

Panshin, Alexei. *Heinlein in Dimension*. Chicago: Advent, 1968.

Platt, Charles. *Dream Makers: The Uncommon People Who Write Science Fiction*. New York: Berkley, 1980.

Reginald, Robert. *Science Fiction and Fantasy Literature: A Checklist 1700–1974*. 2 vols. Detroit: Gale Research, 1979.

Scholes, Robert, and Eric S. Rabkin. *Science Fiction: History, Science, Vision*. New York: Oxford University Press, 1977.

Slusser, George E., and Eric S. Rabkin, eds. *Hard Science Fiction*. Carbondale: Southern Illinois University Press, 1986.

Stasz, Clarice. *American Dreamers*. New York: St. Martin's, 1988.

Toupence, William F. *Frank Herbert*. Boston: Twayne, 1988.

Tymn, Marshall B., and Mike Ashley, eds. *Science Fiction, Fantasy, and Weird Fiction Magazines*. Westport, CT: Greenwood Press, 1985.

Underwood, Tim, and Chuck Miller, eds. *Jack Vance*. New York: Taplinger, 1980.

Walsh, Chad. *From Utopia to Nightmare*. New York: Harper, 1962.

Warrick, Patricia. *Mind in Motion: The Fiction of Philip K. Dick*. Carbondale: Southern Illinois University Press, 1987.

Wolfe, Gary K. *The Known and the Unknown: The Iconography of Science Fiction*. Kent, OH: Kent State University Press, 1979.

Wollheim, Donald A. *The Universe Makers*. New York: Harper, 1971.

INDEX

INDEX

INDEX

INDEX

INDEX

INDEX

INDEX

INDEX

INDEX

INDEX

INDEX

INDEX

INDEX

INDEX

Whorf, Benjamin Lee 237, 245
Wiener, Norbert 43, 62
"Wilderness, The" 51, 56
Wilhelm, Kate 177, 186–187
Williamson, Jack 20–21, 27, 28–29, 114, 143
Wilson, Robin Scott 178
Witch World 184–185
Wolfe, Bernard 43–44
Wolfe, Gary 17, 52, 88
Wollheim, Donald A. 24–25, 32–33, 40, 41, 206–207, 214, 234, 237
Woman a Day, A 143
Woolf, Virginia 211
Wordsworth, William 210
World Aflame, The: The Russian-American War of 1950 43
World Jones Made, The 112
World of Null-A, The 21, 176
World of Science Fiction, The 213
"World Well Lost, The" 143
Worldcon 16, 179, 202
Worlds of If 234
Writer 179
Wylie, Philip 40, 97, 145
Wyndham, John 41

Yeats, William Butler 210

Zamiatin, Yevgeny 56, 251
Zelazny, Roger 234, 248–250, 251
Zola, Emile 34